YOU, TOO, COULD
WRITE A POEM

YOU, TOO, COULD

WRITE A POEM

Selected Reviews and Essays, 2000–2015

DAVID ORR

PENGUIN BOOKS

PENGUIN BOOKS

An imprint of Penguin Random House LLC
375 Hudson Street
New York, New York 10014
penguin.com

Some of the reviews and essays in this book originally appeared in *The New York
Times*, and to the extent they are reprinted here, they are reprinted with
permission. Inquiries concerning permission to reprint any column or portion
thereof should be directed to PARS International, 253 West 34th Street, 7th
Floor, New York, NY 10001. The following selections originally appeared in
The New York Times: "You, Too, Could Write a Poem," "The Age of Citation,"
"Vendler's Yeats," "Hit Parade," "The Style of Luis de Góngora," "The Happy
Couplet," "The Great(ness) Game," "Oprah's Adventure's in Poetryland,"
"Annals of Poetry," "School of Verse," "The Virtues of Poetry: Longenbach and
Papageorgiou," "Louise Glück's Metamorphoses," "The Obscurity of Michael
O'Brien," "Too Close to Touch: Thom Gunn's *Selected Poems*," "Tomas
Tranströmer and the Art of Translation," "Rough Gems: The Uncollected Work
of Elizabeth Bishop," "The Letters of Ted Hughes," "The Dream Logic of
Matthea Harvey," "Jack Gilbert's Daily Devotions," "The Neglected Master,"
"*The Trouble with Poetry*," "James Franco, Poet," "On Robert Hass," "Christopher
Gilbert's Improvisations," "Matthew Zapruder and Rachel Wetzsteon," "The
Raw and the Cooked: Frank Stanford and Devin Johnston," "The Collected
Poems of Louise MacNeice," "Versions of Zbigniew Herbert," "The Poetry of
Nabokov," "Mary Jo Bang's *Elegy*," "Jorie Graham, Superstar," "*The Notebooks of
Robert Frost*," "Donald Justice," "On Carl Phillips," "Richard Wilbur's
Anterooms," "Frederick Seidel, Scary Guy," "Marie Ponsot."

"Bad Guys," "Poetry and, of, and About," "Beach Reading," and "Public
Poetry: Four Takes" originally appeared in *Poetry*.

"The State of Contemporary American Poetry: An Allegory" originally
appeared in *Virginia Quarterly Review*.

"How Far Can You Press a Poet?" originally appeared in *The Believer*.

ISBN 9780143128199

Printed in the United States of America
10 9 8 7 6 5 4 3 2 1

Set in Simonicini Garamond • Designed by Ginger Legato

For my family

· CONTENTS

Introduction, as a List of Things I Don't Like • 1

On Poetry

You, Too, Could Write a Poem • 13

Bad Guys • 19

The Age of Citation • 33

Vendler's Yeats • 39

Hit Parade • 45

The Style of Luis de Góngora • 51

Virtuosity • 57

The Happy Couplet • 74

The Great(ness) Game • 80

Oprah's Adventures in Poetryland • 91

Annals of Poetry • 97

Poetry and, of, and About • 103

School of Verse • 121

The Virtues of Poetry: Longenbach
     and Papageorgiou • 127

Beach Reading • 134

The Tunnel • 147

Volta

The State of Contemporary American Poetry:
     An Allegory • 165

On Poets

Louise Glück's Metamorphoses • 175

The Obscurity of Michael O'Brien • 184

Too Close to Touch: Thom Gunn's
     Selected Poems • 190

Tomas Tranströmer and the Art of Translation • 196

Rough Gems: The Uncollected Work of
     Elizabeth Bishop • 203

The Letters of Ted Hughes • 210

The Dream Logic of Matthea Harvey • 216

Jack Gilbert's Daily Devotions • 222

The Neglected Master · 229

Public Poetry: Four Takes · 235

The Trouble with Poetry · 259

James Franco, Poet · 265

How Far Can You Press a Poet? · 271

On Robert Hass · 291

Christopher Gilbert's Improvisations · 297

Matthew Zapruder and Rachel Wetzsteon · 303

The Raw and the Cooked:
    Frank Stanford and Devin Johnston · 309

The Collected Poems of Louis MacNeice · 316

Versions of Zbigniew Herbert · 323

The Poetry of Nabokov · 329

Mary Jo Bang's *Elegy* · 337

Jorie Graham, Superstar · 341

The Notebooks of Robert Frost · 347

Donald Justice · 353

On Carl Phillips · 359

Richard Wilbur's *Anterooms* · 364

Frederick Seidel, Scary Guy · 370

Marie Ponsot · 376

Acknowledgments · 383

YOU, TOO, COULD
WRITE A POEM

INTRODUCTION, AS A LIST

OF THINGS I DON'T LIKE

I don't like introductions to collections of criticism. A piece of criticism says, "Here is a way to think." An introduction to an assortment of such pieces says, "Here is how to think about the ways I asked you to think." Introductions like this one are like picture frames for picture frames, or a prescription-strength sheet of glass mounted in front of a rack of bifocals.

◼

I DON'T LIKE INTRODUCTIONS that are premised on a negative—"things I *don't* like"—which plays into the assumption that critics are motivated by resentment. There is an old saying, often wrongly attributed to Michelangelo, the gist of which is that sculpting an elephant is easy: you just cut away everything that doesn't look like an elephant. Criticism is what cuts those pieces away when the elephant is an art form. There's no resentment in that—or, at least, there's more than resentment in that.

•

I DON'T LIKE INTRODUCTIONS that are premised on the critic's individuality—"things *I* don't like"—which plays into the assumption that critics are motivated by vanity.

•

I DON'T LIKE POETRY. I do like—very much—certain poems and poets. Poetry is a lot like America, in the sense that liking all of it means that you probably shouldn't be trusted with money, or scissors.

•

I DON'T LIKE POETRY criticism, unless it's written by someone who cares about criticism almost as much as he cares about poetry, and who in the moment of writing cares more about the sentence he's constructing than about either one of them.

•

I DON'T LIKE HEARING that some person or attitude or undertaking is "good for poetry," which is a categorization that occurs with surprising frequency. Here is a list of things that have been good for poetry, in the sense that they almost certainly led individual poets to write better poems: prison, the death of a parent, catastrophically failed romance, the death of a child, violent political upheaval, religious persecution, the death of a spouse, depression, tuberculosis, devastating physical injury, the death of a friend, cancer, alcoholism, war, decades of loneliness, fantastic sex. Unless the person recommending something as "good for poetry" is offering the last item on that list, poets should check for exits.

■

I DON'T LIKE HEARING that poetry is dying or dead. I particularly don't like it when it's clear that the person making the claim hasn't bothered to so much as glance at any contemporary writing. That said, I also don't like hearing that such claims can be safely ignored because they've been repeated over and over for eighty years. Poetry is an ancient art. Were it to die, it wouldn't vanish overnight. It would vanish like a town in a glacier's path—by inches, over lifespans.

■

I DON'T LIKE MEMORIZING poetry, unless it happens by accident, as it sometimes does. Memorizing it on purpose makes me flash back to first grade and the Pledge of Allegiance.

■

I DON'T LIKE THE word "serious," particularly when it's followed by "criticism." The concept behind "serious criticism" is fine—everyone likes thoughtful writing—but in practice it's often a way for people who read a great deal of poetry and poetry criticism to congratulate themselves at the expense of people who read very little (most of their fellow citizens, in other words, including a large number of people who are more intelligent and interesting than anyone currently inhabiting the poetry world). It's always good to remember that no art form gets to determine its own standing—that judgment will be rendered over time by readers on the art's periphery, who are always choosing among the temptations of many entertainments, many possible experiences.

·

I DON'T LIKE THE assumption that where poetry is concerned, explanation is the highest form of criticism. American poetry does not currently suffer from a dearth of people keen to explain it.

·

I DON'T LIKE THE distance between me and my much younger self, who once carried around Robert Hass's book *Praise* as if it were a talisman. Couldn't I see that the sentimentality of "Meditation at Lagunitas" isn't lessened by being acknowledged? That this actually makes it more sentimental?

·

I DON'T LIKE THE way my older self feels the need to correct my younger self. Let the kid be a kid, Dad.

·

I DON'T LIKE THAT when I asked several accomplished younger poets to give me the names of living poets they considered "great" (for the essay in this volume called "The Great(ness) Game"), the only poet their lists had in common was John Ashbery. Ashbery is a very fine writer, to be sure, but he's also eighty-nine years old. It's as if you surveyed poets in 1963 and the only name anyone could muster was Robert Frost.

I DON'T LIKE THAT the work in this volume almost certainly overpraises several poets.

I DON'T LIKE THAT the work in this volume is almost certainly too critical of several poets.

I DON'T LIKE THAT I've never written a full-length essay on Philip Larkin, a figure who appears here so often that I may as well have called the book *Selected Prose, as Enabled by Philip Larkin*.

I DON'T LIKE THAT I'll probably never be able to convey the delight I feel every time I read the end of Elizabeth Bishop's "The Map": "More delicate than the historians' are the map-makers' colors." I'm always interested to see whether a reader thinks the most interesting thing about this line is the word "delicate" or the syntax. (I'd say the latter.)

I DON'T LIKE THAT I've invoked this poem partly because its conclusion relates as much to criticism as it does to poetry.

·

I DON'T LIKE THAT I've never written a full-length essay on the Irish (and now American) poet Paul Muldoon. I also don't like that one of my more embarrassing poetry-related experiences occurred in front of Muldoon, although I doubt he remembers it. I ran into him one morning in Princeton, New Jersey, when I was in my early twenties, having come into town to see a mutual friend the night before. I'd been an English major at Princeton, where Muldoon teaches, so I'd met him a couple of times, but I didn't really know him at all. My friend was quite familiar with him, though. He and Muldoon stopped to greet each other, and Muldoon turned to me after my friend mentioned we'd had dinner the previous night. "Weryauten the tine, then?" he said, his accent carrying the intonation up like a hot-air balloon trailing sandbags. "Sorry?" I replied. He repeated, "Weryauten the tine?" Then—and I recall this as one of those fascinating and horrifying moments in which one is simultaneously in one's body and yet completely separate from its functioning—I said, "I'm sorry?" again. And then, after he repeated the phrase, again. And again. ("The tine?" I kept thinking. "Like a fork?") Muldoon's previously benevolent gaze was beginning to harden, and my companion, sensing disaster, had just begun to interject, when suddenly it dawned on me. "Yes!" I nearly yelled. "Yes! We were out on the town! The town! We were out on it, yes."

■

I DON'T LIKE THAT the format I've chosen for this introduction makes it difficult for me to point out that the anecdote above is a metaphor for the critical process.

■

I DON'T LIKE THAT "the critical process" is the kind of description one finds oneself writing after fifteen years as a critic, when what is really meant is "not understanding things, and then trying to figure them out, and then sometimes saying if you like them."

■

I DON'T LIKE THAT when covering Barack Obama's inauguration in 2008, *The Daily Show* did a segment on the difficulty the enormous crowd posed. "How do you clear 2.5 million people off the Washington Mall," Jon Stewart asked—and then the show immediately cut to Senator Dianne Feinstein saying, "I have the distinct pleasure of introducing an American poet."

■

I DON'T LIKE THAT the studio audience immediately burst out laughing. I don't like that I also started laughing, and that when I looked up the segment for purposes of this introduction, I laughed again, even harder.

■

I DON'T LIKE THAT it's hard for me to imagine that joke simply not making sense, as it wouldn't have made sense when Robert Frost read at Kennedy's inauguration.

I DON'T LIKE THAT so few people will ever know what it means to be bothered by a poem, let alone strengthened by one.

I DON'T LIKE THAT when the American poetry world talks about "loving poetry," the affection in question is often of a placid, reverent, subtly condescending sort, as if the love object were better than the lover could ever hope to be and yet also something that deserves (and needs) the lover's charity. It's like the love one feels for a toddler or a dog.

I DON'T LIKE READING a new book of poetry and not wanting to return to it. This is the case most of the time, and the situation could hardly be otherwise—as Randall Jarrell once said, "The good, in poetry, is always a white blackbird; an abnormal and unlikely excellence." In the same piece ("Introduction to a Poetry Roundup"—and anyone who's ever written such a roundup knows how depressing they are), Jarrell also observed that "disliking what is bad is only the other face of liking what is good." What is interesting about Jarrell's suggestion is that it implicitly acknowledges the role that litotes plays in criticism, or at least in a certain kind of criticism. Litotes is an old rhetorical ploy in which an affirmative is stated by negating its opposite—for instance, "not bad" for "good." It's usually thought of as leading to understatement ("We are not amused," said the queen) and the tone is often ironic, since the figure depends upon tangling together the implications of endorsement and rejection. I've always been drawn to it. For me, litotes means restraint, resistance, wiliness—qualities that point, not toward some glittering purity (which as Dickinson knew, might blind us), but toward the shadow such a purity might cast; not toward love, but toward the trail of foam in love's wake. Of course, to think this way is to elevate the ideas of purity and love, in however roundabout a fashion. But that's not such a bad thing for a critic to do. Or a poet, for that matter.

ON POETRY

YOU, TOO, COULD
WRITE A POEM

It's autumn again, the time of year when small gnats mourn among the river sallows, when the ovenbird says the early petal fall is past, when the wind moves like a cripple among the leaves—and when some beleaguered editor attempts to cobble together 250 pages of new poetry that will pass muster with shoppers at Barnes & Noble. Yes, it's time again for the Best American Poetry, the legendary series that is now in its eighteenth edition, including Harold Bloom's "best of the best" version from 1997. As poetry fans know, each edition offers all the finest poetic moments of the past year, so long as they come in the form of one poem each by around seventy writers of varying skill, as chosen by an editor who is a famous poet with favors to trade and axes to grind. In the past, this simple yet elegant formula has produced such editorial highlights as Bloom's assault on the selections made by Adrienne Rich ("of a badness not to be believed"), the appearances of several editors' spouses, the appearances of many editors' buddies, and the inclusion of poems by John Ashbery or Donald Hall in nearly every volume, including the one compiled by John Ashbery himself (*l'état, c'est moi!*).

The editor this time is Lyn Hejinian, who seems to represent a departure for the series (not where Ashbery's concerned, though; you'll find him here between "Arnold, Craig" and "Bang, Mary Jo"). Hejinian is a Berkeley professor often identified with American "experimental poetry," a catchall for an assortment of avant-gardists who take their cues from Gertrude Stein, Ezra Pound, some lesser known modernists, various French theorists, and the Language poetry movement of the 1970s and '80s. These writers embrace fragmentation and the deliberate use of nonsense, they generally resist traditional forms (unless they're using them in untraditional ways), and they often think of themselves as opposing a "mainstream" poetry culture that supposedly remains devoted to moist lyric epiphanies. Considering that the Best American series is about as mainstream as poetry gets, it's tempting to view Hejinian's editorship as a signal that the guerrilla fighters are now riding into town to become sheriffs.

There are several problems with this picture, though, and the first is one that has long troubled American poets: for the average, engaged reader (the Best American's target audience), even fairly accessible poems can be maddeningly arcane. The second problem, which is related to the first, is that in the poetry world even the insiders are outsiders. As it happens, poets who could reasonably be called "experimental" currently are sitting in chancellors' seats at the Academy of American Poets, occupying faculty lounges from Buffalo to Berkeley, and, of course, editing the Best American Poetry. To the extent there's a poetry establishment, these writers have been as much a part of it as anyone else for decades now.

Still, not all parts view the whole the same way. For most poets, the notable distinction of this Best American edition will be that it contains nothing from such traditional sources as *Poetry*, the *Paris Review*, or the *Yale Review* and is instead chock-full of work from newer magazines like *Shiny* and *POOL* and *No: A Journal of the Arts*. To put the adventurousness of this editorial decision in perspective, however, consider that the circulation of *POOL* is approximately one thousand, for the *Yale Review* it's seven thousand, and for *Cat Fancy* it's four hundred thousand. And if this year's editor has scorned the *Paris Review*, she hasn't exactly passed up the known for the unknown: of the seventy-five writers here, forty-one have previously appeared in a version of Best American Poetry, a typical ratio for the series.

As for the poems themselves, they run the usual gamut from very good to slightly dull to "what were you thinking?" with a few more in the latter two categories than usual. Hejinian has favored assertively avant-garde writing but made an effort to include writers from other camps as well—Kim Addonizio, John Hollander, and Robert Pinsky, for example. The poems range from twenty-two words (Carl Rakosi) to thirteen pages (Fanny Howe); they are, as you might expect, rarely written in traditional forms (Frederick Seidel's disturbing "Love Song" is an exception); and they're often more interested in peculiar surface effects than in constructing a reliable voice ("'Let's be logical.' / Your panties.") This is poetry short on anecdote, long on implied quotation marks. And while much of the work is preoccupied with the idea of playfulness, the best poems are the ones that actually know how to play. Consider Olena Kalytiak Davis's moody and engaging "You Art a Scholar, Horatio, Speak To It," a twenty-nine-couplet poem that begins:

> *You say you walk and sew alone?*
> *I walk and sew alone.*
>
> *You say you gape and waver?*
> *I am mostly dizzy, most open-mouthed.*
>
> *You say you taste it with each dish?*
> *I drink it and I spit it up.*
>
> *You say it lays you face-down?*
> *I kiss the dirt.*

Oni Buchanan's macabre poem "The Walk" and Aaron Fogel's "337,000, December, 2000" are similarly vivid and unforced.

When the poems here are less successful, it's often because a preprogrammed wonkiness has prevented them from offering us the challenge they'd like to make. Instead, the poem will fall upon its own cutting edge in a way that recalls the

uncomfortable moment in *The Matrix Reloaded* when it becomes obvious that beneath the supercool trench coat of Mor-
pheus beats the heart of a very nerdy man. This is a persistent
problem for self-consciously avant-garde writing. One of the
most heralded experimental poems is Michael Palmer's "Sun"
(*The Best American Poetry 1989*), which includes such observations as, "For a dollar I will have text with you and answer three
questions." Don't trust the Oracle, Neo; she's been reading way
too much Barthes.

Which leads to the question we ask every year: can this
really be the "best" poetry in America? Like the previous editors in this series, Hejinian has her doubts: "Certainly no single poem in this volume is definitive," she writes, "not of
'bestness,' nor of what's 'American,' nor of 'poetry.'" Anyone
who thinks about these concepts for more than two seconds realizes this is true, if only because poetry has never distributed its
"bestness" equally among seventy-five writers in a given year.
What this series stands for isn't excellence, aesthetic or otherwise, but the idea of poetry as a community activity. "People are
writing poems!" each volume cries. "You, too, could write a
poem!" It's an appealingly democratic pose, and it has always
been the genuinely "best" thing about the Best American series.
The only problem is that poetry isn't really an open system; it's a
combination of odd institutions, personal networks, hoary traditions, talent, and blind luck. It's both an art and a guild, in other
words. And if basic participation is possible for anyone with a
heartbeat and a laptop, the requirements for the deluxe

plan—the true "Best American" plan, if you will—are obscure to all but a handful. The negotiation between what we now call the "best" and what we'll later call the "great" never ends; each year the Best American Poetry offers a new compromise, and each year the truce is broken, the sides are marshaled, and the oldest argument begins again.

BAD GUYS

I.

In response to the question, "Can a bad man be a good poet?" there are only two things to be said: "yes" and "obviously." In part, that's because the poetry world sets the bar fairly low for "badness"—when we say a poet was a "bad man," we don't mean that he was a shotgun-toting, baby-kicking monster; we mean that he was unpleasant, disturbed, or a jerk. And considering that poetry's history is thick with unpleasant, disturbed jerks, the question would seem to answer itself. Still, smart readers continue to bemoan the disgraceful behavior of poets and to ask how it possibly can be reconciled with their art. In a recent *New York Times* review of Philip Larkin's *Collected Poems*, for example, Stephen Metcalf tells us that "poets are expected to be more than first-rate talents," and then asks, "How do we square this with Larkin, with his bitterness, his commitment to masturbatory solitude and his slide into gross political reaction?" In raising this question, Metcalf, a Larkin fan, is simply acceding to critical reality—if you're going to review a Larkin book, you're going to do a lot of sighing over the poet's racial slurs, spiteful quips, and dirty magazines. But why is that? Why do we feel the need to judge a Larkin or a Lowell or a Pound—or at least to judge them morally? What do we mean by "bad," anyway? And why continue to ask a question about poetic morality whose answer—"yes, obviously"—has been proven over and over and over again, century after century, from Blake to Shelley to Rimbaud to Frost?

II.

THE FIRST LAW OF poetic morality could be stated as follows: how we read determines how (and whom) we judge. We like to talk about "bad men" and "good poetry," but we're the ones handing out the gold stars and demerits, and we may be "good" or "bad" ourselves in ways that affect our views of others. Thus Baudelaire, no stranger to nastiness, throws his sins like a shroud over audience and writer alike ("Hypocrite lecteur, — mon semblable, —mon frère!"), and even the empyreal John Ashbery reminds us, "The poem is you." Often our reading habits play a relatively obvious and uncomplicated role in determining who we consider "bad." If we like a poet's work, for example, we're more forgiving of his sins, and if we don't, we're not. But the way we read can affect our evaluation of a poet's "real life" activities in quieter and more obscure ways as well. Consider the way we position ourselves in relation to the speaker of Pound's canto 81:

> *Zeus lies in Ceres' bosom*
> *Taishan is attended of loves*
> *under Cythera, before sunrise,*
> *and he said, "Hay aquí mucho*
> *catolicismo—(sounded catoli*thismo)
>   *y muy poco reli*Hion"
> *and he said: "Yo creo que los reyes desaparecen"*
> *(Kings will, I think, disappear)*
> *That was Padre José Elizondo*
>   *in 1906 and in 1917*
> *or about 1917*

Whoever is talking here, it certainly isn't "one of us." For
one thing, the speaker doesn't seem to know whether we understand Spanish—otherwise, why comment on an idiosyncrasy of
local pronunciation (which would be interesting only if we knew
the language), but then translate an entire line into English
(which would be useful only if we didn't)? In canto 81 we're being allowed to overhear; we aren't being engaged.

Although we might at first consider it insignificant, the gap
between speaker and reader is essential to our judgment of poetic misbehavior. We may understand intellectually that "the
speaker" is neither "the reader" nor "the poet," but when we're
in the business of casting stones and erecting pillories, we've
already gone far beyond the realm of things we know, deep into
the murky territory of things we feel. We're more often crying
out than criticizing. Of course, even in ordinary circumstances,
greater distance between speakers and readers creates greater

emotional distance between the poet and his audience—an effect demonstrated by the scarcity of college students who finish *The Cantos* saying, "You know, that's exactly how I feel too." But when sin is on the line, the significance of that distance increases. Think about the following remarks, which were broadcast by Pound from Italy on April 23, 1943:

> Of course, for you to go looking for my point—points of my bi-weekly talk in the maze of Jew-governed American radio transmissions—is like looking for one needle in a whole flock of haystacks. And your press in not very open. . . . Had you had the sense to eliminate Roosevelt and his Jews or the Jews and their Roosevelt at the last election, you would not now be at war.

Now, this is "bad" any way you look at it. But given the way we read poems like canto 81, we're in little danger of getting our own interests (or our own selves) confused with Ezra Pound's or his voices'. Our condemnation of Pound may be self-righteous or excessive, but it probably won't involve the blinkered emotion of a betrayed fan. We might say, for example, "This is terrible"; we probably won't say, "This makes me ashamed," or "This is so revolting that I'm going to throw up." Imagine, though, how we would feel if the above broadcast had not been made by Pound but had instead been delivered by the author of these lines:

I CELEBRATE myself,
And what I assume you shall assume,
For every atom belonging to me as good belongs to you.

Whitman is "ours" and his statements are ours in a way that Pound and his work aren't. Not because Whitman is a better writer than Pound, but because of the relationship that develops among reader, speaker, and poet in Whitman's poems. If we were to discover that Whitman had written a series of newspaper articles in which he asserted, à la Pound, that a "dirty gang of kikes and hyper-kikes" had caused the Civil War, the reaction—even today—would be for many readers something along the lines of, "I think I'm going to puke."

III.

WHICH BRINGS US TO the intriguing case of Philip Larkin. As many poetry readers will recall, Larkin's biography and *Selected Letters* revealed that a poet who generally had been considered a wry, self-deprecating everyman had in fact been the kind of guy who called Morocco "coonland," viciously belittled his peers, lied to his various lovers, and collected pornography. As Martin Amis noted in a 1993 article, the critical reaction to these revelations concerning Larkin's private life took on a very particular cast:

Thus the reception of [Andrew Motion's biography of Larkin] was marked by the quivering nostril and by frequent recourse to the pomaded hanky, the smelling salts and the sick bag. Writing in *The Times*, Peter Ackroyd attributed "a rancid and insidious philistinism" to the "foul-mouthed bigot". Similarly, Bryan Appleyard saw, or nosed, "a repellent, smelly, inadequate masculinity" in "this provincial grotesque". . . . A.N. Wilson, in a piece graciously entitled "Larkin: the old friend I never liked", said that "Larks" was a "really rather nasty, prematurely aged man", and "really a kind of petty-bourgeois fascist", and "really a nutcase".

"Rancid," "repellent," "smelly," "grotesque," "nasty," "really a nutcase"—this isn't the language of either artistic criticism or moral judgment; it's the patois of disgust. As Martha Nussbaum reminds us, disgust is a peculiar and irrational sensation: "Disgust appears to be an especially visceral emotion. . . . Its classic expression is vomiting; its classic stimulants are vile odors and other objects whose very appearance seems loathsome." In the sociopolitical theater, Nussbaum argues, disgust is a means of separating ourselves from undesirables, of making sure that "we" are considered normal while establishing that the object of disgust remains firmly in the camp of the abnormal. But why would Larkin's boorishness inspire this particular response, rather than simply irritation or impatience or disappointment? After all, the critics mentioned above presumably read about worse unpleasantness every day in the newspaper without having to hustle to the bathroom with their hands over their mouths. They've probably even read about worse behavior by Larkin's peers—a letter in response to Amis's article, for example, asserts that Anne Sexton's "emotional and sexual abuse of her daughter, Linda, is surely more 'unforgivable' than Larkin's hole-in-corner bigotry and misogyny."

Again, though, the difference lies in our reading habits. We are unlikely ever to see ourselves in Sexton's poems—her work insists on being the product of an unrepresentative consciousness. (This is why readers are almost never disgusted by confessional poetry: someone who is confessing to us is unlikely also to be us.) Larkin's poetry, however, is more determined to engage the reader's sympathy than the work of any other major twentieth-century poet. His diction, his syntax, his calculated shifts from the first person to the third person plural, his tone, his humor, even (as Stephen Burt has pointed out) his use of the word "fuck"—all of these factors encourage the reader to take sides with Larkin's speakers, despite the unappealing conclusions that those speakers often reach. Think of the beginning of "Sad Steps":

> *Groping back to bed after a piss*
> *I part think curtains, and am startled by*
> *The rapid clouds, the moon's cleanliness.*
>
> *Four o'clock; wedge-shadowed gardens lie*
> *Under a cavernous, a wind-picked sky.*
> *There's something laughable about this.*

The colloquial language immediately links speaker and reader—we may not all know what Pound means by "Zeus lies

in Ceres' bosom," but we have certainly taken a piss. This is the
Larkin persona at work: the protagonist remains quirky (or
cranky) enough to be distinct, yet average enough to establish a
rapport with the typical reader.

That rapport, which involves a careful manipulation of distance, is Larkin's greatest achievement. In the average Larkin
poem, not only is the reader encouraged to identify with the
speaker, but the distinction between the poet and the speaker
is blurred—an effect so subtle that many critics simply assume
that the speaker of, say, "Dockery and Son" is Larkin himself. As Larkin readers know, that poem involves a speaker who
attends a funeral for a former college classmate named Dockery,
and who afterward reflects on the paths that led them to different ends—"For Dockery a son, for me nothing." Prior to the
publication of the biography and *Selected Letters*, the poem
was taken by some critics to be a relatively straightforward tran-
scription of Larkin's own thoughts, proceeding from ruefully
observed social detail to philosophical conclusion without complication. After Larkin's dirty laundry was aired, this critical
misconception wasn't corrected; instead it was duplicated—but
in reverse. In an article published shortly after the biography
and *Selected Letters*, Marjorie Perloff, ordinarily a penetrating
and persuasive reader, offered her new interpretation of "Dockery and Son":

> To invent characters named Dockery and Son and then
> to allow those characters no role but to represent the
> bourgeois choice of "increase," is itself, I would argue,

a form of prejudice very like the racism, sexism, or xe-
nophobia Larkin practiced in his life.

There are many profound problems with this theory, but
the most obvious is that Perloff, like Larkin's early critics, falla-
ciously connects the poet himself to one technical aspect of the
poem at the expense of all the others. Why, for example, can we
find the truth about Larkin's attitude toward other people in the
speaker's alleged attitude toward Dockery but not in the poem's
relatively simple diction, straightforward syntax, and accommo-
dating tone? After all, those qualities could be seen as generous
and democratic. Perloff elsewhere says that Larkin was "eager to
have the hypothetical reader sympathize" with him, and she be-
littles him for this supposed eagerness. But isn't the desire to be
understood by other people a way of empowering those people?
Don't Larkin's poems demonstrate nothing so much as the desire to belong—to someone, anyone?

Larkin is often called a "poet of solitude," but he doesn't
write out of solitude (as does, say, Stevens), but rather about
solitude. His poetry is obsessed with acceptance and exclusion,
and consequently also with abnormality and its attendant emotions, shame and disgust ("Love again: wanking at ten past
three"). As Nussbaum tells us, "All societies contain a composite
image of the 'normal' person that is actually embodied, as a
whole, by more or less nobody. . . . People who lack any of those
desirable characteristics are made to feel shame; so more or less
all of us feel shame about something." When Larkin's defenders
and detractors find themselves debating whether the poet can

speak "for us"—whether he is, in essence, "normal"—they're acting out a script written by the poet himself, who all along has been less interested in aphoristic wisdom than in dramatizing the individual's emotional relationship to the group. Larkin's poems demand a personal connection, and responding to them with disgust is every bit as personal as responding to them with love. Pound, in many ways a less complicated poet than Larkin, never forces us to relate to art in this way—when we ask, in reference to Pound, "Can a bad man be a good poet?" we aren't covertly wondering about our own normalcy. But when we ask the same question about Larkin, we're often really saying, "Could we too be anything like this?" He needs to be bad so we can stay good.

IV.

THIS THEATRICAL ELEMENT IN Larkin's writing is related to what we might call the second law of poetic morality: how a poet acts can be as important as what he does. We want poets to play particular roles, and we're less forgiving of poets' misbehavior if the misconduct also seems to be a departure from these personae. In this, we're not unlike William Bennett, the famous moralist, Clinton assailant, and slots player. As Richard Posner writes in *An Affair of State*, his book on the Clinton impeachment scandal,

> Bennett wants the nation's chief executive to behave
> and present himself in such a way as will make him an

exemplary figure. . . . Bennett desires this not because
a better performance in the head of state role might
enhance a President's effectiveness as the head of the
government, but because a President who personifies
the nation's moral aspirations can inspire the people to
be better. Bennett, the stern moralist, has at root a theatrical conception of the Presidency.

Most of us—the wise and tolerant poetry reading
audience—have a similarly theatrical view of the Poet. Admittedly, the role we have in mind isn't the same as the part Bennett
wanted the president to play, but it is a role—it has nothing to do
with the basic function of a poet, which presumably is to write
poetry. Of course, this kind of thinking has more to do with gut
impulses than measured conclusions. When we think carefully
about who poets actually are, and what they actually do, and
who actually listens to them, then our ideas about the Poet tend
to be less theatrical. But the point is that we usually don't think
carefully; we're fans, and unexamined assumptions are nine-
tenths of the joy of fandom. The contemporary poetry reader's
view of the Poet therefore remains a combination of old and
sometimes discordant ideas: the Poet is immensely learned (Eliot) but also an innocent (Blake) and possibly a kind of idiot
(Plato); he can't help but speak the truth (Plato again), although
his natural territory is fiction (Stevens); he has a heroic public voice (Emerson), despite being deeply private (Dickinson);
and he's a kind of aristocrat (Shelley), yet still a common man
who understands common concerns (Whitman). Generally

speaking, we want poets to be active and righteous; if only sub-consciously, we often agree with Carlyle that "the Poet who could merely sit on a chair, and compose stanzas, would never make a stanza worth much."

These ideas may seem scattershot, but they're often specifi-cally related to the way we interpret poets' misbehavior. Take Larkin's alleged misogyny, for example. Assume for the moment that the case against the poet could be stated as follows: he punched his first wife in the face and broke her nose, threw a subsequent lover on the floor and tried to strangle her, deserted his second wife and their child for another woman, and then appropriated his second wife's letters (written under the stress and pain of desertion) into a book of poems addressed to his third wife. Given this dismal record, you could see why some critics would be tempted to accuse Larkin of hating women, no matter how pleasant his poems were.

But the above incidents weren't part of Larkin's life; they were part of Robert Lowell's (the last was borrowed from Adri-enne Rich's review of Lowell's later books). Collected versions of both Larkin's and Lowell's poems were released this year; many of Larkin's major print reviews involved the word "mi-sogyny," but not one of Lowell's did. The point here is not to suggest that Lowell should have been called a misogynist—he shouldn't—but to show that we view different poets' behavior differently, depending on the way in which the misbehavior seems related either to the poet's art or to one of our ideas about the Poet. In this case, Lowell's work often has to do with mad-ness, excess, and violence, so it isn't particularly surprising to find that he could be mad, bad, and dangerous to know. And as most recent reviews of Lowell's *Collected Poems* demonstrate, critics are still at least as in love with an idea of Lowell as they are with his poems. Lowell performed a version of the Poet that we like—that of the raging, aristocratic hero—and he never broke character. Larkin played a part we thought we might like—the common man—yet he did things we don't want to think are common at all. That, we find hard to forgive.

V.

BUT WOULD WE REALLY want Larkin to be forgiven? When we ask, "Can a bad man be a good poet?" we're also reinforcing our belief that poetry is an active moral force: that it can make things happen. Every day we spend arguing over a poet's dirty doings is a day in which the writer in question avoids the oblivion of mild approval—we give far more power to poets when we consider them too wicked to be read than when we find them too boring to be bothered with. Perhaps, then, the most disturbing thing about the question of bad men and good poetry is how seldom those men turn out to be women. We might say that's because the great female poets of the twentieth century have been, on the whole, pretty nice people, at least as compared to the men. We might also suggest that female poets are less vulnerable to delusions of Shelleyhood and hence less inclined to behave badly for no reason. But what about Plath? Or Millay? Or Sexton? It seems that some part of us (but, now, who are "we"?) may still be reluctant to accept the idea that female

writers can be just as lousy as men—and, by extension, just as
good as men. It may seem perverse to want to see a critic argue
for the immorality of Elizabeth Bishop, but wouldn't that be
preferable to William Logan's recent description of her work (in
a review of Robert Lowell, no less) as "charming and endlessly
resourceful. . . . So much charm and not a particle of intellect"?
Or Adam Kirsch's description of her poetry (also in a Lowell
review) as "modest"? Are we comfortable with the idea that
Pound, Larkin, and Lowell are capable of sin but that Bishop is
capable only of being charming? Perhaps when we're making
our judgments—and carefully not making our judgments—we
should bear in mind the wisdom of someone who thought more
about morality than most of us, Friedrich Nietzsche: "It is not
enough to possess a talent: one must also possess your permission to possess it—eh, my friends?"

THE AGE OF CITATION

I magine that this essay began not with the sentence you're reading but with the following observation, attributed to Wittgenstein: "A picture held us captive. And we could not get outside it, for it lay in our language and language seemed to repeat it to us inexorably." A little oblique for an opening gambit, you might think, but presumably it will pay off shortly. Imagine further, however, that the Wittgenstein quotation was immediately followed by quotes from Simone Weil, the Upanishads, and the Hungarian poet György Petri. At this point, you might find yourself wondering, "Okay, when is the actual author going to actually give me something he actually wrote?"

Right now, actually. And it is this: the above scenario is one that occurs with surprising frequency in books of contemporary poetry. Consider Liz Waldner's recent collection, *Trust*. First we're presented with epigraphs from Lewis Carroll and Karl Marx that are presumably meant to cover the book as a whole;

then we have an epigraph from Samuel Johnson that's meant to apply to section 1; and, finally, we have an epigraph from Plato's *Symposium* in the first poem. That's four writers we've encountered before we've read one line from the author.

To be fair to Waldner, this tally is by no means unusual: a quick survey of recent collections on my bookshelf yields opening pronouncements from Wallace Stevens, Walter Benjamin, Shakespeare, Karl Marx (again), James Schuyler, Don De-Lillo, Gertrude Stein, Chekhov, Ovid, Dickinson, Sappho, the *Wumen guan*, Theodore Roethke, and the eighteenth-century art historian Johann Joachim Winckelmann. Randall Jarrell said his generation lived in the age of criticism; we apparently live in the age of citation.

Why is that? In part, our abundance of epigraphs is simply a function of poets doing what poets have always done. Chaucer opened "The Knight's Tale" with a quotation from the Roman poet Publius Papinius Statius; Alexander Pope began the 1743 version of *The Dunciad* with an epigraph from Ovid; and Keats prefaced his *Poems* with a quotation from Spenser (as well as a drawing of Shakespeare's head). But while epigraphs have always been a part of poetic tradition, they do seem to be unusually thick on the ground these days, and not just in America. As the Canadian poet and critic Carmine Starnino wryly noted in the January issue of *Poetry* magazine, "Lately it seems no book of Canadian poetry can be put to bed without an epigraph to tuck it in."

Some of the credit (or blame) for this peculiar ubiquity probably belongs to the continuing and often underestimated influence of T. S. Eliot. Eliot is, after all, the master quotation dispenser of Anglo-American letters, with almost half the poems of his maturity sporting some preliminary wisdom. *The Waste Land*, for instance, begins with the following excerpt from Petronius, which Eliot helpfully declines to translate: "Nam Sibyllam quidem Cumis ego ipse oculis meis vidi in ampulla pendere, et cum illi pueri dicerent: Στβμλλ τί Θέλεις; respondebat illa: άπσΘνειν Θελω." (Roughly, "Sorry about *Cats*.") Along with his sidekick Pound, Eliot inspired a generation of midcentury poets to offer up little appetizers from the illustrious dead, and it's interesting to see so many poets today working from the same menu.

But if the epigraph's prevalence is a product of history, it also reflects the specific needs of our own literary moment. In *Paratexts: Thresholds of Interpretation*, the theorist Gérard Genette claims four basic functions for epigraphs. The first two are straightforward: an epigraph can comment on the title of a given work, or it can apply to the work's body. But after that, matters get a little more "oblique," as Genette diplomatically puts it. For one thing, he says of the epigraph, "Very often the main thing is not what it says but who its author is, plus the sense of indirect backing that its presence at the edge of a text gives rise to." The point, then, isn't Karl Marx's wisdom; it's Karl Marx. In addition, the epigraph can be "a signal . . . of culture, a password of intellectuality." With it, Genette says, the author "chooses his peers and thus his place in the pantheon." So if you were wondering where my work belongs in the greater scheme of things, look right here: Pascal, Dickinson!

That last function is the most relevant one for contemporary poetry. Like all literary genres, poetry is constantly in the business of positioning itself—of reminding us what poems are and how they're to be read. And as Eliot understood, epigraphs can assist in this process by acting as a shorthand for tradition. But traditions aren't all the same size or shape. When T. S. Eliot quotes Dante and Heraclitus, it's because Eliot wants to be seen as binding together thousands of years of Western culture. When a contemporary poet quotes the same authors, however, it's more likely that he wants to be seen (whether he knows it or not) as T. S. Eliot. That's not a bad thing, of course. But it does reflect a change in the way that Eliot's signature device is being deployed: once a symbol of ambition, the epigraph is now more likely to be an indication of community. It tells us less about whom a poet hopes to equal and more about where he'd like to hang out.

In this sense, the epigraph reflects a larger trend in American poetry. Partly as a result of the art form's academic attachment, poets are increasingly knit together in complicated patterns based on mentorship, instruction, or just basic university proximity. These structures can encourage a kind of association via pedigree that greatly resembles association via epigraph. In *Laureates and Heretics: Six Careers in American Poetry*, for example, the critic Robert Archambeau smartly traces poets including Robert Pinsky and Robert Hass through their connection to Yvor Winters at Stanford. It's a project that wouldn't work (or at least not quite so well) with Eliot or Frost or Williams, simply because times have changed. That said, some of the interdependence in today's poetry world isn't a function of modernity but of insecurity, which is why you'll occasionally find writers claiming to be, for example, fourth-generation New York school poets, as if latching on to your great-grandfather's avant-garde were something to be proud of, rather than sheepish about. Presumably it feels better to be a poet carrying on a venerated tradition than just a plain old poet talking to the void.

Which brings us, finally, to the question of audience. As Genette points out, the epigraph is often a token of literary fashion, but because fashions vary from group to group, the ones you follow say a great deal about whom you expect to meet. So it's interesting that Eliot himself appears so rarely in contemporary poetic epigraphs, despite his responsibility for their popularity. Indeed, to judge again from a quick tour of my bookshelf, Wallace Stevens beats Eliot by a count of something like fifteen to none. That disparity has nothing to do with the relative abilities of the two poets (both are brilliant) and everything to do with the expectations of the contemporary poetry world, in which Stevens has been a fashionable name to drop for decades, whereas Eliot . . . well, weren't we sick of him by 1940? When poets quote Stevens but not Eliot (or Frost, for that matter), the implication is they expect a potential reader to be the sort of person who considers Stevens the Acceptable Name.

And yet Eliot is one of the few poets the average reader actually knows. So the contemporary poet can please either the universe he inhabits (a smart thing to do, as it's the only one he can be sure of) or he can play to the taste of an audience that probably doesn't exist. It's a hard choice. And it very likely explains one of the more distinctive and inevitable epigraphic tactics of our era, which you might call the Janus approach. This is when a poet pairs epigraphs from very different cultural realms, as when William Matthews opened his 1995 collection *Time & Money* with quotes from Stevens (naturally) and Fats Waller ("One never knows, do one?"). The quotes have little to do with each other, or with the book as a whole, but there's a wistfulness in their pairing that recalls the delicate yearning for connection of a Victorian poet circa 1850. It's almost enough to make you think that time present and time past might both be present in time future. As someone may have said.

VENDLER'S YEATS

The critic is the only artist who depends entirely upon another art form, which means that part of his job is to determine the nature of that relationship. Should he be an advocate? A policeman? A curator? A hanging judge? A mostly loyal but occasionally snippy personal assistant? The decision is an unconscious one, perhaps, but once it's made, the critic's writing will be colored by his chosen role in the same way that our voices carry the accents of our birthplaces.

Helen Vendler is one of the most powerful poetry critics of our time, and her relationship with her art is as simple as it is peculiar: She's a steward. If contemporary poetry were a great manor house, then Vendler would be its long-serving and unshakable manager, monitoring the stable hands, restocking the wine cellar, preventing the chambermaids from swiping the jewelry, and, above all, keeping immaculate the high chambers to which the lords and ladies retire at nightfall. It's an unusual position—unlike Vendler, most poetry critics are poets themselves—and it comes with its own curious set of virtues and vices. On one hand, Vendler is an astonishingly thorough and patient reader whose devotion has influenced the way we read Stevens, Herbert, Shakespeare, and many others. On the other hand, her work occasionally demonstrates the flaws that come from feeling that one is obligated to ensure the right poets are read the right way.

W. B. Yeats is, of course, one of the rightest poets imaginable. Vendler's new book, *Our Secret Discipline: Yeats and Lyric Form*, is an attempt to explain, as she puts it, "the inner and outer formal choices Yeats made, the cultural significance his forms bore for him, [and] the way his forms . . . became the material body of his thoughts and emotions." That's no small task: Yeats was a technician's technician whose massive output is a blizzard of stanza shapes and metrical variations. Fortunately, Vendler relishes the nitty-gritty of douzains and dizains, and the result is a meticulous, enlightening, and strangely flawed study that adds plenty to the Yeats canon. If you're looking for a general introduction to the poet, this isn't the book for you (it's 375 pages and drier than chalk dust), but scholars will find years of material here. Vendler's method is straightforward: each chapter takes up one of Yeats's potential formal quandaries—the Byzantium poems, the sonnets, the sequences, and so forth—and then attempts to determine why and how Yeats made the technical choices he did, often with helpful reference to biographical or historical facts.

The results can be impressive. Vendler is especially

persuasive when tracing the evolution of a poem; one of the book's first studies is a detailed analysis of "After Long Silence" in which Vendler carefully walks us through Yeats's development of the poem, in particular the lines, "Unfriendly lamplight hid under its shade, / The curtains drawn upon unfriendly night." She's also very good at explaining what different forms meant to Yeats. In her discussion of the twelve-poem sequence "Supernatural Songs," for instance, Vendler notes that the sequence ends with a Shakespearean sonnet that seems at odds with the more primitive forms that precede it. But for Yeats, as she explains, the sonnet represents an ultimate refinement of artistic poise, which makes it the perfect vehicle to reflect the tension between "ascetic life" and "sexual life" that animates the entire sequence. It's an intriguing and well-argued point.

Yet while there's much to admire in *Our Secret Discipline*, there are also considerable problems with it (aside from the inadvertently whips-and-cuffs title). In general, these problems stem from the same source: Vendler treats poems as if their elements could be isolated and measured for expressiveness. For instance, she argues on several occasions that a particular form is ideal because when the poem is "rewritten" in another form, it sounds "off." So she offers a version of "Easter, 1916" in tetrameter quatrains ("I have met them at close of every day / Coming abroad with vivid faces"), and then claims that "we recognize the contrast between the rapidity and intensity of the trimeter quick-march . . . and the more sedulous and deliberate step of such tetrameters." Well, maybe. But it's more likely that we "recognize the contrast" simply because we're familiar with Yeats's poem as it currently exists (and, of course, had Yeats wanted to express the same concepts in tetrameter, he'd likely have used completely different words).

Along the same lines, Vendler repeatedly commits variations on what has been called "the enactment fallacy." Basically, this is the assignment of meaning to technical aspects of poetry that those aspects don't necessarily possess. For example, in an otherwise excellent discussion of Yeats's use of ottava rima (a type of eight-line stanza), Vendler attributes great effect to "the pacing" allegedly created by "a fierce set of enjambments" followed by a "violent drop" in the fourth stanza of the poem "Nineteen Hundred and Nineteen." Here's the stanza in question:

> *Now days are dragon-ridden, the nightmare*
> *Rides upon sleep: a drunken soldiery*
> *Can leave the mother, murdered at her door,*
> *To crawl in her own blood, and go scot-free;*
> *The night can sweat with terror as before*
> *We pieced our thoughts into philosophy,*
> *And planned to bring the world under a rule,*
> *Who are but weasels fighting in a hole.*

"With each new verbal or participial theater of action of the stanza," Vendler writes, "there arrives a new agent . . . making the clauses scramble helter-skelter after one another. The headlong pace is crucial." Since the stanza involves words like

"dragon," "nightmare," "murdered," "blood," and "fighting,"
it's easy to see what she's thinking here. But to make a more
modest use of Vendler's rewriting trick above, what if we kept
the same enjambments, syntax, rhyme scheme, and basic rhythm
yet changed some of the words? We might get this (with apolo-
gies to I. A. Richards for adapting one of his examples):

> *Now days are slow and easy, the summer*
> *Sighs into fall: a purring bumblebee*
> *Can leave the flower, softened to a blur,*
> *To soak in the noon sun, and fly carefree;*
> *The night can breathe with pleasure as once more*
> *We weave our visions into poetry*
> *And seek to bring our thoughts under a rule,*
> *Who are the mindful servants of the soul.*

Not so "helter-skelter" now, is it? In a book review or essay,
committing this particular fallacy is a minor error. Most critics
do it regularly (I certainly have). In a book that sets out to explain why a poet makes particular formal choices, however, the
mistake is more serious, because it replaces the complex relationships among a poem's elements with just-so stories in which
it always turns out—surprise!—that meaning has been mirrored by shape and sound. Think of it this way: we don't enjoy a
bowl of gumbo because it "feels" exactly the way it "tastes";
rather, we find the combination of "taste" and "feel" pleasing.
Similarly, a particular stanza arrangement can reinforce our

experience of a poem (part of which is the poem's semantic meaning), but only because that arrangement is working in harmony with the poem's other aspects.

If *Our Secret Discipline* isn't as strong as it could be, then, it's because Vendler has thought deeply about Yeats's use of form but not about form apart from Yeats. And this isn't surprising, really—her great strength has always been her close reading of individual poets. If that causes her occasionally to find correspondences that don't exist, well, what steward hasn't wanted to find a world perfected in the venerable stones of the master's great house?

HIT PARADE

In late 2002, the radio host Garrison Keillor committed an act of inadvertent but undeniable depravity: he published a poetry anthology for average readers that sold pretty well. Anthologies are often troubling for poets (who likes being left out?), and many serious writers are ambivalent about popular success, but the combination of these concerns—a popular anthology—can create a near perfect storm of psychic distress.

In the case of Keillor's collection, the modestly titled *Good Poems*, the trouble came to a head in a rare double review in the April 2004 issue of *Poetry* magazine. The first review, by the poet and critic Dana Gioia, was a reasonable and amiable appraisal that said, in essence, this book is surprisingly okay. The second, by the poet August Kleinzahler, was a different story— or as they might say in Lake Wobegon, a whole 'nother pan of casserole. Kleinzahler began by suggesting Keillor be locked in a Quonset hut and tortured to convince him never again to stray from "Lutheran bake sales" into the realm of art. After that, Kleinzahler got mean. He claimed that Keillor "makes no demands on his audiences, none whatsoever." He accused him of "appalling taste," of hosting an "execrable" show, of compiling a "rotten collection," and of having a weird speaking voice ("that treacly baritone, which occasionally releases into a high-pitched, breathless tremolo"). Not content simply to wallop Keillor, Kleinzahler then turned his megaphone on every target within soapbox range, accusing the MFA system of being filled with "dispirited, compromised mediocrities" and asserting that "American poetry is now an international joke."

It was a performance to savor. According to Christian Wiman, *Poetry*'s editor, the response to the double review— mostly to Kleinzahler's polemic—was "enormous." The magazine ran over a dozen letters from readers about the reviews ("just the tip of the iceberg"), with reactions ranging from amusement ("funny and true") to annoyance ("tired and cliché") to double annoyance ("I need look no farther than *Poetry* magazine to find a reason for poetry's decline"). The controversy hit the Internet, and later became the focus of David Lehman's introductory comments for *The Best American Poetry 2005*. As Lehman wrote, "It was as if one of the two reviews of *Good Poems* was in favor of civilization and one in favor of its discontents; as if one spoke with the adjudicating voice of the ego, while the other let loose with the rebellious rant of the id."

Whatever Freud might think of that comparison, Keillor doesn't seem to have been too troubled by all the shouting, because *Good Poems* has now been joined by a sibling anthology,

Good Poems for Hard Times. Like its predecessor, *Good Poems for Hard Times* consists of about three hundred poems previously read on Keillor's public radio show *The Writer's Almanac* and sorted into thematic sections. The poems themselves range from classics of English verse (Marvell's "Thoughts in a Garden") to the best of modern American writing (Elizabeth Bishop's "At the Fishhouses") to a large number of amiable and frequently forgettable contemporary efforts. In his unabashedly personal introduction, Keillor recounts his childhood theft of a poetry anthology from a department store, talks about how his dad's work as a carpenter had "the cadence and fervor of poetry," and delivers a grumpy-old-man rant about the "shallow knowingness" of today's culture, as opposed to the truehearted-ness he finds in Poetryland. According to Keillor: "Poetry is the last preserve of honest speech. . . . All that matters about poetry to me now is directness and clarity and truthfulness. All that is twittery and lit'ry: no thanks, pal." Well, fair enough, pal. Of course, in the literary world directness and clarity and truthfulness are themselves matters of artifice, but a man is entitled to his preferences. There's plenty to admire about this anthology and the spirit in which it was undertaken.

On the other hand, there's also plenty to question. The most obvious problem with *Good Poems for Hard Times* is that it proposes that "the meaning of poetry is to give courage." That is not the meaning of poetry; that is the meaning of Scotch. The meaning of poetry is poetry. But a more subtle and intractable difficulty is that Keillor's taste isn't just limited, it's limited within its limitations. He likes plainspoken writing that is long on sentiment, short on surface complication—a defensible aesthetic, if one that occasionally condescends to its subject matter and audience. But rather than emphasizing the strongest writers in this mode (James Wright and Sterling Brown, for instance), Keillor favors soggy tough guys like Raymond Carver and Charles Bukowski, as well as a host of small-scale epiphany manufacturers, almost all of whom appear to be, as they say, white. (Lake Wobegon, where all the children are above average, and all the colored people are in somebody else's anthology.) Moreover, you could hold nine of Kleinzahler's Lutheran bake sales in the gap between the best and worst poets in these collections, a fact that seems to bother their editor not one bit. Indeed, "The pleasure of making this book," Keillor wrote in *Good Poems*, "is the chance to put poets such as Jennifer Michael Hecht and C. G. Hanzlicek and April Lindner and Ginger Andrews and Louis Jenkins into a club with Frost and Dickinson and Burns and Shakespeare." The comparison is unnecessary and silly. One of the more interesting things about Keillor's project is that it quietly emphasizes poems over poets—a social, craft-centered approach that has fallen by the wayside in the age of Harold Bloom. But when Keillor claims to be putting Ginger Andrews "into a club with Frost" (instead of a good poem by Andrews beside a good poem by Frost), he not only undermines his credibility as an editor; he sets Andrews up for an annihilating failure.

So which way do we turn? Do we agree with Kleinzahler that art is meant to be an entertainment for the select few, by the select few? Or do we sign on with Keillor and embrace poetry as a means of creating a common life, even if we lose a few high-brow writers along the way? The truth is, it was never a real choice to begin with—a fact neatly demonstrated by the extent to which Keillor's and Kleinzahler's own careers are mixtures of high and low, lone wolf and average bear. After all, Keillor may praise the homely world of Wobegon, but he is a sophisticated writer with *New Yorker* credentials and possesses an angry wit rarely heard on Main Street. Similarly, Kleinzahler isn't anyone's idea of an avant-garde poet; his work is published by a major house and is easily appreciated by a smart but untrained reader. This isn't real confrontation; it's Narcissus chewing out his own reflection.

Yet even if the arguments are taken at face value, both Keillor (playing populist) and Kleinzahler (playing elitist) are hoping to hold back waters that can't be dammed. When Keillor writes that poetry "is entirely created by peasants" and that "the intensity of poetry . . . is not meant for the triumphant executive, but for people in a jam—you and me," he's assuming that poetry is a tool to be used, rather than a force capable of doing a little using of its own, not all of it wholesome. And he's assuming, along the same lines, that "you and me" are bound to like a certain kind of thing, that "we" won't turn out to be as strange and unknowable as all those "lit'ry" poems out there. Similarly, as a talented poet, Kleinzahler would like to believe that poetry is split between "real originality" and pointless mediocrity; in an art so divided, there's little doubt where a strong writer like Kleinzahler would end up. But great poets often produce mediocre work, bad poets can be surprisingly good, and very good poets are frequently no better than consistently above average—all of which is to say that it's far more difficult to isolate "great poetry" than Kleinzahler (and most critics) might like to believe. We're forced to live with a chaos of styles and a muddle of best guesses. This makes everyone uncomfortable; we're much happier when we can have well-worn arguments about populism and elitism, about *Good Poems* and high brows. But what Elizabeth Bishop once said about knowledge may be equally said of poetry itself, that it is "dark, salt, clear, moving, utterly free"; not a sure matter of sides, but a fleeting balance of currents. The best we can do—the best we have ever been able to do—when faced with the words "good poems" in a book's title, is to turn the page hoping to say yes they are, or yes they were, or yes (believe it or not) they will be.

THE STYLE

OF LUIS DE GÓNGORA

"But what is this poem about?" This dread question stalks almost every poetry classroom, and it's vanquished only to return with a tenacity that would intimidate Michael Myers. Most recently, Ernie Lepore, a professor at Rutgers, took a swing at it in the *New York Times*'s philosophy blog, *The Stone*. Lepore is interested in what's sometimes called "the heresy of paraphrase"—the idea that what a poem is really about is best represented by the poem itself. He concludes that while the usual reasoning behind the heresy claim is suspect, the idea itself is basically right. Poetry, Lepore argues, is not just about its paraphrasable data (and what we might make of that data) but also about the way that data is articulated. So Frost's "Mending Wall" is about a not-so-bright farmer, a bunch of rocks, and their various symbolic accouterments; yet it's also about the break between the word "balance" in line 18 and "Stay" in line 19.

Lepore's conclusions have the side effect of illuminating an

essential point about style. If we come to believe—either because of intuition or a philosopher's reasoning—that poetry is
distinguished by its emphasis on vehicles of articulation, then
we may find ourselves thinking that poetry highlighting extremities of form, sound, or typography is more "poetic" than poetry
that works differently. And in practice this is indeed what we
often do. For example, a phrase like "Words of the fragrant por-
tals, dimly-starred" sounds like poetry to most people in a way
that a phrase like "Now when I walk around at lunchtime" does
not. Yet both lines come from poems (by Wallace Stevens and
Frank O'Hara, respectively) and are therefore poetic to the
same degree. It's a subtle but important point, and it helps explain why so many debates over the meaning of poetry—in particular, debates over the perceived difficulty or simplicity of
poetry—are often really arguments over style.

And these arguments occur over and over again. Consider the case of Luis de Góngora, whose major long poem, *The
Solitudes*, has recently been translated by Edith Grossman.
Góngora is one of the most significant figures in Spanish early
modern literature—he was born in 1561, three years before
Shakespeare—and his work is generally associated with the idea
that, as Grossman puts it in her foreword, "language itself, not
its emotive referent or expressive content, is the intrinsic aesthetic component of poetry." As one might expect, then, his poetry is ornate and occasionally impenetrable, thick with classical
allusions and metaphors sprawling into one another like rose-
bushes planted too closely. This approach earned Góngora the

enmity of perhaps his most talented contemporary, Francisco de Quevedo, whose own work was distinguished by its wit, plain diction, and fencer's balance. Naturally, the two poets discussed their differences in the measured tones typically assumed by great artists, which is to say, Quevedo wrote a sonnet making fun of Góngora's nose.

To an extent, the view that Góngora was especially interested in "language itself" reflects the misunderstanding discussed above, which we might call the pure poetry fallacy. The truth is, every poem is about its own manner of expression, no matter how limpid that articulation may seem. One can foreground this peculiar fact, as Góngora does with his outrageous layers of verbal frosting, or one can obscure it, as Quevedo does. But these are just different tactics deployed toward the same end: creating a poem that's interesting to read and that says more than its words mean.

Fortunately, *The Solitudes* is intriguing (if frequently baffling) even in translation. Góngora intended the poem to be in four parts, but only two sections, of roughly a thousand lines apiece, exist, the second of which is unfinished. The plot, such as it is, is fairly straightforward. In the first part, a young man is shipwrecked; he meets a band of shepherds (in the countryside of the late sixteenth-century poem, you couldn't swing a stick without clobbering twenty-five dubiously employed shepherds); and he attends a rural wedding. In the second part, the same young man loiters with a group of fishermen before sighting some noblemen hunting with falcons. But plot doesn't tell you much about *The Solitudes*, because the true point of the poem is style. And what a style it is. Here is Góngora describing, as they pass, part of the rural company with which his pilgrim shelters:

> *And so they all passed by, and in good order*
> *as at the equinox we see furrowing*
> > *through oceans of open air*
> > *not flights of galley ships*
> > *but flocks of swift-sailing cranes,*
> *moons perhaps waxing, perhaps on the wane*
> > *their most distant extremes,*
> *perhaps forming letters on the pellucid*
> > *paper of the heavens with*
> *the quill feathers of their flight.*

If you're counting metaphors, the people are walking by like (1) a group of cranes flying through the air, which could be compared to (2) galleys passing over the ocean, which is (2a) like the sky, as the ends of the cranes' formations expand and contract (3) like the moon and also seem (4) to create writing across the sky with their feathers, which are (5) like quills. Mind you, this is just a bunch of guys walking among some trees near a stream. Reading Góngora is like traveling by hot-air balloon—you'll get somewhere eventually, but all the pleasure is in the elevation, and occasional vertigo.

The challenges in translating a writer like this are obviously considerable. Given these difficulties, Grossman's version is

remarkably lucid, and her lines often achieve a mesmerizing
shimmer that would surely have pleased her subject. Góngora's
poem was written in a form called the *silva*, which consists of
stanzas of varying length using seven- and eleven-syllable lines,
most of which are rhymed. Grossman has forgone rhyme but
kept the basic syllabic structure, and her translation generally
sticks close to Góngora's text. (This is in slight contrast to the
approach taken by John Dent-Young, whose looser version of
the "First Solitude" in his *Selected Poems of Luis de Góngora*
provides a nice accompaniment to Grossman's interpretation.)
There are also some very necessary footnotes, my favorite of
which is probably the one that frankly admits, "The word 'there'
is ambiguous." It's hard to imagine a better effort to capture a
poem that was difficult in Góngora's time and teeters on the
edge of impossible in our own.

But like most difficult poems, this one is often preoccupied
with simplicity. This shouldn't surprise us where Góngora is
concerned; as Alberto Manguel points out in his introduction to
the translation, Góngora often departs from his baroque style to
write with "heartbreaking plainness." Yet the fascination of
what's simple (as Yeats might put it) often characterizes difficult
poetry more generally. Writing around the same time as Góngora, George Herbert asks, in "Jordan (I)," why certain poets
write as if everything must "be veil'd, while he that reads, di-
vines,/Catching the sense at two removes?" And he contrasts
this with his own decision to "plainly say, *My God, My King*."
But the intentional irony is that for all the straightforwardness

of its conclusion, "Jordan (I)" involves an impressive and sophisticated manipulation of metaphors and rhymes. Plainly saying entails not plainly saying, which is perhaps why even our cleverest philosophers grapple with the question of what poetry is about, what it means for an art form to manage such complicated simplicity, such difficult ease.

VIRTUOSITY

The question for every performer is how to pull a crowd, and the answer is usually assumed to be, "Do something very, very well." But it could also be, "Do something very, very badly." Consider, for instance, two species of video that have been astoundingly popular on aggregating sites for the past fifteen years. The first is what I think of as the technical extravaganza. These videos are recordings of musicians (generally young musicians) playing torrid versions of extremely difficult classical or heavy metal songs, often in imitation of one another. The musicians typically deemphasize their faces—or obscure them entirely by, say, looking down and wearing a baseball cap—and the camera lingers on hands and feet, on strings and pedals. The prototypical example here is "Canon Rock," a wizardly electric guitar take on Pachelbel's Canon that has been viewed over nineteen million times. The second sort of video is the fail, which in its purest form is a pratfall—for instance, a person trying to jump onto a moving treadmill and being sent flying. The most popular videos of this kind don't involve serious injury, and while the episode is obviously embarrassing for the person in question, that embarrassment seems dispersed into a cloud of universalized humiliation: the failure itself is more important than the fact that this person in particular has been upended. (The progenitor of the Internet fail is the television show *America's Funniest Home Videos*, and that "America" is notable.)

So we like to see people succeeding, and we like to see people falling flat. We like to see plans brought to fruition and plans bursting like balloons. We like to be confirmed in our expectations, and we like to be startled. But there's more to it than that—we like to see individual success in which the identity of the person doing the succeeding somehow becomes effaced, and we like to see individual failure in a way that speaks to a generalized (or generalizable) sense of humanity. We want to see the tree as a forest, and the forest as a tree. And this, I think, says something odd but essential about the concept of poetic technique and, more specifically, about technique's golden child, virtuosity.

■ ■ ■

"Virtuosity" is now a generic term for excellence of nearly any sort ("Richard Moxon: A virtuoso of vaccinology," announces an article in the *Lancet*), but for much of the nineteenth and twentieth centuries, it was a hotly disputed subject in the world of classical music. "A distinctive feature of present-day musical life," wrote the French musicologist Marc Pincherle in 1949, "is the almost constant controversy stirred up by virtuosity." The problem, basically, was showing off. Nonimprovised music always involves a kind of overlay: there is the score, and then there is the rendition of the score. In that divide lies the potential for considerable tension, especially if the instrumentalist comes to regard his own skill as deserving the spotlight. (As anyone who has ever heard an over-the-top rendition of "The Star-Spangled Banner" knows, it's often all too easy to distinguish the singer from the song, whatever Yeats may have thought.)

At various points in the long history of Western music, the idea of virtuosity has resided more on one side of this division than the other, but by the late eighteenth century, the title "virtuoso" had settled on the performer. This didn't sit well with composers who were not themselves great instrumentalists. Wagner, for example, complained:

> The highest merit of the executant artist, the Virtuoso, would . . . consist in a pure and perfect reproduction of that thought of the composer's; a reproduction only to be ensured by genuine fathering of his intentions, and consequently by total abstinence from all inventions of one's own. . . . Unfortunately however, this very reasonable demand runs counter to all the conditions under which artistic products win the favour of the public. This latter's first and keenest curiosity is addressed to art-dexterity; delight in that is the only road to notice

of the work itself. Who can blame the public for it? Is it not the very tyrant whose vote we sue? Nor would things stand so bad with this failing, did it not end by corrupting the executant artist, and make him forget at last his own true mission.

So for Wagner, the essence of music is "that thought of the composer's," and it is the job of the performer simply to reproduce that conception without introducing "inventions of one's own." Putting aside whether this is actually possible, Wagner's criticism sets forth the main elements in—or maybe the main issues with—the standard notion of virtuosity. There is (1) a performance that is (2) based on something else (in this case, Wagner's compositions), and that (3) has the potential to highlight the virtuoso's individuality ("inventions of one's own"), but that is also (4) inextricably bound to the expectations of the broader public ("this latter's first and keenest curiosity is addressed to art-dexterity").

■   ■   ■

THIS WOULD AT FIRST seem to have little to do with poetry—or with Internet videos, for that matter. The public performance of poetry, after all, is at best a minor, trailing aspect of the art: the tuft of hair at the end of the lion's tail. We don't think of poems as being acted out; we think of them as being read, and usually in private. In poetry, then, virtuosity must be mostly, if not entirely, a matter of composition—the province of Wagner, not of the violinist playing Wagner. And if that's the case, it seems reasonable to wonder whether virtuosity has any special meaning where poetry is concerned. Perhaps being a virtuoso poet means nothing more than simply being a very good poet, much as being a virtuoso mechanic means being very good at fixing Volvos.

Yet this doesn't seem quite right, in part because it's not hard to think of poets who are very good indeed, but who don't seem particularly virtuosic. It seems unlikely to me, for instance, that most readers are drawn to Christopher Smart or Stevie Smith or even Walt Whitman by a quality those readers would call virtuosity. When we think about virtuosity, we think about mastery, fluency, ease, range—the feeling we get from certain poets that they could write about nearly anything, in nearly any way, and make it sound at least moderately interesting. But poets like Smart don't give us the sense they could write anything. On the contrary, it seems they could write only *one* thing—but that one thing happens to be astonishing. We admire these writers not for their "art-dexterity," as Wagner put it, but for what you might call their "art fixedness": part of their appeal is that they appear completely devoted to projects only they can fulfill. This is in contrast to the response we have to poets like Auden and Swinburne, who are routinely referred to as virtuosos, and who, in addition to performing their own projects, seem to be simultaneously making a show of something else—something outside themselves, something whose contours we recognize, something that lends itself to words like "mastery" and "range."

That something, of course, is technique. Technique is a notoriously difficult subject to discuss, let alone define; indeed, it's become a catchall term for any number of aspects of poems, from line breaks to rhyme to euphony to diction. Nonetheless, it does seem to me that when poets say things like "she has good technique" they have a concept in mind that is stable, though not fixed. We might call it "generally acknowledged areas of basic good practice." A technical consideration isn't merely a convention—it seems wrong, for instance, to talk about the "technique" of putting titles above poems instead of below them. But there is always something conventional about any given technique, in the sense that it involves audience expectations: we have to know what a technique should look like to say whether it was executed well or poorly. Technique is a smaller concern than style, which takes in nearly everything a poet does, and a larger concern than form, which a poet may or may not engage with (and if she does engage with a form—the sonnet, say—the dictates of the applicable technique will immediately spring up like automated hurdles). Or, to put it another way, a poet can have admirable technique while not working in anything that could be called a "form," and a poet can have an intriguing style and pedestrian technique.

All of this is probably best illustrated by example. Consider the beginning of "The Electric People," by a twenty-year-old Paul Muldoon, a poem that probably qualifies as juvenilia:

> *The early electric people had domesticated the wild ass.*
> *They knew all about falling off.*
> *Occasionally they would have fallen out of the trees.*
> *Climbing again, they had something to prove*

To their neighbors. And they did have neighbors.
The electric people lived in villages
Out of their need of security and their
*   constant hunger.*
Together they would divert their energies

To neutral places. Anger to the banging door,
Passion to the kiss.

I'd guess that most poets would say the technique here is questionable, if not poor. The rhythm is very start-and-stop, for no apparent good reason, and the lines are larded with redundancies ("To their neighbors. And they did have neighbors."), also for no apparent good reason. But while one can feel the technical infelicities inhibiting the poem, one can also sense that something stylish and unusual is going on in this bizarre fable. "The early electric people had domesticated the wild ass." What? Tell me more.

But now consider the following lines, from a twenty-five-year-old Philip Larkin:

To write one song, I said,
As sad as the sad wind
That walks around my bed,
Having one simple fall
As a candle-flame swells, and is thinned,
As a curtain stirs by the wall
—For this I must visit the dead.

There's nothing wrong with the technique here: the rhythm is nicely managed, the meter is consistent but not oppressive (the one line that clearly exceeds three beats does so to accentuate the word "swells"), the rhymes are competent if unsurprising, and so on. And yet this excerpt is also derivative (of Yeats), overly poetic (wind, candles, sadness, etc.), and pretentious ("For this I must visit the dead"). The lines aren't bad, but they also aren't exceptional. They're just, you might say, an exercise. We know what we should be getting, and we get exactly that— but nothing more.

■ ■ ■

AND THIS, OF COURSE, is a frequent criticism of virtuosity. It is empty. It is soulless. It is simply a matter of moves made with unreflecting proficiency in the chill of a vacuum, as if the artist weren't a person but a machine. Against this we could set a slightly different but equally prevalent criticism of virtuosity: that it is preening, narcissistic, a spectacle in which the artist tries to raise himself above his art, and thereby "forget[s] at last his own true mission," as Wagner puts it.

The two criticisms are in tension, if not actual opposition, since the first suggests that virtuosity is depersonalizing, while the second portrays virtuosity as personality run amok. But this is inevitable given virtuosity's dependence on technique. Technique, after all, leads a double life. On one hand, it arises from the expectations of many people over time, and it can therefore work against the sense of individuality in any poem that foregrounds it. On the other hand, the social, conventional nature of technique can allow a kind of electric instantiation of the poet's own presence, should he manage to do something exceptional by playing on those expectations. (To stand out from the crowd, it helps to have a crowd to stand out from.) A poet who accentuates technique, then, presents us with something like the old optical illusion of the duck-rabbit. The poet vanishes into technique, reemerges, vanishes again, and so on. The figure is the ground, the ground is the figure, and technique is the border that makes each shift of perception not only possible but unavoidable.

■ ■ ■

WHICH HAS MORE TO do with Internet videos than one might suppose. If technique is a manner of performing, it is also, as I've tried to indicate, a thing that is performed. But in terms of getting and holding our attention, the performance of technique isn't strictly a matter of succeeding or failing at the relevant procedure: there can be successful failures and failed successes. Consider, for example, the incredible popularity of the so-called parking fail. These videos, many of which have over five hundred thousand views on YouTube, are nothing but recordings of comically inept attempts by hapless drivers to squeeze into or out of parking spaces. Parking is something we have definite ideas about—almost everyone has had to maneuver a car into an awkward spot at some point, and almost everyone recognizes that there is a more or less proper way to go about it. So spectacular failure to park is a failure we easily understand (as we would not understand, for instance, failure to correctly collimate a Newtonian reflecting telescope), and a failure that allows us to sympathize with the driver, if only a little, even as we mock him. Or as we mock *her*—we may never even see the driver in a parking fail, which places the emphasis on the action itself, on the failure of technique. And yet we know someone must be driving, which returns us again to the individual. The duck is a rabbit, the rabbit is a duck, and there is something appealing about that alternation of implication and release, of confinement and escape.

Though it may seem counterintuitive, this is equally true of technical extravaganzas—those videos in which a musician blazes a trail through, for instance, the solo from Megadeth's "Tornado of Souls." (Clips dedicated to this undertaking alone have been viewed well over three million times.) One might think that these videos are popular simply because they're impressive demonstrations of musical agility. But there's often more to it than that. As I mentioned earlier, many of these performers exhibit, as the writer Virginia Heffernan put it in an article for the *New York Times* on "Canon Rock," "a kind of anti-showmanship": the focus is entirely on the technique, not the musician. The guitarist at the center of Heffernan's piece, Lim Jeong-hyun, says, "I think play is more significant than appearance. Therefore I want the others to focus on my fingering and sound." But, to focus on "fingering and sound" is also to focus on the person responsible for both of these phenomena. In the case of "Canon Rock" and videos like it, however, our gaze is diverted to hands (which could be anyone's) and an instrument (which could also be anyone's), which makes us even more eager to see the individual, and so on. The duck is rabbit; the rabbit is a duck. But imagine if, rather than averting his gaze, Lim had looked straight at the camera while mugging outrageously. Now the duck is merely a duck, and it's hard to imagine a writer for the *New York Times* tracking the guitarist down to get his thoughts on the nature of performance. (In fact, shred videos—recordings in which a guitarist intentionally overdubs terrible playing over a live performance from a guitar master like Paco de Lucía—are mockeries of exactly this kind of egotism.)

Technique writ large, then, isn't just a matter of doing something correctly or incorrectly. It's a matter of holding our attention by manipulating expectations and desires, such that we feel we're watching something utterly different from us that is somehow also a part of us. In this sense, the antics of the clown, who overturns our expectations through failure, can be just as compelling as the progress of the hero, who confirms our expectations through triumph.

■ ■ ■

THIS IS WHY THERE are really two models of poetic virtuosity, not one. Both models foreground technique, of course: this is the precondition for any virtuoso performance. But they foreground it in different ways, and the easiest way to talk about this difference is to talk about two poets who helpfully embody it, James Merrill and Paul Muldoon.

Merrill has been praised and faulted for his virtuosity from the very beginning. "Merrill's early poems," writes Charles Simic, "read like virtuoso performances by a prodigy who still hasn't discovered that there is life outside literature." Whether or not one agrees with this criticism, it seems fair to say that Merrill is undaunted by even the densest thickets of technique. Sonnets, couplets, sestinas, envelope stanzas—really any form at all—slant rhyme, identical rhyme, internal rhyme, alliteration ("I have lit what is left of my life," he famously declares in "The Broken Home"), assonance, abecedarian structures: every challenge in poetry's vast wilderness is expertly surmounted in Merrill's writing. And surmounted with equanimity—if some poets give us a sense of straining, breathless effort, Merrill makes the reader feel that another dozen sapphic stanzas would be no trouble at all, really, simply a matter of sitting down with a fresh pad of paper.

Merrill's virtuosity, then, is premised on successfully executing whatever technical tasks a given poem takes on (I'm aware that may seem like saying that his height is premised on tallness, but bear with me). When that virtuosity is appealing—as it often is—that success takes on the same kind of figure-ground uncertainty we find so compelling in "Canon Rock" and its cousins. Consider his delicately potent short poem "A Renewal":

> *Having used every subterfuge*
> *To shake you, lies, fatigue, or even that of passion,*
> *Now I see no way but a clean break.*
> *I add that I am willing to bear the guilt.*
>
> *You nod assent. Autumn turns windy, huge,*
> *A clear vase of dry leaves vibrating on and on.*

We sit, watching. When I next speak
Loves buries itself in me, up to the hilt.

The technical merits of this poem should be fairly clear. We have an unobtrusive and unusual *abcd, abcd* rhyme scheme in paired stanzas that mirror the two protagonists. We have subtle slant rhymes ("passion," "on and on") and carefully managed rhythm. We have images that seem to have been custom-made by a team of experts at the Autumnal Sorrow Institute ("A clear vase of dry leaves"), and a climax, perfectly timed, that conjures sex, death, and rebirth all at once by playing wittily on a cliché ("to the hilt").

But of course, the poem isn't merely a technical spectacle; it's also an affecting depiction of the shocking force of a change of feeling. This comes from the final line, which seems to arrive out of nowhere. To that point, all of the poem's technical resources (except, notably, the title) are devoted to convincing us that we're going to get a final line that is compatible with the muted emotions that often accompany the end of an affair, much like Hardy's "Neutral Tones" ("And a pond edged with grayish leaves"). But instead we get a reversal of this expectation, which we then realize is actually a confirmation of a different set of expectations for another type of poem entirely. The poem isn't about feelings that wither as an affair draws to a close; it's about feelings that unexpectedly erupt (and perhaps the affair isn't ending after all). And the surprise of this revelation comes with, as I suggested earlier, a sudden and appealing instantiation of the poet's presence. This is *Merrill*, we think. But also: this is so perfectly written. The duck is a rabbit; the rabbit is a duck. The virtuosity here is a kind of ultimate refinement of technique, a success that is greater than the success we anticipated.

But as I said, there is another kind of virtuosity. Like James Merrill, Paul Muldoon has been referred to as a virtuoso for much of his career, and for much the same perceived strengths and flaws. Muldoon "began as a prodigy and has gone on to become a virtuoso," declares Michael Hofmann, and Adam Kirsch concurs on the label, though not on its connotations ("But if virtuosity is all that a poet can display . . . then he has in some sense failed."). And like Merrill, Muldoon is renowned for daring structural and formal exploits: double sestinas, 250-page poems about failed utopian societies, every species of rhyme, interlocking haikus, and so on. One might expect, then, that the two poets would, if not actually resemble each other, at least share a basic approach to questions of technique.

They do not. If Merrill offers a virtuosity of success, Muldoon gives us a virtuosity that often looks quite a lot like failure. Here is "Holy Thursday," which I've picked for its similarity in theme and tone to "A Renewal":

> They're kindly here, to let us linger so late,
> Long after the shutters are up.
> A waiter glides from the kitchen with a plate
> Of stew, or some thick soup,
>
> And settles himself at the next table but one.
> We know, you and I, that it's over,

That something or other has come between
Us, whatever we are, or were.

The waiter swabs his plate with bread
And drains what's left of his wine.
Then rearranges, one by one,
The knife, the fork, the spoon, the napkin,
The table itself, the chair he's simply borrowed,
And smiles, and bows to his own absence.

What's most remarkable about this remarkable poem is not its refinement but its clumsiness. In the first stanza alone, Muldoon not only rhymes "up" with "soup"—hitting a comic note that would seem poorly suited to a poem about the death of love—but he drags "soup" in as part of a throwaway narrowing of detail: "Of stew, or some thick soup." What would seem fine in conversation feels superfluous in a sonnet. On top of that, the poem's meter is nonexistent, its rhyme scheme is more of a hunch (a rhyme for "napkin," please?), and the language is choked with dead phrases like "something or other" and "one by one." This is virtuosity? Can anyone imagine James Merrill rhyming "late" with "plate"?

Yet where the performance of technique is concerned, success and failure are more like opposite sides of the same coin than like opposite outcomes in a race or a fight. As I've suggested, we can be drawn to a technical failure just as much as to a success, especially when, as with parking fails, we understand the requirements that are being bungled. (There are at least three anthologies devoted to bad poetry, and all of them rely heavily on bad verse, which is the sort of poetry most people think of as poetry.) The virtuoso of failure takes advantage of this fact; in effect, he gives us a performance of a bad performance. Of course, for us to understand that the failure *is* a performance, he needs to signal to us that he does, in fact, know what he's doing. In "Holy Thursday," Muldoon communicates this in small ways: the pleasing alliteration of "let us linger so late / Long after . . ."; the line break at "between / Us," which enacts what it describes; the way the poem observes the sonnet's traditional turn after the octave, shifting its focus to the waiter and his private theatrics. In this context, Muldoon's failures take on a humble, almost democratic cast—the impression one gets is that while he could easily have written the poem with intimidating elegance and precision, he has instead written it in a way that invites the attention of people who routinely say "something or other" and who fixate on soup. Most of us, in other words. We're drawn in, we're invited, and then we notice the great skill, the virtuosity, with which the invitation has been delivered.

■   ■   ■

IN 1843, HEINRICH HEINE, who, in addition to being a poet, was an occasional commentator on the violin virtuoso Paganini, wrote the following about the distinctive qualities of the violin:

> In the case of the violinists, their *virtuosity* is not altogether the result of finger-dexterity and of pure technical

skill, as with the piano-players. The violin is an instrument which has almost human caprices, and has, so to speak, sympathetic relations with the mood of the performer. The smallest discomfort, the lightest disturbance of the spirits, a breath of emotion, finds in it an immediate echo, and such may be the case because the violin, pressed close to the breast, participates in the beatings of the heart. This, however, is only the case with artists who really have a heart in the breast which does beat, and also, above all, have a soul.

Poetic technique is even more sensitive than the violin; it has no wood, no strings; it is nothing but expectation, agreement, recognition. The poet who emphasizes it, who performs it—the poet who takes on the challenge of virtuosity—will always face the same paired criticisms: a lack of soul or an excess of self. But when he succeeds, he will seem to bring self and soul into such perfect union that we won't understand what hybrid creation draws our eyes. We will only know that we can't look away.

THE HAPPY COUPLET

Weddings, as everyone knows, are extraordinary—which is to say, they're occasions to do things you wouldn't usually do, like wear a boutonniere, eat a five-pound lump of cake, or pledge your eternal soul to a person from Delaware. But they're also one of the few events at which you're likely to hear (or possibly even read) a poem. According to a recent study by the Poetry Foundation, "Poetry is most often experienced at private ceremonies such as weddings . . . with 80 percent of nonusers and more than 90 percent of poetry users reporting that they've been exposed to poetry at one of these private occasions." Granted, this makes poetry sound like a combination of heroin and the Marburg virus (most nonusers were exposed at private ceremonies, were they?). But the foundation's report does make a point worth remembering: although poetry is often belittled as obscure and unpopular, it's an art form we turn to when we need to bear not only the weight of our own promises of eternal fidelity but also the scrutiny of all our relatives.

Which makes sense, because poetry has been connected to weddings in the Western world for more than two and a half millennia. Wedding poems are technically known as epithalamia, and they were written by Greek and Roman poets to be sung outside the bedchamber of the happy couple. Yes, the bedchamber. During the Renaissance, the form became less sexual (or at least less obviously sexual) while continuing to draw on both classical sources and the Song of Solomon. Among earlier poets, Donne, Herrick, and Jonson all wrote notable wedding poetry; the master, however, is Edmund Spenser. Spenser's "Epithalamion," written for his own marriage, promises to be "for short time an endlesse moniment," and it follows through on that pledge with an impressively complicated numerical structure. Among its many quirks, the poem consists of twenty-three stanzas plus an envoy (to symbolize the twenty-four hours of the day), and includes 365 long lines (to symbolize the days of the year). How did Spenser love his wife? Let him count the ways.

If you're planning to read poetry at a wedding today, many of these older poems will work fine with a little tweaking. But for your own ceremony, you don't need a wedding poem so much as a love poem. You could use a traditional piece from, say, John Fletcher ("but ever live with me, / And not a wave shall trouble thee") or a modern lyric like Robert Creeley's "Love comes quietly, / finally, drops / about me, on me, / in the old ways." For something longer and more complex, you might try Derek Mahon's "Preface to a Love Poem," which takes the instability of language as its starting point and concludes, "This is a way of airing my distraught / Love of your silence; you are the soul of silence." Even better would be to read Mahon's poem back-to-back with John Ashbery's "Paradoxes and Oxymorons" ("And the poem / Has set me softly down beside you. The poem is you").

The problems kick in, however, when you're asked to read at someone else's wedding. Traditional epithalamia are designed for precisely this situation, of course, but they tend to involve words like "troth" and can therefore (depending on the crowd) be tricky. And your modern English language options are limited. One possibility is to turn a poem that has nothing to do with weddings into an epithalamium by force. For instance, if you don't mind a little irony (not to mention comparing the wedding couple to Moses), you could use Louise Glück's "The Undertaking":

> *The darkness lifts, imagine, in your lifetime.*
> *There you are—cased in clean bark you drift*
> *through weaving rushes, fields flooded with cotton.*
> *You are free. The river films with lilies,*
> *shrubs appear, shoots thicken into palm. And now*
> *all fear gives way: the light*
> *looks after you, you feel the waves' goodwill*
> *as arms widen over the water; Love,*
>
> *the key is turned. Extend yourself—*
> *it is the Nile, the sun is shining,*
> *everywhere you turn is luck.*

Glück's poem is lovely, but it's also a rarity—even the experts have trouble locating up-to-date verses with which to salute the bride and groom. Consider *Into the Garden: A Wedding Anthology*, edited by Robert Hass, a former poet laureate, and Stephen Mitchell. There's some modern English-language writing here—"The Dance," by Wendell Berry, and Richard Wilbur's "Wedding Toast," for example—but these pieces are the exception, not the rule. Half the poems are translations (Rilke gets a real workout), and only ten out of more than one hundred could be considered contemporary, even under the most flexible definition. That's not to fault the editors—*Into the Garden* is a thoughtful collection—but the world of the poets in this anthology is not, for the most part, the world of the people who might be picking it up at Barnes & Noble.

This disconnect is especially curious when you consider how easy it is to find poetry to read at a funeral. If epithalamia are rare, elegies are so common nowadays that it's actually surprising to run across a poet who hasn't written one or two. A partial explanation for this disparity might be that the contemporary elegy gives poets more room to maneuver—after all, it isn't so much a form as a broad mode of expression. (In the much-quoted opening to "Meditation at Lagunitas," Robert Hass writes, "All the new thinking is about loss. / In this, it resembles all the old thinking"—and man, he isn't kidding.) Yet the greater flexibility of the elegy can't entirely explain the situation; instead it seems that something that used to bind together poetry and weddings has weakened, loosened, and very nearly fallen away.

Could that quality be happiness? Is the problem simply that weddings are joyous, and modern poetry largely isn't? Maybe: Henry de Montherlant famously claimed that "happiness writes white—it doesn't show up on the page," which isn't exactly true but sounds like it should be. Along the same lines, many poets would agree with Eliot's characterization of contemporary history as an "immense panorama of futility and anarchy"; it's easy to see how such writers might not be drawn to a ceremony that implies pleasure and permanence. Still, these explanations don't quite cover it. For one thing, you don't have to look too hard for poetry that is, in some way or another, celebratory. Whether it's Frank O'Hara having a Coke or James Wright breaking into blossom, our poets haven't been reluctant to describe moments of fulfillment, even if those moments haven't often occurred in front of a crowd of friends and family.

And that, perhaps, is the difference. Modern poetry is often talked about in terms of its relation to "the personal," either because the writing in question embraces specific facts from the poet's private life (as in much confessional work) or because it rejects that sort of disclosure (as in many theory-driven poems). In debating "the personal," however, it's easy to lose sight of a related issue—poetry's trembling, uncertain relationship with "the public." To borrow from Eliot's tellingly awkward "Dedication to My Wife," weddings necessarily involve "private words addressed to you in public." They require the sanction of a society. In this sense, they differ from funerals, which are usually closer to private assemblies than true public events.

A classic epithalamium bridges this private-public

divide—if a lyric love poem imagines an "I" and a singular "you," a wedding poem implies a "we" and a plural "you." It reaches back to the origin of "public" in the Latin *populus*: "a people, a host." And while it would be excessive to argue that modern poetry has lost the ability to speak publicly in this sense, it's probably fair to say that most poets no longer view such occasions as natural outlets for their work. This isn't to criticize contemporary poets by any means—if our poetry has lost some of the public presence it once enjoyed, it's gained a subtle, shifting private force that might well be worth the trade. Even so, it's hard not to regret the diminishment of the wedding poem, and not to wince a little at this year's Pulitzer Prize for Poetry, which was given to Claudia Emerson for a book about (you guessed it) divorce.

THE GREAT(NESS) GAME

In October of this year, John Ashbery became the first poet to have an edition of his works released by the Library of America in his own lifetime. That honor says a number of things about the state of contemporary poetry—some good, some not so good—but perhaps the most important and disturbing question it raises is this: what will we do when Ashbery and his generation are gone? Because for the first time since the early nineteenth century, American poetry may be about to run out of greatness.

That may seem like a strange (and strangely fraught) way of putting things. But the concept of greatness has a special significance in the poetry world that it often lacks elsewhere—after all, in most areas of life, greatness is to be cherished, but it isn't essential. The golf world idolizes Tiger Woods, sure, but duffers will still be heaving nine-irons into ponds long after Woods plays his last major. Poetry can't be as confident about its own

durability. Poetry has justified itself historically by asserting that
no matter how small its audience or dotty its practitioners, it
remains the place one goes for the highest of high art. As Byron
put it in a loose translation of Horace: "But poesy between the
best and worst / No medium knows; you must be last or first; /
For middling poets' miserable volumes / Are damned alike by
god and men and columns." Poetry needs greatness.

Or so the thinking goes, anyway. The problem is that over
the course of the twentieth century, greatness has turned out to
be an increasingly blurry business. In part, this is a reflection of
the standard narrative of postmodernism, according to which
all capital-letter-sporting ideals—Truth, Beauty, Justice—must
come in for questioning. But the difficulty with poetic greatness
has to do with more than the talking points of the contemporary
culture wars. Greatness is—and indeed, has always been—a
tangle of occasionally incompatible concepts, most of which depend upon placing the burden of "greatness" on different parts
of the artistic process. Does being "great" simply mean writing
poems that are "great"? If so, how many? Or does "greatness"
mean having a sufficiently "great" project? If you have such a
project, can you be "great" while writing poems that are only
"good" (and maybe even a little "boring")? Is being a "great"
poet the same as being a "major" poet? Are "great" poets necessarily "serious" poets? These are all good questions to which
nobody has had very convincing answers.

Still, however blurry "greatness" may be, it's clear that segments of the poetry world have been fretting over its potential
loss since at least 1983. That's the year in which an essay by

Donald Hall, the US poet laureate from 2006–7, appeared in the *Kenyon Review* bearing the title "Poetry and Ambition." Hall got right to the point: "It seems to me that contemporary American poetry is afflicted by modesty of ambition—a modesty, alas, genuine . . . if sometimes accompanied by vast pretense." What poets should be trying to do, according to Hall, is "to make words that live forever . . . to be as good as Dante." They probably would fail, of course, but even so, "the only way we are likely to be any good is to try to be as great as the best." Pretty strong stuff—and one wonders how many plays Shakespeare would have managed to write had he subjected every line to the merciless scrutiny Hall recommends.

And yet many of Hall's points are still being wrangled over more than twenty years later. In 2005, *Poetry* magazine published a roundtable discussion entitled (naturally) "Ambition and Greatness," in which participants were alternately put off by the entire idea of "capital-G Greatness" (as the poet Daisy Fried put it) or concerned that, as the scholar Jeredith Merrin suggested, the contemporary poetry world might be trying "to re-write 'great' as small." What no participant did, though, was question the implicit premise that greatness isn't something American poets can take for granted but rather something they should subject to the analysis of a panel. No one, for instance, said, "Well, obviously we are living in an age of great and hugely ambitious American poetry, so let's talk about [insert name(s)] and how we all admire and envy [insert work of timeless relevance]." No one even mustered the contrarian hyperbole with which William Carlos Williams greeted *The Waste Land*: "It wiped out our world as if an atom bomb had been dropped upon it and our brave sallies into the unknown were turned to dust." Instead, the panelists bickered mildly over Elizabeth Bishop (dead for thirty years) and Frank O'Hara (who was born fifteen years after Bishop but died in 1966), with Adam Kirsch concluding, "Good and enduring as they are . . . there is something not quite right in calling them great, in the sense that Eliot and Whitman and Dickinson are great."

Not exactly a ringing endorsement for either poet. And yet the ambivalence over Bishop's status in particular is worth pausing over for two reasons. One relates to the structure of the poetry world, and we'll get to it shortly. The other has to do with the fact that, as I touched on above, words like "great" have a tendency to get a little squirrelly when applied to complex disciplines like poetry. In relatively straightforward activities, such words aren't as much of a problem. If we're looking at a series of footraces, for example, it's not hard to see who finished first the most times (or had the highest average finish), and as a result, whether we call a given runner "great" or "excellent" or "terrific," we'll generally have the same thing in mind. Not so with poetry. A list of "great" poets will look quite a bit different from a list of "perfect" poets, which may have almost no overlap with a list of "spectacular" poets, which in turn may be completely different from a list of "sublime" poets. When we talk about poetic greatness, we're talking about style and persona, even when (or, maybe, especially when) we think we aren't.

Our largely unconscious assumptions work like a velvet rope: If a poet looks the way we think a great poet ought to, we

let him or her into the club quickly—and sometimes later wish
we hadn't. If a poet fails to fit our assumptions, though, we
spend a lot more time checking out the poet's outfit, listening to
the poet's friends importuning, weighing the evidence, waiting
for a twenty, and so forth. Of course, this only matters for poets
whose reputations are still at issue. It may have taken Emily
Dickinson a hundred years to get into the club, but now that
she's there, she's there. For contemporaries and near contemporaries, though, falling on the wrong side of our intuitions can
mean trouble, because those intuitions give rise to chatter and
criticism and scholarship that can take decades to clear away.

What, then, do we assume greatness looks like? There is no
one true answer to that question, no neat test or rule, since our
unconscious assumptions are by nature unsystematic and occasionally contradictory. Generally speaking, though, the style we
have in mind tends to be grand, sober, sweeping—
unapologetically authoritative and often overtly rhetorical. It's
less likely to involve words like "canary" and "sniffle" and "wid-
get" and more likely to involve words like "nation" and "soul"
and "language." And the persona we associate with greatness is
something, you know, exceptional—an aristocrat, a rebel, a
statesman, a prodigious intellect, a mad-eyed genius who has
drunk from the fountain of Truth and tasted the fruit of Knowledge and . . . Well, anyway, it's somebody who takes himself very
seriously and demands that we do so as well. Greatness implies
scale, and a great poet is a big sensibility writing about big
things in a big way.

It's risky, then, to write poems about the tiny objects on

your desk. But that's exactly what Bishop did—and that choice helps explain why she was for a long time considered obviously less great than her close friend Robert Lowell. As the poet David Wojahn noted in a letter in response to *Poetry*'s panel, Lowell was "probably the last American poet to aspire to Greatness in the old fashioned, capital-G sense." Lowell had the style: his poetry is bursting with vast claims, sparkling abstractions, and vehement denunciations of the servility of the age. And Lowell had the persona: he was a thunderbolt-chucking wild man from one of America's most famous Bostonian lineages. Bishop, on the other hand, had neither. Her poems open with lines like "I caught a tremendous fish," and she's invariably described by critics as shy, modest, charming, and so forth. Yet it's Bishop's writing, not Lowell's, that matters more in the poetry world today. "What is strange," writes the poet-critic J. D. McClatchy, "is how her influence . . . has been felt in the literary culture. John Ashbery, James Merrill, and Mark Strand, for example, have each claimed Bishop as his favorite poet. . . . Since each of them couldn't be more different from one another, how is it possible?"

It's possible, one might answer, because Bishop was a great poet, if we take "great" to mean something like "demonstrating the qualities that make poetry seem interesting and worthwhile to such a degree that subsequent practitioners of the art form have found her work a more useful resource than the work of most if not all of her peers." But our assumptions about how greatness should look, like our assumptions about how people should look, are more subtle and stubborn than we realize. So in certain segments of the poetry world, the solution has been to make Bishop what you might call "great with an asterisk." In particular, there has been a persistent effort to pair her with the less-talented but greater-looking Lowell, a ploy that resembles the old high school date movie tactic of sending the bookish plain Jane to the prom with the quarterback (when her glasses are slowly removed by the right man, she's revealed to have been, all along, totally hot!). In reviewing *Words in Air: The Complete Correspondence Between Elizabeth Bishop and Robert Lowell* for the *New York Times Book Review* recently, William Logan carried this tendency to its logical if dubious conclusion, depicting the two poets as star-crossed lovers despite the fact that (a) Bishop was a lesbian and (b) Lowell's only romantic overture to Bishop in their thirty-year friendship—and this was a man who would've made a pass at a fire hydrant—was met with polite silence by its intended recipient. Yet while this flight of fancy is unfair to both writers, it does give us a workable if unwieldy model of greatness. Bishop wrote the poems, Lowell acted the part, and if you simply look back and forth fast enough between the two while squinting, it's possible to see a single great poet staring back at you.

Which brings us to the point I mentioned earlier, about the structure of the poetry world. Greatness isn't simply a matter of potentially confusing concepts; it's also a practical question about who gets to decide what about whom. Our assumptions about poetic greatness are therefore linked to the reputation-making structures of the poetry world—and changes in those structures can have peculiar effects on our thinking. For most of the twentieth century, the poetry world resembled, well, a country club. One had to know the right people; one had to study with the right mentors. The system began to change after the GI Bill was introduced (making a university-level poetic education possible for more people), and that change accelerated in the 1970s as creative writing programs began to flourish. In 1975 there were eighty such programs; by 1992 there were over five hundred, and the accumulated weight of all these credentialed poets began to put increasing pressure on poetry's old system of personal relationships and behind-the-scenes logrolling. It would be a mistake to call today's poetry world a transparent democracy (that whirring you hear is the sound of logs still busily rolling away), but it's more democratic than it used to be—and far more middle class. It's more of a guild now than a country club. This change has brought with it certain virtues, like greater professionalism and courtesy. One could argue that it also made the poetry world more receptive to writers like Bishop, whose style is less hoity-toity than, say, Eliot's. But the poetry world has also acquired new vices, most notably a tedious careerism that encourages poets to publish early and often (the Donald Hall essay I mentioned earlier is largely a criticism of this very tendency). Consequently, it's not hard to feel nostalgic for the way things used to be, or at least the way we imagine they used to be. And this nostalgia often manifests as a preference for a particular kind of greatness.

The easiest way to see this phenomenon in action is to look at a peculiar development in American poetry that has more or less paralleled the growth of creative writing programs: the lionization of poets from other countries, especially countries in which writers might have the opportunity to be, as it were, shot. In most ways, of course, this is an admirable development that puts the lie to talk about American provincialism. In other ways, though, it can be a bit cringeworthy. Consider the way in which Robert Pinsky describes the laughter of the Polish émigré and Nobel-winning dissident Czesław Miłosz: "The sound of it was infectious, but more precisely it was commanding. His laughter had the counter-authority of human intelligence, triumphing over the petty-minded authority of a regime." That's one hell of a chuckle. The problem isn't that Pinsky likes and admires Miłosz; it's that he can't hear a Polish poet snortle without having fantasies about barricades and firing squads. He's by no means alone in that. Many of us in the American poetry world have a habit of exalting foreign writers while turning them into cartoons. And we do so because their very foreignness implies a distance—a potentially "great" distance—that we no longer have from our own writers, most of whom make regular appearances on the reading circuit and have publicly available office phones.

In addition, non-American writers are the perfect surface upon which to project our desire for the style and persona we associate with old-fashioned greatness. One hesitates to invoke the dread word "colonialism" here, but sometimes you've got to call a *Mayflower* a *Mayflower*. How else, really, to explain the reverse condescension that allows us to applaud pompous nonsense in the work of a Polish poet that would be rightly skewered if it came from an American? Miłosz, for instance, was regularly congratulated for lines like "What is

poetry which does not save / Nations or people? / A connivance
with official lies, / A song of drunkards whose throat will be cut
in a moment, / Readings for sophomore girls." Any sophomore
girl worth her copy of *A Room of One's Own* would kick him in
the shins.

It may be starting to sound as if greatness isn't all that great,
that it's simply another strategy for concealing predictable preju-
dices that poets should forswear on their path to becoming wise
and tolerant twenty-first-century artists. That is, however, almost the opposite of the truth. Yes, greatness narrowly defined
to mean a particular windily dull type of writing is something
we could all do without, and long may its advocates gag on their
pipe smoke and languish in their tweeds. But the idea that poets
should aspire to produce work "exquisite in its kind," as Samuel
Johnson once put it, is one of the art form's most powerful lega-
cies. When we lose sight of greatness, we cease being hard on
ourselves and on each other; we begin to think of real criticism
as being "mean," rather than as evidence of poetry's health; we
stop assuming that poems should be interesting to other people
and begin thinking of them as only being obligated, maybe, to
sort of vaguely interest our friends—and, finally, not even that.
Perhaps most disturbing, we stop making demands on the few
artists capable of practicing the art at its highest levels. Instead,
we cling to the ground in those artists' shadows—John Ashbery's is enormous at this point—and talk about how rich the
darkness is and how lovely it is to be a mushroom. This doesn't
help anyone. What we should be doing is asking why a poet as
gifted as Ashbery has written so many poems that are boring or

repetitive (or both), because such questions will allow us to better understand the poems he's written that are moving and funny and beautiful. Such questions might even allow other poets—especially younger poets—to find their own ways of writing poems that are moving and funny and beautiful. Which for people who read them, for people who believe in them, would be a very great thing indeed.

OPRAH'S ADVENTURES

IN POETRYLAND

The signs of the coming apocalypse are many, but none is starker than this web headline in the April issue of *O, The Oprah Magazine*: "Spring Fashion Modeled by Rising Young Poets." Yes. Spring fashion. Modeled. By rising young poets. There follows a photo montage of attractive younger women— some of whom are rising poets mostly in the I-get-up-in-the-morning sense, but all of whom certainly look poetic—in outfits costing from $472 to $5,003. This is all part of *O*'s special issue celebrating National Poetry Month, edited by noted verse aficionado Maria Shriver and including interviews with "all-star readers" like Bono, Ashton Kutcher, the gossip columnist Liz Smith, and someone named James Franco, who is apparently an actor.

Let's get a few things out of the way. First, only a snob or an idiot complains when the magic wand of Oprah is flourished in his direction. (I have a book about poetry for general readers out next month, and my publisher broke land-speed records attempting to get copies to Oprah's people before their issue closed. Alas, we were too late, which means the world will never know how I look in a Kiton suit—for the record, the answer is "grateful.") Second, *O* has been running an intelligent and professional book section under the direction of the former *Publishers Weekly* editor Sara Nelson for some time now, using excellent critics like Francine Prose. You could do considerably worse than get your book news from *O*. Finally, it's all too easy for Important Literary Folk to sneer at anything involving fashion. It's so *girly*, you know, and real writers are never *girl*—ah. So the lingering gender biases of the literary world are often at play when readers cringe at the pairing of poetry with the stuff of women's magazines. There is also a regrettable tendency to underestimate the wit and perceptiveness of the fashion industry—which is a silly business, true, but certainly no sillier than publishing, as anyone who's read the book *The 4-Hour Body* should be aware. (*The New York Times*'s own *T Magazine* has outfitted the poet Terrance Hayes in Dolce & Gabbana.)

And yet. "Spring Fashion Modeled by Rising Young Poets." The words are heart sinking. For some readers, this will be because poetry represents a higher form of culture that can only be debased by the commentary of Oprah Winfrey and the pencil skirts of L'Wren Scott. But this isn't quite right. Any critic knows there are dozens of poetry collections published every year that are considerably less culturally valuable than Winfrey's many enterprises and that could only be improved by pencil skirts, preferably by being wrapped in several of them and chucked in the East River. The problem is that poetry can't approach the world inhabited by *O* and fashion design—that is, the world of American mass culture—with the same swagger as other fields. When Terrell Owens holds forth on poetry in *O* (yes, he does), much of the audience knows that Owens is a football player, and has at least a vague idea of what football is, what it means, and why it inspires otherwise reasonable people to put Styrofoam cheese slices on their heads. But poets and poetry readers . . . We can't bring our context with us. We're at the mercy of someone else's display. The sad thing about "Spring Fashion Modeled by Rising Young Poets" is not that the photos are a debasement of art. The sad thing is that they capture an inevitable and impossible yearning. The chasm between the audience for poetry and the audience for *O* is vast, and not even the mighty Oprah can build a bridge from empty air.

But at least her magazine makes an effort, sort of. Sure, the issue includes plenty of stuff that does credit neither to poetry nor to readers of *O*—there's a bunch of talk about using poetry to overcome personal challenges (if it worked as self-help, you'd see more poets driving BMWs); there's the aforementioned Ashton Kutcher; and roughly a fifth of the coverage is devoted to Mary Oliver, about whose poetry one can only say that no animals appear to have been harmed in the making of it. But there are at least two admirable features. The first is a profile of W. S. Merwin by the magazine's editor, Susan Casey. Casey obviously likes Merwin, has read him, and makes a genuine effort to talk about one of his poems despite her presumed unfamiliarity with the byzantine rituals of contemporary American poetry. If more journalists would try things like this, the chasm would still gape, but maybe less widely. The second is a list of "20 books no reader's library should be without." The list is idiosyncratic, to say the least—Rumi but not Shakespeare or Yeats?—but as a starting point it's not bad.

The magazine also encourages a number of poets to discuss the art, although mostly in one- or two-sentence asides. Unfortunately, they're opining on topics like "where poems come from," and this is exactly the kind of abstract speculation that summons forth magical poetry talk—comments that make poetry sound like God's own electric Kool-Aid acid test—from even the smartest writers. Easily the most peculiar remark in the "all-star" section comes not from any of the bold-name celebrities but from the only actual poet, Margaret Atwood. She declares that "the question, 'What is the role of poetry' is like asking 'What is the role of eating?'" I'm both an Atwood fan and a poetry critic, but even for me, it's hard not to notice that people who don't read poetry seem generally to be healthy and happy, whereas people who don't eat seem generally to be dead.

Yet one must fill the yawning chasm with something: magical poetry talk, a fashion shoot, some lists, the wisdom of Sting, whatever. I wish, though, they had found space for someone—not a critic, necessarily, just someone willing to be honest—to talk about the actual experience of reading a poem. Not why poems are good at rehabilitating people. Not where poems come from. Not what they can help us do or forget or remember. Not what the people who write them are wearing. Just what reading one of them is like to one person. If the chasm is to be ever so slightly narrowed, it seems to me this is how it will be done. I find myself turning again to the fashion shoot: there is Anna Moschovakis, whose work I know. She's a fine writer, a translator, an editor at the thoroughly admirable Ugly Duckling Presse (publisher of the dryly antic Eugene Ostashevsky, among others), and she's wearing a "supple suede jacket (Haute Hippie, $995)." It's impossible to say what Moschovakis was thinking during this shoot—I certainly hope one of her thoughts was, "I better get to keep this damn jacket"—but perhaps we can guess. Here is the end of her poem "Untitled":

> *I wish I could be inanimate,*
> *banged-up and appreciated*
> *for all my surface qualities*
> *without ethics getting in the way. I seem to remember*
> *being ethical. I seem to act along some kind of line*
> *albeit a kinky one. I wonder when kinky became*
> *pornographic and whether that aspect is*
> *subtractable. I don't remember my grammar*
> *rules. I don't think English is very good*
> *for a certain kind of inventioning. I gather*
> *some readers don't like being*
> *confronted with the language in every word.*
> *I want to be a word. I would be abstract*
> *with an inscrutable ending.*

But that's precisely the trouble: for the overwhelming majority of the culture, almost every poem has an inscrutable ending, even the ones that aren't actually inscrutable. How can we *seem* inscrutable when we *are* inscrutable? The chasm is vast; it yawns. All poets and their readers can do is stare half-longingly, half-fearfully across that great divide at the golden palace of mass culture (portcullis, Fendi, $4,500) and sigh. Oh, Oprah. Oh, poetry.

ANNALS OF POETRY

The history of American poetry, like the history of America itself, is a story of ingenuity, sacrifice, hard work, and sticking it to people when they least expect it. Whether it's Ezra Pound dismissing his benefactor Amy Lowell as a "hippopoetess" (an insult he borrowed from the poet Witter Bynner) or Yvor Winters accusing his friend Hart Crane of possessing flaws akin to a "public catastrophe," you can count on the occasional bushwhacking in the land of what Horace called "the touchy tribe."

The most recent such assault—the most surprising in years—took the form of a sixty-five-hundred-word article in the *New Yorker* last month by the poet Dana Goodyear, who is also a *New Yorker* editor. Goodyear's subject was the Chicago-based Poetry Foundation, which received an unexpected (to put it mildly) bequest of roughly $200 million from Ruth Lilly about five years ago. The article focuses on the Poetry Foundation's

president, John Barr, but Goodyear also takes on *Poetry* magazine, its founder Harriet Monroe, the Poetry Foundation website, legal proceedings relating to Lilly's bequest, Ruth Lilly
herself, the various objects collected by Ruth Lilly's father (toy
soldiers, gold coins), the price of real estate in Chicago, and
the stuff rich people wear at parties (a "crisp white shirt" or
"coral lipstick," apparently). It is a very long article.

It's also a slick production whose craftsmanship any critic
would respect. Goodyear wants to portray the Poetry Foundation as a culturally conservative, slightly tacky enterprise led by
a dilettantish, ex–Wall Street fat cat—"what people these days
call a 'businessman-poet'"—who's itching to sell poems the way
Frito-Lay sells Cool Ranch Doritos (and, no, not by making
them deeeeeelicious). So she fills her piece with references to
advertising, buying and selling, and ostentatious wealth—John
Barr has "a twenty-five-acre estate in Greenwich," the charity's
website has a budget of "more than a million dollars." And she
quotes many poets making critical remarks about Those People
and All That Money (the poet J. D. McClatchy says the foundation has an "aura of mediocrity"). Many readers might figure
that Goodyear has done a fine thing by exposing this bunch of
crisp-white-shirt-wearing yahoos.

The instinct wouldn't necessarily be misplaced. After all,
the Poetry Foundation does have big money, and some of John
Barr's observations (regarding, say, the alleged careerism in
MFA programs) deserve a thoughtful response. But that response already has been made—for months now—on blogs, in
print, and in the letters section of *Poetry* magazine itself. (In the

interest of disclosure, I've reviewed for *Poetry*). As a result, Goodyear's article has a strangely punitive cast—for example, only one poet, Billy Collins, is quoted saying anything remotely positive about the Poetry Foundation's many enterprises. That's funny, since those enterprises are hardly uniform. Indeed, many of the piece's critical voices have appeared in *Poetry* themselves (McClatchy shows up in the March issue); these writers presumably are making judgments about specific aspects of the foundation, not wholesale denunciations. Yet Goodyear doesn't clarify. On the contrary, she leaves things blurry—at best. In an especially confusing decision, she includes a cutting remark by the writer Joel Brouwer about the marketing of poetry, and claims the comment was "an obvious reference" to the Poetry Foundation. But Brouwer, as he confirmed by e-mail, wasn't talking about the foundation at all. Which makes sense, of course, since Brouwer is a regular contributor to *Poetry*, a detail Goodyear's readers probably wouldn't know.

Similarly, the article treats a range of sometimes contradictory anxieties as if they were a unified critique. Goodyear quotes "the director of a nonprofit literary group" complaining that the foundation is trying to "take credit for things that are already going on." By this, the director means that the foundation's efforts to popularize poetry are only continuing a process begun by the Academy of American Poets (responsible for National Poetry Month) and the Poetry Society of America (responsible for poems on the subway). It's a reasonable point. But then Goodyear shifts to a series of comments from poets who are upset about the very popularizing the director is describing. In combination, the criticisms become incoherent. You can complain the foundation is late to the party, or you can argue that the party itself is a mistake—but you can't do both at the same time.

More than anything, though, it's curious that in an article purportedly dealing with the future of American poetry, Goodyear says nothing about actual poems. But maybe that's to be expected—after all, about a decade ago the *New Yorker* essentially stopped covering contemporary poetry. Granted, you'll see the occasional collection in the magazine's "Briefly Noted" section, but you'd have to go back to the midnineties to find a full-scale review of a poet under the age of seventy. And since the turn of the century, the magazine has limited its coverage to poets who are, so to speak, dead—with one exception, Richard Wilbur's *Collected Poems*, which the magazine reviewed in 2004. Wilbur is eighty-six.

Indeed, the *New Yorker* now treats poetry almost exactly as Goodyear suggests the Poetry Foundation does—as a brand-enhancing commodity. Rather than actual discussions of poetry as an art, the *New Yorker* offers "profiles" of poets, which are distinguishable from profiles of, say, United States senators only in that the poets' stories potentially include more references to bongs. That's not to knock the authors of those profiles—often they're a pleasure to read. They just have nothing to do with poetry.

And then there's the question of the poems the magazine chooses to run. Granted, picking poems for a national publication is nearly impossible, and the *New Yorker*'s poetry editor,

Alice Quinn, probably does it as well as anyone could. (Quinn is also liked personally, and rightly so, by many poets.) But there are two ways in which the *New Yorker*'s poem selection indicates the tension between reinforcing the "literariness" of the magazine's brand and actually saying something interesting about poetry. First, the *New Yorker* tends to run bad poems by excellent poets. This occurs in part because the magazine has to take big names, but many big names don't work in ways that are palatable to the *New Yorker*'s vast audience (in addition, many well-known poets don't write what's known in the poetry world as "the *New Yorker* poem"—basically an epiphany-centered lyric heavy on words like "water" and "light"). As a result, you get fine writers trying on a style that doesn't suit them. The Irish poet Michael Longley writes powerful earthy yet cerebral lines, but you wouldn't know it from his *New Yorker* poem "For My Grandson": "Did you hear the wind in the fluffy chimney?" Yes, "the fluffy chimney."

The second problem with the *New Yorker*'s poem selection is trickier. This is what you might call "the home job": the magazine's widely noted fondness for the work of its own staffers and social acquaintances. The most notorious examples of this tendency were the three poems the *New Yorker* published by Manhattan doyenne Brooke Astor in 1996–97 (one more than Robert Creeley managed in his whole life). Some representative lines: "I learned to take the good and bad / And smile whenever I felt sad." Even more questionable, however, is the magazine's taste for its own junior employees. In 2002, for instance, the poet who appeared most frequently in the magazine was the assistant to David Remnick, the editor—that assistant's name, coinciden-tally, was Dana Goodyear. In fact, since 2000, Goodyear (who is thirty) has appeared in the *New Yorker* more than Czesław Miłosz, Jorie Graham, John Ashbery, Derek Walcott, Seamus Heaney, Wisława Szymborska, Kay Ryan, and every living American poet laureate except for W. S. Merwin. She's already equaled Sylvia Plath's total.

The problem with behavior like this is not that it violates some sacred duty of fairness (the *New Yorker* is a business, not a charity for whiny poets). No, the problem, to borrow a quota-tion from Goodyear's article, is that such behavior "signals a lack of ambition and seriousness that may ultimately be fatal." Poets may get frustrated with the Poetry Foundation; they may complain; they may disagree with certain projects. But the Po-etry Foundation, however misguided or impolitic, hasn't given up on poetry. The question is: has the *New Yorker*?

POETRY AND, OF, AND ABOUT

The anthology on my desk is titled *Poetry of the Law: From Chaucer to the Present*. I'm both a lawyer and a poetry critic, so asking me to discuss this book would seem to present an especially harmonious pairing of subject and analyst—like handing an animal cracker recipe to a zoologist–pastry chef. And, indeed, flipping through, I find plenty of work that appeals to me as a reader of poems who is also, when necessary, a filer of briefs. We have some well-chosen passages from Spenser ("Then up arose a person of deepe reach, . . . / That well could charme his tongue, and time his speech"); we have an intriguing poetic performance from the seminal jurist William Blackstone ("The Lawyer's Farewell to his Muse"); and we have a number of more recent efforts that, while mixed in quality, manage to give the reader a sense of the ways in which contemporary poetry can encompass legal subjects. Lawrence Joseph's "Admissions Against Interest," for example, nicely captures the atmosphere of nervous, chilly efficiency that permeates American corporate law, as in the beginning of the second section:

> *Now, what type of animal asks after facts?*
> *—so I'm a lawyer. Maybe charming,*
>
> *direct yet as circumspect as any other lawyer*
> *going on about concrete forces of civil*
>
> *society substantially beyond anyone's grasp*
> *and about money. Things like "you too*
>
> *may be silenced the way powerful*
> *corporations silence, contractually"*
> *attract my attention.*

Not the warmest way in which to regard legal thinking, but, then, the average lawyer's existence rarely bears much resemblance to the life of Ben Matlock, let alone Atticus Finch. Poems by Browning, Kenneth Fearing, and the underrated William Empson are similarly successful at engaging with legal concepts and language. As with any anthology, there are a few pieces that don't quite come off ("Why does a hearse horse snicker / Hauling a lawyer away?" asks Carl Sandburg, inviting prosecution for felony anthropomorphizing). But the project as a whole is a pleasure for the casual reader, as any collection of good poems ought to be.

And yet something here is slightly troubling. Not the book itself—or at least not this book in particular. Rather, there's something unsettling in the preposition that anchors this anthology's title: *Poetry of the Law*. The phrasing is an interesting choice. One can understand, of course, the practical reasoning behind it; for one thing, that "of" permits the inclusion of poems whose relation to the law is, to put it mildly, tenuous. For instance, John Ashbery's "Ignorance of the Law Is No Excuse" begins:

> *We were warned about spiders, and the occasional famine.*
> *We drove downtown to see our neighbors. None of them*
> > *were home.*
> *We nestled in yards the municipality had created,*
> *reminisced about other, different places—*
> *but were they? Hadn't we known it all before?*

Title aside, this poem isn't "about" the law in any meaningful sense; it could just as easily have been called "Déjà vu Redux" or "Concerning the Halibut, However, We Were Sadly Uninformed." We'd read it exactly the same way. But if we say the poem is "of" the law rather than simply "about" the law— well, surely that provides more room to maneuver. And it's comforting, isn't it, to suppose that pursuits like law and poetry aren't really "about" each other in the almost aggressive way that instruction manuals are about food processors but rather are as delicately interrelated as sea and shore, or bees and roses.

■   ■   ■

ARE THEY, THOUGH? AND what does that "of" really signify, anyway? In order to answer that question, it's first necessary to recognize that an anthology like this one isn't simply positioned between two subjects, but two audiences. The first is the one I mentioned earlier: the general, casual reader—the person who picks up a book called *Poetry of the Law* because he's a lawyer who's always liked Whitman, or because he's a poetry reader whose beloved Uncle Ralph was a public defender in Gatlinburg. The second potential audience consists of scholars and, more particularly, as the editors of *Poetry of the Law* put it, of "scholars of law and literature."

That description may require some explanation. Most people probably would assume that the phrase "scholars of law and literature" is meant to refer to scholars of law and also, separately, to scholars of literature. But what the editors actually have in mind here is a specific movement in the legal academy known as (bingo!) "law and literature." As they put it,

> In 1973, James Boyd White's *The Legal Imagination* inaugurated the scholarly study of law and literature. Since then, it has burgeoned as an academic field, yielding dozens of books, hundreds of articles, and several specialized journals.

They aren't kidding. The past two and a half decades have given us *Law and Literature* (a journal edited at Cardozo School of Law), *Law and Literature* (a book by Richard Posner), *Law and Literature: Text and Theory* (by Lenora Ledwon), *Law and Literature: Possibilities and Perspectives* (by Ian Ward), *A Critical Introduction to Law and Literature* (by Kieran Dolin), and

Law and Literature: How to Respond When the Epistolary Novel Files a Motion to Dismiss Pursuant to FRCP 12(b)(6) (okay, maybe not that one). In any case, there's a lot of material out there. "Yet for all the richness of this scholarship," as the editors observe, "[the law and literature movement] has focused almost entirely on fiction and drama." So part of the goal of *Poetry of the Law* is to demonstrate that poetry, like its sister arts, can provide "considerable new matter worthy of study."

And who wouldn't want that? But when we're talking about new matter worthy of study, we should acknowledge that the project taken up by *Poetry of the Law* is different from that of anthologies about, for instance, bicycles or birthday parties. This is a distinction that gets elided, however, when the editors assert that this book

> fill[s] a striking gap in the universe of contemporary poetry, which includes, after all, multiple collections of poems focused on such central human concerns as love, war and politics, as well as more specialized topics like travel, dogs, cats, birds, flowers, mothers, father, and poetry itself.

That sounds reasonable. But an anthology of poems about love might include work from Rilke, Szymborska, and Li Po; the same goes for an anthology about travel. *Poetry of the Law*, though, includes only poets from the United States, Great Britain, and Ireland and could therefore be more accurately titled *Poetry of the Common Law Tradition, Extending into Modern*

American Jurisprudence or, more simply, *Poetry for the Modern American Law School*. It's not entirely correct, then, to say that this book intends to give us poems about a "central human concern" (like love) or about interesting things that pretty much everyone can look at or participate in (like roller coasters or weddings). This is, rather, a book that aims at something a little more peculiar: uniting the specific, local incarnations of two modern practices. It's a book about combining academic disciplines.

■   ■   ■

AND WITH THAT, THE dread word "interdisciplinary" descends. Before going any further, though, I'd probably better explain what I mean by referring to poetry as "an academic discipline." As countless letters to *Poetry* magazine have demonstrated, the academic status of poetry is a subject that gets poets riled up—and while being riled up is often a fine thing, especially for poets, it's usually best to save that sort of energy for subjects that deserve it. So the claim here is modest and, I think, inarguable: at present, the single largest institutional factor in the world of American poetry is the American university system (as opposed to, say, the world of corporate publishing or the nonprofit arts sector). Poets are largely employed by universities or are trying to become so; the audience for poetry, such as it is, exists largely within the university; and a large part of the distribution of poetry in the United States is handled by universities, typically by means of academic presses. The art form, as Mark McGurl put it recently in *The Program Era*, "has been all but absorbed by institutions of higher education."

For reasons I'll explain shortly, I believe the "all but" in McGurl's characterization is an essential qualifier. But for now the point is simply that poetry exists in large part as a manifestation of creative writing departments (and, again, I'm neither praising nor condemning this structure, merely acknowledging that this is the lay of the land). As such, poetry is now exposed to the same anxieties that all academic practices face, one of which is simply the anxiety that comes from realizing that one's fellow practitioners are modern academics arranged in (or maybe confined in) a discipline. The critic Louis Menand believes this anxiety helps account for the intense popularity of interdisciplinary studies, the university trend that motivates and sustains books like *Poetry of the Law* and has given rise to such academic subspecialties as the philosophy of physics and evolutionary psychology. Interdisciplinarity is, as Menand puts it in *The Marketplace of Ideas*, simply "the name for teaching and scholarship that bring together methods and materials from more than one academic discipline," and "there are few terms in twentieth-century higher education with a greater buzz factor. . . . No one, or almost no one, says a word against it. It is evoked by professors and deans with equal enthusiasm." Menand himself is skeptical about this excitement, however, and speculates (this is a long quote, but bear with it):

> Maybe, in the case of the academic subject, self-consciousness about disciplinarity and about the status of the professor . . . is a source of anxiety. . . . Academics have been trained to believe that there must be a

contradiction between being a scholar or an intellectual and being part of a system of socialization. They are conditioned to think that their workplace does not operate like a market, even as they compete with one another for status and advantage. Most of all, they are ambivalent about the status they have worked so hard to achieve. Interdisciplinary anxiety is a displaced anxiety about the position of privilege that academic professionalism confers on its initiates and about the peculiar position of social disempowerment created by the barrier between academic workers and the larger culture.

So the desire to reach toward other disciplines often isn't so much a way of combating the limits of one's own methods as a manifestation of a deeper concern over privilege and isolation. We feel trapped in what we are, and we think that if we could meet some other practice halfway, we'd be . . . renewed? Transformed? Made whole? For once, then, something. But beyond all this, Menand suggests,

> We want to feel we are in a real fight, a fight not with each other and our schools, which is the fight that outsiders seem to be encouraging us to have, but with the forces that make and remake the world most human beings live in.

We want to matter, that is. And one way to matter is to find something that's unquestionably important to "the forces that make and remake the world most human beings live in" and then to find some way of mattering to that. One stands close to the general, hoping to share in the glamour of command. Aside from the inducement of making a quick if small buck, this is a primary motive behind the deluge of poetry anthologies about everything from love to lizards. Does nature matter? Does it speak to you? Well, poets have thought about it! And sports! And horses and depression and music and war! Yet significant as these things are, they're only concepts for the most part, not disciplines. If you really want to "make and remake the world," if you really want to do something meaningful with your inter-disciplinary project, then you're going to want to pair up with something a little less abstract. You want something rigorous. Powerful. Organized. Regimented, even. And preferably within walking distance.

■ ■ ■

THE LAW SCHOOL, FOR example. Law is an attractive interdisci-plinary target for poets for several reasons. First, legal practice consists mostly of saying things or writing things down, and since poets have generally claimed a special authority over lan-guage, the match seems a natural one. (We'll set aside, for the moment anyway, the validity of this particular assumption, which is not generally shared by attorneys.) Second, law makes things happen. Even the lowliest lawyer has the power to force someone to respond to a legal summons, thereby exerting more influence on society than any American poet but Jimmy Carter, or possibly Jewel. So it's easy to see why poets might be pleased by a book like *Poetry of the Law*. It implies a relationship almost perfectly designed to sooth the anxieties of poetry as an academic discipline: if lawyers can think about poetry, then poets can think about, and maybe even shape, the law. And suddenly the mirror through which the Lady of Shalott perceives the world seems to exert force rather than simply providing reflection. Maybe it's now even possible to imagine the title of the anthology in reverse: *The Law of Poetry*.

But poetry is attractive to law as well—or at least to the legal academy. Because while law's academic status may seem unassailable from the perspective of an adjunct professor of creative writing, the legal professoriate often views its position quite differently. As the Yale Law professor Jack Balkin puts it in "Interdisciplinarity as Colonization,"

> These days there is a profound sense of questioning about the purposes of legal scholarship, a profound sense of concern about the fracturing of legal scholarship into mutually incomprehensible camps, and a profound sense of worry about the increasing and, for many, undesirable isolation of legal scholarship from the concerns of the legal profession, the bench and the bar.

So Balkin sees the same anxiety in law schools that Menand finds in the English department. As Balkin goes on to observe, given the uncertainty over legal education, interdisciplinary projects might actually seem to be "a threat to the self-identity of the law professor and the legal academy." And yet at the same time, such projects are enormously attractive, and are, in fact, essential for tenure at many law schools. At most elite schools (which provide the majority of legal faculty throughout the United States), there is a sort of constant, low-intensity skirmishing, as various interdisciplinary factions struggle to earn more space on each school's agenda. For the past several decades, the most successful of these by far has been the movement known as "law and economics," which, as you might guess, attempts to use economics to explain, analyze, and predict the legal system. That movement is, unfairly or not, often identified with conservatism and libertarianism, so it should come as no surprise that its methods are often opposed by legal scholars who favor law and literature (as well as scholars specializing in feminism and what's sometimes known as critical race theory). But it's hard to fight without allies, so, as Balkin and Sanford Levinson write in "Law & the Humanities: An Uneasy Relationship,"

> Contemporary law and literature scholars offer the humanities as an antidote to a form of legal professionalism that they believe has become too technocratic and divorced from any human values, save economic efficiency.

One way to look at *Poetry of the Law*, then, is as evidence of a quietly arranged alliance. Faced with the Huns, the humanistically inclined segment of the legal faculty calls in the poets for last-minute assistance. Of course, as most poets know, we aren't necessarily very effective against Huns, let alone economists, but who's going to complain if the lawyers decide to pay attention? After all, it's not as if many other people do.

■   ■   ■

AND THAT, PERHAPS, BRINGS us back to the significance of the phrase "all but," in Mark McGurl's claim that poetry has been "all but absorbed by institutions of higher education." "All but" means "almost completely," but it also means "not quite." That difference matters, I think, and in ways that many poets may not fully appreciate. One of the main points that Balkin makes about interdisciplinarity and the law is that no matter how confused the legal academy may become, or how frequently it may be invaded by offshoots of other disciplines (economics, political science, philosophy, etc.), no one ever manages to dominate it. This is because law schools are continually being pulled back to their primary duty of educating people who are going to be lawyers, not scholars. The legal world that exists outside of school has its own rules, and demands that law schools never completely forget them.

This should strike a familiar chord for poets. Creative writing is not, on the whole, a strong discipline in the way that the university conceives of such things. It lacks a coherent methodology, shared assumptions about its own materials, perspective on its relationship with other academic departments, and often any kind of historical sense. It can be pretty loosey-goosey stuff. But it's also supposed to be loosey-goosey stuff. As McGurl observes, "It is precisely an unresolved tension between the 'confinement' of institutionality and the 'freedom' of creativity that gives creative writing instruction its raison d'être as an institutionalization of anti-institutionality." Creative writing is both of and, significantly, not of the university—and that's the core of its identity as a university department. In this sense, a young poet in a creative writing class is arguably closer to being a law student than a PhD candidate. Both the poet and the lawyer are, at least in theory, constantly feeling the force of a world outside the quad. For the lawyer, that force is the bench and the bar; for the poet, it's the reader.

Again, at least in theory. One of the more frustrating spectacles in the American poetry world is the seemingly never-ending bickering over whether poets are or aren't, or should or shouldn't, be more involved in "the real world" that potential readers supposedly inhabit, and in particular whether teaching somehow prevents this involvement from occurring. This bickering typically settles into two positions, neither of which is persuasive. On the one hand, people regularly complain about poetry's academic status as if it were obvious (a) that no one involved in university life could ever think about anything but university problems, and (b) that there are no benefits to being employed by a university—like, say, health insurance—that might conceivably outweigh the liabilities. On the other hand, it is depressingly easy nowadays to find poets who behave as if the only audience that matters is the one signed up for fall term, and who seem to believe that poets and critics who bother to speak to anyone else are engaged in a kind of quaint pretense, like wearing a smoking jacket. Often these poets will make noises about how poetry's audience has "always been tiny" (as if it were sensible to compare the United States circa 2010 with Elizabethan England), while simultaneously ignoring the question of why, if poetry is a magical flower that needs no tending in order to flourish, anyone should be paid thousands of dollars to teach it.

Both attitudes aren't so much wrong in theory as mistaken in fact. For practical reasons, it makes little sense to complain about the academic status of poetry: that ship has not only sailed but is probably halfway through the Strait of Magellan, which is a good thing in many ways. (Frost may not have been entirely right when he claimed that "the best audience the world ever had . . . is the little town-and-gown audience that we get in the little college towns in the U.S.A."—but he wasn't entirely wrong, either.) Yet it's also incorrect to assume that poetry can exist as a purely academic enterprise, not simply because the arguments to the contrary above are unconvincing, but because it is precisely the perception that the art form is unacademic that allows it to flourish in the university in the first place. Why, for instance, don't we teach serialized novel writing in American universities? Because serialized novel writing no longer exists in the world outside of American universities. And the moment at which poetry ceases to be meaningful to nonprofessors—to doctors and lawyers and engineers and basketball coaches—isn't the moment it will become a purely academic discipline; it's the moment it either will be abandoned by academia or (more likely) quietly absorbed by the English Department. This, as Balkin reminds us, happens regularly in our cordially interdisciplinary universities: "Interdisciplinarity results when different disciplines try to colonize each other. If the takeover is successful, work is no longer interdisciplinary; rather, it is seen as wholly internal to the discipline as newly constituted." Poets, the bell tolls for thee.

■   ■   ■

In "Two Tramps in Mud Time," Robert Frost outlines a scene in which a speaker who is happily splitting wood is approached by two tramps who'd like to do the wood-splitting job for money. They need the work, and he doesn't. Frost then meanders into three stanzas of seemingly unrelated disquisition on the unpredictability of weather in April before returning to the tramps' entreaty in the poem's well-known conclusion:

> *Nothing on either side was said.*
> *They knew they had but to stay their stay*
> *And all their logic would fill my head:*
> *As that I had no right to play*
> *With what was another man's work for gain.*
> *My right might be love but theirs was need.*
> *And where the two exist in twain*
> *Theirs was the better right—agreed.*
>
> *But yield who will to their separation,*
> *My object in living is to unite*
> *My avocation and my vocation*
> *As my two eyes make one in sight.*

Only where love and need are one,
And the work is play for mortal stakes,
Is the deed ever really done
For Heaven and the future's sakes.

The question for writers, always, is never simply "What must I do, in order to write?" It is, as *Poetry of the Law* and "Two Tramps in Mud Time" both suggest, albeit in different ways, "What does it mean for my writing to be of my life, and my life of my writing?" How can "love" and "need" be one? One answer, obviously, is that you can get paid for doing what you love. This is not, alas, generally an option for poets. Another answer is that you can do something reasonably close to what you love and hope that some of the love bleeds into it. This is more or less the idea behind university arts programs, and it isn't a bad one. But it's not always a good one, either. It exposes artists to the problems faced more generally by academics—the anxiety that troubles Menand, for instance—and it can lead to confusion over which needs are getting met, and which loves are getting slowly left behind.

Perhaps a more useful way to think about these questions comes, not from the essayistic conclusion to "Two Tramps in Mud Time," but from the odd three stanzas about April weather that precede it. These stanzas don't, on the face of it, make much sense in the broader context of the poem. Here's the first:

The sun was warm but the wind was chill.
You know how it is with an April day
When the sun is out and the wind is still,

You're one month on in the middle of May.
But if you so much as dare to speak,
A cloud comes over the sunlit arch,
A wind comes off a frozen peak,
And you're two months back in the middle of March.

What do we make of this? Not much, some would say. Hayden Carruth, for instance, claims Frost simply "appears not to know what to do with his opening. The poem wanders into further unnecessary description: the April day, the bluebird, the snow and water. . . . One can see clearly, I believe, how he had deserted his own imagination and how he tried to make up the deficiency through conscious manipulation and force."

The reaction is understandable but misjudged. Throughout his poems and prose, Frost is drawn to digressions, awkwardness, and wrong notes—but in the way that, for instance, a champion athlete might pause in the middle of a race to juggle chainsaws before going on to win by a yard. It's a display of confidence and lazy power. In an era in which Eliot was busily putting together systems from which his work might emerge as a luxury good—many of which are very much still with us—Frost was happy to undermine anything settled, regular, or authoritative in the name of one of his favorite words, "play." The three out-of-place stanzas in "Two Tramps in Mud Time" are, in fact, illustrative of the poem's broader point: it's exactly the pleasure of doing what one wants that allows the poet to chop wood, or to spend twenty-four lines talking about bluebirds and snow for no particular reason. The poem celebrates its own autonomy.

Which is something poems, and poets, should always celebrate. However anxious the poetic life may become; however
difficult it may be to resist pressures from the forces, institutional and otherwise, that surround the art; however awful it
may be to know that there are panels being organized even now
in which poetry will be discussed as if it were a combination of
baseball statistics and sloppy philosophy; however bad all this
may be, there is always room for confidence in poetry's own lazy
power. Wherever one works, wherever one lives, there is always
a way to write poems about bluebirds that aren't about bluebirds. And with due respect to kindly motivated projects like
Poetry of the Law, such work will never be truly "of" anything.
It'll just be poetry—which has always been more than enough.

SCHOOL OF VERSE

The difficulty of teaching poetry to a lay audience can be summarized by a single, diabolical name: Robin Williams. Williams, as you may recall, played the free-thinking English teacher John Keating in the 1989 movie *Dead Poets Society*, a film that established once and for all the connection between learning about poems and killing yourself while wearing a silly hat. In the movie's first depiction of poetical pedagogy, Williams/Keating instructs his students to open their textbook—a dry, dully diagrammatic primer by "Dr. J. Evans Pritchard"—and then, with the insouciant panache of Lord Byron (or possibly Patch Adams), tells them to rip out the introduction! Yes! Riiiip! "Armies of academics going forward, measuring poetry," cries the righteous Keating. "No, we will not have that here!" Instead, the class is told to embrace a philosophy of "carpe diem," and sic transit J. Evans Pritchard. Significantly, however, while Keating subsequently teaches his students how to stand on their desks, how to kick a soccer ball with gusto, and how to free-associate lamely about Walt Whitman ("a sweaty-toothed madman with a stare that pounds my brain!"), he's never shown actually teaching them anything about the basics of form—basics they'd need to know in order to appreciate half the writers he's recommending.

This is to be expected. As Samuel Johnson put it over 250 years ago, anyone attempting to discuss "the minuter parts of literature" usually ends up either "frighting us with rugged science, or amusing us with empty sound." That is, in trying to avoid being a technique-obsessed pedant (like Pritchard), the teacher of poetry can easily become a slogan-spouting windbag (like Keating). Or vice versa. Seen in this light, the famous text-ripping scene from *Dead Poets Society* doesn't show us a helpful new way of relating to poetry so much as the two standard, unhelpful approaches colliding. Of course, this dilemma isn't unique to poetry. Any discipline with a complicated set of rules—baseball, for instance—is equally vulnerable to being reduced to limp statistics or inflated into a George F. Will column. But poetry has a problem that baseball doesn't: it exists both as an art and as a metaphor for certain kinds of experience. It's both poetry and Poetry.

When people use the word "poetry" as a metaphor—when it's Poetry—they're usually thinking about one of two related concepts. First, they're talking about a kind of exemplary expression of a particular craft, a sort of "art of the art." So, for example, different audiences might describe a performance by Cecilia Bartoli or Tiger Woods or Ferran Adrià or Zakk Wylde as "pure poetry." Second, people tend to associate poets with outrageousness, rebellion, and the "deliberate disorientation of the senses," as Rimbaud puts it. This helps to explain why so many rock stars (as opposed to country singers) get called "poets"; it also helps explain why Keating asserts that his youthful encounters with Shelley's verse were bacchanalia in which "spirits soared, women swooned, and gods were created!" Regardless, because so many readers become used to thinking about the word "poetry" in one of these metaphoric senses, they often come to an actual poem expecting either to be awed by excellence or overwhelmed by the Raw Passion of It All.

And they're usually disappointed. Neither of these possibilities has much to do with the way most readers respond to real, unmetaphorical poetry—which is, after all, an art form and not a trope. While it's true that some aspects of poetry transcend the nuts and bolts of technique, it's equally true that many more do not. Consequently, only rarely do lay readers experience poems as a cross between an orgasm and a heart attack; usually the response is closer to "What?" or "Eh" or, at best, "Hm." This doesn't mean that other reactions aren't possible, but such reactions generally come (as with any other complex practice) from learning what the hell is going on. And you don't learn what's going on by kicking a soccer ball and shouting a quote from Shelley. You learn what's going on in poetry by reading carefully and devotedly, questioning your own assumptions, and sticking with things even when you're confused or nervous. Then you can kick the soccer ball.

This is where it's useful to turn from Robin Williams to

another actor, Stephen Fry. Fry, who's known in Britain as a novelist, actor, commentator, and all-around interesting dude (and in America as the guy who sometimes collaborates with the guy from *House*), has written a book with the cheerfully awful title, *The Ode Less Travelled: Unlocking the Poet Within*, which purports to teach all of us "how to have fun with the modes and forms of poetry as they have developed over the years." Or to put it another way, this is J. Evans Pritchard as rewritten by the man who played the sublimely obtuse General Melchett in the *Blackadder* series; which is to say, this is something very odd indeed.

It's also oddly effective. *The Ode Less Travelled* is at once idiosyncratic and thoroughly traditional—it's filled with quips, quirks, and various Fryisms (sestinas are "a bitch to explain but a joy to make"), yet still manages to be a smart, comprehensive guide to prosody. The book is organized in three main sections—meter, rhyme, and form, with exercises suggested for each—and a smaller concluding section in which Fry gives some general thoughts about contemporary British poetry. It also has a practical, good-natured glossary. (Sample entry: "Choliamb—a kind of metrical substitution, usually with ternary feet replacing binary. Forget about it.") The key to the book's success is its tone, which is joking, occasionally fussy, sometimes distractingly cute, but always approachable. If Fry thinks the meter of a Keats couplet "can safely be said to suck," he'll tell you so, and he's more than happy to admit when his own effort at a ghazal is "rather a bastardly abortion." As is to be expected in any book taking on such a complicated subject, there are a few minor errors. For instance, in a discussion of hendecasyllabic lines (that is, lines that have eleven syllables), Fry includes Frost's "And like the flowers beside them, chill and shiver" (count for yourself). But such mistakes are negligible. On the whole, the book is ideal for anyone who's interested in learning more about poetic forms but who doesn't have an obsessive assistant professor living next door.

So why does *The Ode Less Travelled* work when many books with more responsible titles have failed? First, Fry avoids the poetry-as-metaphor trap. He does so by acknowledging upfront what anyone who's ever taught poetry to a nonspecialist audience will recognize as "the fear." This is, in Fry's words, the general reader's sense that

> poetry lies in inaccessible marshland: no pathways, no
> signposts, just the skeletons of long-dead poets poking
> through the bog and the unedifying sight of living ones
> floundering about in apparent confusion and mutual
> enmity. Behind it all, the dread memory of classrooms
> swollen into resentful silence while the English teacher
> invites us to "respond" to a poem.

Rather than pull a Keating, and attempt to turn poetry into a Doors concert circa 1969, Fry's goal is to demystify the art without deadening it, to make it seem as open to the interested amateur as "carpentry and bridge and wine and knitting and brass-rubbing and line-dancing and the hundreds of other activities that enrich and enliven the daily toil of getting and spending." This attitude may annoy certain segments of the American poetry world, to which one can only say, good.

Second, the book works because it gives us a strong perspective without sounding pinched or dogmatic. Fry is a stickler for form: he believes you don't really understand poetry unless you understand at least some of the history of English verse technique. But if he's in favor of form, he's also "far from contemptuous of Modernism and free verse, the experimental and the avant-garde or of the poetry of the streets." It's also to Fry's credit that alongside the sonnet and quatrain, you'll find the Japanese senryu, the Filipino Tanaga and the Vietnamese *luc bát*. In the end, what comes through most vividly in *The Ode Less Travelled*, and what makes it work so well for the amateur, is Fry's belief that "poetry, like cooking, derives from love, an absolute love for the particularity and grain of ingredients." Here he's unconsciously echoing John Dewey, who argued that "craftsmanship . . . must be loving" and that the form of art "unites the very same relation of doing and undoing, outgoing and incoming energy, that makes an experience to be an experience." Poetry, then, isn't a symbol for a type of behavior; it's an experience on its own—and the reader who is properly taught (by Stephen Fry, maybe) won't need to stand on his desk to know it.

THE VIRTUES OF POETRY:

LONGENBACH AND PAPAGEORGIOU

The audience for poetry is like a vastly reduced version of the audience for college football—superstitious, gossipy, and divided into factions that are no less fervent for having only an occasional idea of what's going on outside their own campuses. It's a hard crowd to write to (or for), and the critic who sets himself up as a color commentator inevitably struggles to find a style that can please Peter without needlessly riling up Paul.

James Longenbach is one of the finest scholar-critics working today, and his method for dealing with poetry's fractious readership is simple: he just tells everyone they're wrong. In *Modern Poetry after Modernism*, he pointed out that we "exaggerate the formal and political idiosyncrasy of postmodern poetry." In *The Resistance to Poetry*, he suggested that "poems have resisted themselves more strenuously than the cultures receiving them." Typically these counterintuitive arguments are delivered in a tone of such thoroughgoing reasonableness that you feel as if you've been not so much corrected as gently nudged into rationality.

Longenbach's new book, *The Virtues of Poetry*, examines "the virtues to which the next poem might aspire," which is a project that will obviously get the attention of poets, but should also appeal to general readers. Each chapter is organized around one or two concepts—"compression," "doubt," "otherness," and so forth—that Longenbach uses as a fulcrum to lift some impressively complex argumentative machinery. The book's opening chapter, for instance, is an examination of restraint and plainness in poetry, qualities that Longenbach describes as arising from a "surrender" that allows a poet to "wither" into his proper style. He means that as a compliment. "The surrender of the will is itself impossible to will," he writes, "and we may struggle with the act of surrender even more than we struggle with the act of rebellion." Because fashion currently favors poems that are frenetic and knowing, the poet whose gift is for the plain style needs to find a way to give in to his own best impulses. (As Longenbach notes, a differently situated writer might need to surrender "to worldliness and excess.")

In making these points, Longenbach covers Proust, early and late Yeats, the aural difference between Germanic and Latinate words, William Blake, Andrew Marvell, and George Oppen, all in about twelve pages. The historical breadth is typical: *The Virtues of Poetry* is meant to provide a perspective on poetry's long tradition that will help readers resist "the renegade engines of taste." So we get a thoughtful treatment of

Pound that leads to Susan Howe and a smart take on intentionally bad writing that moves from *King Lear* to Elizabeth
Bishop. But if Longenbach believes in tradition, he isn't exactly
traditional. A better description might be antireductionist.
Throughout these essays, we're repeatedly asked to consider the
ways in which style A is actually compatible with (or a version
of) style B, and vice versa. The chapter called "Infinitude," for
instance, draws a parallel between Whitman and Louise Glück,
whose approaches are typically assumed to stand in relation to
each other like Jack Sprat and spouse.

But then, typical assumptions are Longenbach's bête noire.
While *The Virtues of Poetry* is a thoroughly civil book, you can
sense the professorial cool beginning to slip whenever Longenbach feels poetry is being sacrificed to conventional wisdom
or clubbiness. He mentions having read a review in which another critic suggests Yeats is "an unlikely model" for today's
writers—to which Longenbach saltily replies, "Why? Because
he arranged syllables into rhythms? Because he didn't live in
Brooklyn?"

Longenbach's exasperation is understandable, but his unhappiness with jargon, ginned-up conflicts, and breakthrough
narratives—all staples in the poetry world's eternal quest to do
something really, really new this time!—can occasionally cause
him to understate differences that actually are different. In a
discussion of "revelation" in the poetry of Elizabeth Bishop and
Robert Lowell, for instance, Longenbach asserts that "the apparently reticent Bishop has been used as a club to beat the apparently revelatory Lowell, much as Lowell was once used as a

club to beat the apparently impersonal T. S. Eliot." He loses me
here at "much as." Lowell and Eliot were born thirty years apart;
Lowell and Bishop were peers. And Eliot and Lowell were both
men. Contrary to the implicit suggestion ("much as"), these are
not small differences. In focusing on poets and poems, Longenbach sometimes moves a little too quickly past questions about
which poets, and *what* poems, and *why*: the very questions that
"renegade taste" confronts, however unsatisfyingly. But this is to
dissent only mildly. The advice that *The Virtues of Poetry* implicitly offers—always read for maximum complexity, and with
maximum patience—is as valuable as it is frequently ignored.

And perhaps the highest compliment you can pay any
poetry critic is to say that you found yourself thinking of his
writing the next time you encountered a good poem—which is
exactly what I did when reading Fani Papageorgiou's discon-
certing and magnetic first book *When You Said No, Did You
Mean Never?* Papageorgiou's poems are small—most come in
under fifteen lines—and composed in a spare but conversational free verse that rarely breaks the rules of everyday syntax
(there's even a poem here called "Modal Verbs"). They often
begin with slightly off-kilter observations ("I'll tell you all about
the battle of Copenhagen"), frequently drift into aphorisms
("The man who stepped out for a paper / and never came back /
lives inside us all"), and generally have identifiable if quirky
subjects: children's games, the Glasgow coma scale, the word
"marasmus," oubliettes, peacock feathers. But what most distinguishes Papageorgiou's writing is its peculiar embodiment of
two concepts Longenbach dwells on at length: compression and

dilation. Compression refers to the sense that a poem's language has been scrupulously pared down; dilation occurs when a poem's language has been allowed to go so slack that it seems almost unpoetic.

Papageorgiou's poetry elides the two concepts, or maybe just tangles them together—and in a very tight space. The poems are intense but enigmatic, as if they were brands burned in with broken irons. Consider "The Watchtower":

> *I am up here*
> *it is raining*
> *I see a cistern with a turtle in it.*
> *This is our life.*
> *I slip down a rung*
> *then another.*
> *This is when accidents happen.*
>
> *The cistern rotates and departs at a slow canter.*
> *Head, limbs and tail withdraw*
> *into the leathery shell of the turtle.*
> *There is rain on my hands*
> *I run towards the sea*
> *there is nowhere else to go.*

The poem is flat ("I am up here / it is raining"), then furiously focused ("This is our life"), then just plain weird ("The cistern rotates and departs at a slow canter"). And it would be hard to separate any part from the other: the banal opening

proves just as "enticing" (Longenbach's term of praise for dilation) as the artfully bizarre conflation of the cistern and the
turtle (notice that Papageorgiou deliberately delays identifying
whose "Head, limbs and tail withdraw"). It's an odd effect that
Papageorgiou manages repeatedly. Here's the beginning of
"Bergmann's Rule" (the rule in question holds that larger animals are found in colder environments):

> *Siberian tigers are bigger than Bengal tigers*
> *and Bengal tigers are bigger*
> *than those in equatorial jungles.*
> *Forget the tiger.*
> *Take the bear.*

The poem continues in a series of repetitions and false
starts:

> *Take turtles and salamanders,*
> *they tend to follow the rule,*
> *with exceptions concentrated in lizards and snakes.*
> *Forget the exceptions—*
> *take what you need.*
> *You can do anything if you're not in a hurry.*

The poem winds through facts ("he published his observations in 1847"), pauses for unsettling maxims ("These are the
comforts of neat enclosure"), and winds up in a very strange
place indeed ("Other people can lie if they want, but not you").

The effect is like looking at a flickering lightbulb and finding yourself unable to distinguish the darkness from the split seconds of illumination.

And this, you might say is the real virtue of poetry. "It was as if the poem were a house I'd lived in all my life without knowing it," Longenbach writes of rereading Marvell's "The Garden." The idea is similar for very good contemporary collections: they feel like houses we've visited before and are happy to return to. And yet as Papageorgiou's curious, delightful book reminds us (and as Dionne Warwick once observed), a house is not a home; it's always just a little unfamiliar, just slightly beyond our easy occupation. Which is precisely what draws us to the door, to the briefly lit windows.

BEACH READING

If you were compiling a list of Places Appropriate for Poetic Thoughts, the beach probably would rank somewhere near the top, on par with "in a dark wood" and well above "in an Outback Steakhouse." In general, of course, this has less to do with the beach as a lived experience (that is, a place you can eat oysters and play skee ball) than with the beach as a concept (a territory that is marginal, shifting, and adjacent to a vast and impenetrable element). Or to put it another way, for most writers the beach is less important than "the beach." Consider, for example, the way the British critic Gabriel Josipovici describes his arrival in Los Angeles in his elegant and peculiar book *Touch*:

> On my first visit . . . I surprised my hosts—and myself—by asking to be taken down to the sea. I found that, more even than wanting to visit the streets down which Philip Marlowe had walked, or any of the city's

great museums, which my hosts were eager to show me, I wanted to dip my hand in the Pacific. We drove out of town and along the coast in the direction of the Getty Museum. They stopped the car and I got out and went across the dirty beach and bent down where the waves lapped the shore. . . . Within a very short while, of course, I could recall nothing of that moment, only my sense of myself hurrying across the sand and the feeling of disappointment that the water did not seem in any way distinctive.

Josipovici isn't interested in the actual "dirty beach"; he's interested in the possibilities the beach represents, in particular the intuition that a "touch" can confirm one's arrival in a place that previously existed only in imagination. Borrowing from the work of the historian Peter Brown, Josipovici concludes that his desire to put a hand in the Pacific related to the ancient belief that pilgrimage culminates in a personal encounter—a shared touch—with the saint whose blessing is sought. It's a pleasingly subtle finale to a subtly pleasing essay.

But it's also incomplete. Whether or not the desire for physical contact relates to the longings of the medieval pilgrim (or the modern essayist), it doesn't explain why Josipovici needed to touch the ocean in particular. After all, if he'd chosen to touch a fish taco instead, he'd still have been in Los Angeles. What is it about the sea—and, more specifically, the way we think about beaches—that makes Josipovici's anecdote moving and persuasive, rather than just another sad tale of tacos forgone? Why does it seem so appropriate that he marked his passage by visiting the shore? And why have so many poets preceded him down to the water's edge, to make their own obscure offerings to the tide?

* * *

"THESE SANDS," SAID THE naturalist Henry Beston of Cape Cod, "might be the beginning or the end of a world." The point is basic, but it matters—whatever else the shoreline may be, it's a boundary between one thing and another (or as Josipovici might say, it's a place at which a touch can occur). And boundaries, as all poets know, are meant to be tested, probed, and, when necessary, crossed. One of the best illustrations of the beach as a site of poetic border blurring occurs in book 4 of *The Odyssey*, in which Menelaus describes his long journey home from Troy. Having been marooned in Egypt for twenty days, Menelaus learns that his escape depends on finagling a solution out of Proteus, the shape-changing god known as the Old Man of the Sea. As Menelaus puts it, getting the better of Proteus involves some slightly gory trickery on the part of Proteus's daughter, Eidothea:

> *back from the waves she came with four sealskins,*
> *all freshly stripped, to deceive her father blind.*
> *She scooped out lurking places deep in the sand*
> *and sat there waiting as we approached her post,*
> *then couching us side-by-side she flung a sealskin*

over each man's back. Now there was an ambush
that would have overpowered us all—overpowering,
true, the awful reek of all those sea-fed brutes!
Who'd dream of bedding down with a monster of the deep?

When Proteus arrives on the beach, he mistakes Menelaus and his men for the seals he usually tends "like a shepherd with his flock." He lies down among the "seals" and falls asleep. At once Menelaus and his companions seize the god, who (as Eidothea had warned) begins rapidly shifting through a multitude of forms—"a great bearded lion," "a serpent," "a torrent of water," "a tree with soaring branchtops." At last, exhausted, he assumes his original shape, and Menelaus is able to force him to explain how the Greeks might return to Sparta.

So here we have (1) men disguised as seals; (2) seals described as sheep; (3) a god portrayed as a man ("a shepherd") who then becomes an array of animals, plants, and elements; and (4) a scenario in which a "true" form and "true" directions are produced only by physical force (a kind of touch). And, of course, it all takes place in an area that's sometimes bare land, other times covered by water. That last fact matters too—just try imagining this episode in the middle of a broccoli patch. The beach isn't simply part of the scene; it's what makes the scene work. Just as Josipovici looks to the shore to officially mark his arrival in a new place (that is, to make a transition), so Menelaus must fight on the sand to return to an old one (that is, to stop making transitions). Either way, the beach is the place where change occurs.

■ ■ ■

THERE ARE TWO WAYS to think about this aspect of the shore as it relates to Menelaus's battle with Proteus. The first is to focus on the fact that the change in question eventually ceases—that a form emerges out of formlessness, meaning is achieved, order is established, and so on. If you favor a systematic approach to literature, this aspect of Menelaus's confrontation probably will appeal to you. But if you're a more disorderly sort of reader, what's more interesting is the humor and strangeness of the piled-up crossings and recrossings of borders—land/sea/man/ animal/god—and the comical, frightening, desperate process that seems, as Keats might say, like being "in uncertainties, Mysteries, doubts," only with a fairly irritable "reaching after fact & reason." It's the struggle, not the struggle's successful conclusion, that stays in the imagination and seems distinctly poetic. Or think of it this way: Menelaus is a hero and king when he wrests a definite form and a clear answer from Proteus; he's a hero and king when he sails the water and when he assumes his dominion on land. But while he's scrambling on the beach, sloughing off a sealskin, clutching a lion that's a serpent that's a stream of water—then he's reading (or writing) poetry.

■ ■ ■

THE BEACH, THEN, IS an area that lends itself to discussions of betweenness, hybridity, and unstable identities—in other words, promising terrain for poets and people who spend a lot of time

thinking about postcolonial theory. But of course, borders aren't
always flexible, and if the shore is a boundary that's constantly
tested by the tide, it remains a boundary nonetheless. Indeed,
the very fact that a beach implies change means that it also implies separation—in order for X to become Y, there must be
a discrete X and Y. This is why beach poems are often about
failure, especially a failure to understand or communicate. For
example:

> I was much further out than you thought
> And not waving but drowning.
>   —Stevie Smith

> The Sea of Faith
> Was once, too, at the full, and round earth's shore
> Lay like the folds of a bright girdle furled.
> But now I only hear
> Its melancholy, long, withdrawing roar.
>   —Matthew Arnold

> We wished our two souls
> might return like gulls
> to the rock. In the end,
> the water was too cold for us.
>   —Robert Lowell

Death, and change, and darkness everlasting,
  Deaf, that hears not what the daystar saith,
Blind, past all remembrance and forecasting,
  Dead, past memory that it once drew breath;
These, above the washing tides and wasting,
  Reign, and rule, this land of utter death.
  —Algernon Charles Swinburne

If the beach is, in daily life, often a cheerful, goofy place filled with waterslides and regrettable swimsuits, in poetry it's more frequently a territory that causes even Whitman to say things like "Nature here in sight of the sea taking advantage of me to dart upon me and sting me / Because I have dared to open my mouth to sing at all."

* * *

THIS IS, AT LEAST in part, because there's something potentially sad about metaphor. After all, if we can only describe one thing in terms of something else, there's no one true, eternal word to be said about anything. And as a place where two elements meet, the beach is a kind of metaphor for the conditions of metaphor—a double failure, then, if you're secretly wishing to be free of comparisons and changes. In his strange beach poem "The Merman," Paul Muldoon is concerned with exactly this kind of disappointment:

He was ploughing his single furrow
Through the green, heavy sward

Of water. I was sowing winter wheat
At the shoreline, when our farms met.

Not a furrow, quite, I argued.
Nothing would come of his long acre
But breaker growing out of breaker,
The wind-scythe, the rain-harrow.

Had he no wish to own such land
As he might plough round in a day?
What of friendship, love? Such qualities?

He remembered these same fields of corn or hay
When swathes ran high along the ground,
Hearing the cries of one in difficulties.

In Muldoon's poem (an updating of Frost's "Mending
Wall"), the beach isn't a place where elements blend, however
violently; instead the shore is a hard line between two realms. If
we think about Menelaus and Proteus, it's not surprising to find
a merman near a beach—as a shared territory it draws shared
forms. But this merman is seen exclusively through the language
of the farmer on shore. As the critic Tim Kendall argues, "Lacking any sense of empathy, the farmer appropriates the merman's
domain to fit his own limited vision. . . . The merman is seen
as different from humankind, unable to share the farmer's values, and his apparently irrelevant response seems only to stress
his ignorance of friendship and of love." As Kendall probably

would agree, though, the most interesting thing about "The Merman" isn't this disjunction but rather the way in which the failures of the farmer's language go beyond simple inappropriateness. What matters—and what makes the poem so strange— is that the two figures aren't merely separate, they're alienated.

The word "alien" stems from the Latin *alius*, meaning "other." In Muldoon's poem—and indeed in many beach poems—the sense of strangeness comes from realizing that in comparing one thing to another, we're making it impossible for the two things to be manifestations of a larger whole. The act of comparison is an act of division, just as the beach will always remind us that the land isn't the sea. Consequently, when Muldoon's farmer tries to make the merman into himself—and fails, as he must—he foregrounds an aspect of language that's already built into the poem's placement. Rather than thinking that the merman is a type of person, we're reminded instead that he is alien, that he is other.

■ ■ ■

THIS LEADS TO AN odd but important question: Why does Elizabeth Bishop have a thing for seals? Or, at least, why does she go out of her way to insert one into "At the Fishhouses"? As you may recall, that poem ends by claiming that sea water

> *is like what we imagine knowledge to be:*
> *dark, salt, clear, moving, utterly free,*
> *drawn from the cold hard mouth*

of the world, derived from the rocky breasts
forever, flowing and drawn, and since
our knowledge is historical, flowing, and flown.

This is a rare instance of Bishop in high style—conspicuously poetic, darkly grand. But before all the talk about knowledge and the "cold hard mouth / of the world," there's the slightly whimsical appearance of a seal:

Cold dark deep and absolutely clear,
element bearable to no mortal,
to fish and to seals . . . One seal particularly
I have seen here evening after evening.
He was curious about me. He was interested in music;
like me a believer in total immersion,
so I used to sing him Baptist hymns.
I also sang "A Mighty Fortress Is Our God."
He stood up in the water and regarded me
steadily, moving his head a little.
Then he would disappear, then suddenly emerge
almost in the same spot, with a sort of shrug
as if it were against his better judgment.

What's a joke about a seal doing in this deadly serious meditation? For the most part, critics have tended to put the seal off as "comic relief" that shows Bishop "nervously relaxing with a little satire of her immersion" (Robert Dale Parker), or as a mere interruption in her "progress toward the sea" (Vicki Graham). Almost everyone thinks the seal is funny.

But it's not—or at least not entirely. In order to see why, it helps to remember that "At the Fishhouses" is, among other things, one of the great beach poems. And just as the beach is neither land nor water—neither self nor other—beach poems often involve a figure that represents or comments on the possibilities that are going to be set in relation without necessarily being committed to any of them. For Homer, this figure is Proteus; for Mathew Arnold in "Dover Beach," it's the speaker's "love"; for Whitman in "Out of the Cradle Endlessly Rocking," it's a mockingbird; for Stevens in "The Idea of Order at Key West," it's Ramon Fernandez; for Muldoon, it's a merman.

■   ■   ■

FOR BISHOP, IT'S A seal. "At the Fishhouses" is a poem about, among other things, our alienation from our own knowledge of the world. While it's true that Bishop could have attempted to make that point by simply writing about water that is "cold dark deep and absolutely clear," she's able to make it much more convincingly by including her supposedly amusing seal. Because, like Muldoon's merman, the seal represents a kind of failure—and again it's a failure of depiction and communication. It matters, first, that the seal is not only a mammal but one associated with the ability to take on human form in stories about selkies from Irish and Scottish folklore. As with Muldoon's merman, this places the seal closer to us and allows us

to think some kind of exchange might be possible. (To understand how deliberate and essential this choice is, try imaging
Bishop singing "A Mighty Fortress Is Our God" to, say, a crab.)
Indeed, the seal is given "judgment," "a sort of shrug," an interest
in music—a series of human characteristics that are likely the reason so many readers have found this section of the poem comic.

But there's something very serious about these anthropo-
morphizations, and about the jarringly light tone in which
they're delivered. The seal, as Bishop knows, is an animal. No
matter how human it may seem, no matter how familiar its gestures may look, there is ultimately no possibility of exchange,
beyond a mutually uncomprehending gaze. The seal is just a
seal. And the curiously "off" tone of this section—its dissonant
jauntiness—is Bishop's admission that she cannot make this
particular other into another form of herself. Despite the Baptist
hymns, she's alone on the beach.

■   ■   ■

THIS IS WHY WE'RE prepared for the more explicit and profound
depiction of alienation with which the poem closes. If the water is
knowledge, it's a knowledge we can barely touch and never hold:

> *If you should dip your hand in,*
> *your wrist would ache immediately,*
> *your bones would begin to ache and your hand would burn*
> *as if the water were a transmutation of fire*
> *that feeds on stones and burns with a dark gray flame.*

Josipovici would understand the fascination and regret that mingle in these lines. No matter how often we approach the sea, Bishop is saying, we can never arrive anywhere but another beach. And like so many poets before us, we are left on the sands, facing the waves, anticipating a meeting toward which we will never stop traveling and at which we will never arrive.

THE TUNNEL

In the mountains just north of Walhalla, South Carolina, there is a tunnel that goes nowhere. The tunnel is over twenty feet high and more than fifteen feet wide—large enough to accommodate a train, which was its original mission—and staring into its entrance, one can easily imagine some newborn, mythic creature emerging from the absolute dark that takes hold within roughly two hundred steps. Or one could imagine the surrounding countryside for miles around (the red maples, the nearby waterfall, the battered trailers and roadhouses) being slowly drawn into the tunnel's mouth and vanishing entirely, to leave an outer emptiness equaling the void within.

These are dramatic thoughts. They are also sexual thoughts, any student of literature would say, and probably thoughts of death as well. But mostly they are thoughts of home. My early childhood was spent in upstate South Carolina, within about forty miles of the tunnel, and throughout my life I've felt claimed by that curious region, which should never be confused with the swampy midlands of the state, much less its sybaritic coast. The upstate is hard, strange, mystical territory. Though it lies more in the foothills than in the mountains themselves, it remains a close cousin to Appalachia: a religious, restless, self-reliant, and aggressive place that is all the more prideful for feeling perpetually looked down upon. And looked down upon not just by the rest of America—that's been true of the South writ large for a century and a half—but by the state's traditional seats of power in the lowlands around Charleston and the central counties that circle Columbia, the capital.

The distinctions among these regions are largely matters of terrain (red clay in the upstate, sand-based soils near the coast) and historical economic patterns (smaller farms versus massive plantations). But they're also philosophical, and even ethnic. As the journalist Ben Robertson put it in 1942 in his upcountry memoir *Red Hills and Cotton*:

> The leading Charlestonians were descended from gentlemen in England, and they actually talked about who was a gentleman born and who was not. We said God help us if we ever became that kind of gentleman; a gentleman with us had to win that title by the quality of his acts. Charlestonians had come to the colony of South Carolina with money and china dishes and English silver. We had come down along the mountains from Pennsylvania with nothing—we had walked.

Editorializing aside, this is essentially correct. Prior to the Revolutionary War, the lower part of South Carolina was populated by the English, and the northwestern corner was held by the Cherokee, who maintained an uneasy peace with nearby settlers who had recently arrived on foot from the north. (The waterfall beside the tunnel is called Issaqueena Falls, and comes accompanied with a variant on the Pocahontas legend.) These settlers were largely what Americans refer to as Scotch-Irish— that is, they were Scots who had relocated to Ireland as tenant farmers and laborers, and then migrated to America in search of their own land. They were "improved Scots of Ulster extraction," as Robertson rather proudly puts it. And they had indeed walked, winding their way down from Pennsylvania along a trail now heavily populated by stoned backpackers, but then a daunting passage menaced by bears, wolves, mountain lions, and a frequently hostile native population. To complete such a journey, you needed to be fairly dangerous yourself.

Which the Scotch-Irish were to nearly everyone, including their own kin. As David Fischer recounts in his study of early British and Irish immigration, *Albion's Seed*, the Scotch-Irish were acquainted with violence—and frankly relished it—in a way that struck even other hardscrabble immigrant populations as unnerving. The story of this ethnicity, as Fischer tells it, is one of border conflict. He views the twice-relocated Scots as one element in a larger pattern of immigration that included their relatives in the disputed territories between northern England and lower Scotland—territory that had been raided and counterraided by Scottish and English monarchs for hundreds of

years. The "borderers," as Fischer collectively calls them, consequently had evolved into a gaggle of guerilla forces and ragtag
militias accustomed to skirmishes, ambushes, and relocating a
moment ahead of a superior force. They relied primarily on family (having no expectation of help from any other quarter), and
their justice was the justice of the blood feud. They were very
proud, very poor, and "void of conscience, the fear of God; and
of all honesty," as an English office put it in 1611, such that the
best way to deal with them often was simply to encourage them
to move elsewhere. This was in fact how a large number of
Scotch-Irish acquired the Irish portion of their designation.
"Many were forcibly resettled in Ireland," writes Fischer, "where
officials complained that they were 'as difficult to manage in
Ireland as in north Cumberland,' and banished them once
again—this time to the colonies." Consequently, the Scotch-
Irish "included a double-distilled selection of some of the most
disorderly inhabitants of a deeply disordered land."

These are, or were, my family's people on both sides. When
they came to America, they headed straight for the frontier, lay-
ing claim to whatever they felt they could keep. The land around
the tunnel became their land.

■ ■ ■

THE STUMPHOUSE MOUNTAIN TUNNEL is a minor tourist des-
tination nowadays, an hour's amusement for SUVs en route to
the cultivated quaintness of mountain towns like Cashiers and
Highlands. But it was originally conceived as the most important step in a scheme to give South Carolina access—or at least,

to give Charleston access—to the expanding markets of the Midwest in the nineteenth century. At that time, goods from Ohio and eastern Tennessee had to travel nearly two thousand miles before they reached South Carolina, because the mountains of the southern Blue Ridge blocked the most direct path to the state. If this obstacle could be overcome, though, the route would be reduced by three-quarters—a difference so enormous that extraordinary measures became worth contemplating. So around 1850 the state granted a charter to a business consortium called the Blue Ridge Railroad Company, with the goal of constructing a series of bridges and tunnels that would traverse the mountains. The biggest challenge lay in northern Oconee County, just above the newly formed town of Walhalla. This was Stumphouse Mountain, hulking over the countryside at roughly four times the height of the Strasbourg Cathedral, then the tallest building in the world. To conquer it, workers would have to tunnel 5,863 feet—well over a mile—straight through granite.

■   ■   ■

TUNNELS DON'T OFTEN APPEAR in poems, and when they do, the treatment is rarely flattering. This is somewhat surprising, considering the poetic popularity of the tunnel's counterpart, the bridge. Bridge poems (and bridge metaphors within poems) are so common that it can sometimes seem as if English-language poets all spent their childhoods puttering around in Venice. "I have stood on the bridge at midnight," writes Longfellow, before delivering a meditation on the spiritual plight of mortal man. "Faith—is the Pierless Bridge," Dickinson tells us, before doing much the same. "I have haunted the river every night lately where I could get a look at the bridge by moonlight," wrote Whitman about St. Louis's Eads Bridge in 1879. "It is indeed a structure of perfection and beauty unsurpassable, and I never tire of it." A bridge is a monument, a crossing, a joining of one thing to another. What poet could ever tire of that?

Yet tunnels, which serve the same purpose, have proved vastly less interesting. In part, of course, this has to do with ancient ideas about the underworld, which is classically depicted as the terminus of an underground passage. One stands on a bridge and looks at the stars or the far shore; one stands in a tunnel and thinks about hellfire and the hungry dead. Even when a poem invokes a tunnel specifically for the purpose of calling up these chthonic associations, as Dante does in the *Inferno*, the tunnel itself generally recedes into the background. When Orpheus descends into the underworld in search of Eurydice, for example, we don't care whether the walls of the tunnel were limestone or granite, or whether water constantly dripped from the ceiling, as it does in the interior of Stumphouse Mountain. The point is not the passage that allows entry into hell, but the fact of that admittance.

The difference between bridges and tunnels, poetically speaking, is perhaps most vividly stated in *The Bridge*, Hart Crane's ruined masterpiece. Most poetry readers are familiar with Crane's ecstatic celebration of the Brooklyn Bridge:

> *O harp and altar, of the fury fused,*
> *(How could mere toil align thy choiring strings!)*

Terrific threshold of the prophet's pledge,
Prayer of pariah, and the lover's cry,

Again the traffic lights that skim thy swift
Unfractioned idiom, immaculate sigh of stars,
Beading thy path—condense eternity:
And we have seen night lifted in thine arms.

"Harp and altar." "Prayer of pariah." Whatever one may think of these effusions, there's no question that Crane intends for the bridge to be a *good* thing. But here is how he describes the subway system in "The Tunnel":

Whose head is swinging from the swollen strap?
Whose body smokes along the bitten rails,
Bursts from a smoldering bundle far behind
In back forks of the chasms of the brain,—
Puffs from a riven stump far out behind
In interborough fissures of the mind . . . ?

Not quite such a good thing, it would seem. This is the tunnel as a proxy for the underworld, accursed and sulfuric. But more interesting than this predictable symbolism, I think, is the racket with which Crane fills "The Tunnel," which includes snatches of overlapping conversations ("if / you don't like my gate why did you / swing on it?") and a medley of instruments and sound effects. As in:

The gongs recur:
Elbows and levers, guard and hissing door.
Thunder is galvothermic here below. . . . The car
Wheels off. The train rounds, bending to a scream,
Taking the final level for the dive
Under the river—
And somewhat emptier than before,
Demented, for a hitching second, humps; then
Lets go. . . . Toward corners of the floor
Newspapers wing, revolve and wing.
Blank windows gargle signals through the roar.

"Gongs," "hissing," "thunder," "gargle": It's a cornucopia of sound. This is partly because the New York subway is a constant clamor. But it's also because a subway is a tunnel. Outside a tunnel, there's nothing to see but a hole in the earth; inside a tunnel, there's nothing to see but whatever you brought with you (subway car windows, as Crane notes, are "blank"). So you dwell on what you hear. In an unlighted tunnel, of course, this effect is heightened. Your eyes can't help you in a place like Stumphouse Mountain, for example; it's far too dark to make anything out. All you can do is listen.

■ ■ ■

WHEN I WAS A young boy, I was afraid to talk to my grandfather, especially on the phone. Not afraid in the way children are typically afraid of older family members—I wasn't worried that he'd get angry, for example, or behave in a way that struck me as confusing or erratic. I was afraid of his voice. Or rather I was afraid of his way of speaking. When he talked, the sound was low, rough, mumbled, and almost absurdly Southern, the syllables arriving in great wobbling exhalations like the benevolent rumbling of some large, patient earth spirit. I understood maybe five words out of ten.

I was too young to fully grasp the concept of embarrassment, so my lack of comprehension registered as simple dread: I was afraid I wouldn't be able to follow what he was saying, afraid he'd realize I hadn't followed, afraid of what that situation would entail, afraid of failure on all sides. The worst of it was that I loved my grandfather. He'd been a textile mill worker all his life, just like my grandmother, and he wore overalls and a decaying baseball cap every time I saw him (I can recall only one exception: at my grandmother's funeral, he put on a black suit that had probably been wilting in a trunk since the Second World War). His favorite thing to do, aside from starting arguments among his vast brood of children and grandchildren, was to go fishing, and to be taken along was the pinnacle of my boyhood.

But I was always afraid I'd misunderstand him. That possibility lay between us like a trip wire, and I eased my way through any exchange with a scout's caution.

■   ■   ■

FROM 1854 THROUGH 1858, the Stumphouse Mountain Tunnel project passed through the ledgers of at least five different companies: Bangs and Company, A. Birdsall and Company, George

Collyer Company, Garret and Junter, Humbird and Hitchcock. A small, impromptu town called Tunnel Hill arose near the tunnel itself, largely populated by Irish workers brought down from New York. These workers frequently clashed with the native inhabitants, who were, as a missionary Catholic priest observed, the sort of men who were happy with "a rifle, a peck of meal, and a dog for the chase." In a paper for the South Carolina Historical Society, Jim Haughey of Anderson University quotes the *Keowee Courier* describing some of the locals as "worthless and drunken, and who live, vampire-like, by preying upon the ignorant and unsuspecting." These were the bad seeds of the Scotch-Irish, the border bandits, the people "void of conscience, the fear of God; and of all honesty." It's clear from the priest's records that he never thought of these men as being Irish themselves, or of Irish descent. They were simply Americans by then.

■　■　■

THE INTRODUCTION TO *The Faber Book of Contemporary Irish Poetry*, edited by Paul Muldoon, isn't an introduction in the ordinary sense. Rather, the poems are preceded by part of the transcript of a conversation between the Irish poets F. R. Higgins and Louis MacNeice that was broadcast by the BBC in 1939. Higgins is quite taken with the notion of Irishness, which he views as determining a poet's writing in the way DNA determines a person's hair color. "I am afraid, Mr. MacNeice," he says, "you, as an Irishman, cannot escape from your blood, nor from our blood-music that brings the racial character to mind. Irish poetry remains a creation happily, fundamentally rooted in rural civilization."

MacNeice—a deeply cosmopolitan writer, a friend (and poetic equal) of W. H. Auden—is skeptical. He replies:

> I think one may have such a thing as one's racial blood-music, but that, like one's unconscious, it may be left to take care of itself. . . . I think that the poet is a sensitive instrument designed to record anything that interests his mind or affects his emotions. If a gasometer, for instance, affects his emotions, or if the Marxian dialectic, let us say, interests his mind, then let them come into his poetry.

For MacNeice, it isn't that his heritage doesn't matter but rather that it "may be left to take care of itself"—that is, it lies somewhere beneath the subjects that the poet deliberately allows to "come into his poetry." So MacNeice wrote reveries from Iceland, spent much of his career in or around London, and when he wrote about Ireland, did so with ambivalence and a cocked eyebrow ("She is both a bore and a bitch"). His poems filled up with trains, electric mops, stalled traffic; as he told Higgins, whatever came in, came in. And as he aged, a black loneliness blossomed beneath this elegantly assembled bric-a-brac.

■   ■   ■

I LOOK BACK AT what I've written here, and much of it seems questionable. I say I feel "claimed" by the upcountry. Do I? In some sense, yes: when I think of what feels like "home," that region is what I imagine. And yet it isn't even where I grew up.

Though we returned to the upstate regularly to visit relatives, my immediate family moved to Columbia when I was five and a half. There I was surrounded, not by rolling, red-streaked hills and masses of kudzu, but by the houses in a typical patchwork of American suburbs, complete with optimistically pastoral names like Greengate, Briarwood, and Spring Valley. I probably spent more time in Spencer's Gifts in the Columbia mall than I ever did with my great-uncle Fletcher's muscadine vines, or in my great-grandmother's tiny, battered house, which had once (or so I was told) been the first stagecoach stop in Pickens County.

And we weren't poor, or even close to poor. My father had grown up the son of two line workers in a textile mill—the same mill that "Shoeless" Joe Jackson had worked in—and he lived with seven brothers and sisters in a nine-hundred-square-foot house with no hot water. My mother was the daughter of a firefighter who had grown up so impoverished himself that he was only ever given one toy—a red plastic car that one of his brothers promptly managed to step on. As a girl, my grandmother, the daughter of sharecroppers, was once embarrassed when she fell off a swing at school and the other children saw that her underwear had been stitched together from flour sacks. She wore her high school ring for most of her life, because she was so proud of having graduated (she was the only one of my grandparents to have done so). This was the poor white South of a dozen pulpy midcentury novels.

But my sister and I—we were middle class, and then upper middle class. We were the children of an increasingly successful lawyer and a woman who'd read every book in every library she'd entered. I never picked cotton, worked a loom, or shot at my own cat ("He tried to take my hunt," my grandfather explained of this boyhood episode). At this point, I've even lost almost all of what was once—as I can tell from VHS tapes of my childhood birthdays—a pungently Southern accent. It survives now only in the smallest of tells, like the *h* I still pronounce in words like "what" or "which." So much of what I've written here seems secondhand, unearned, incomplete, and yet somehow unavoidable—as if I were a tourist condemned to perpetually revisit the same half-abandoned beach town, where each year the placards become a little fainter, a little harder to discern. I'm not even certain the family is Scotch-Irish, though the various surnames make it seem likely. When I think about these things, and when I think about *why* I think about these things, I can't decide whether some part of me is stealing or being stolen.

■   ■   ■

By 1859 THE SOUTH Carolina Legislature had spent over a million dollars on the Stumphouse Mountain Tunnel, and the shaft extended 1,617 feet into the rock. It would go no further. Frustrated with the expense, the occasional graft, and the slow progress, the legislature decided to cancel any further funding. In two years Confederate forces would fire on Fort Sumter in Charleston, and the resulting war would throw much of the region behind a wall of darkness and resentment and poverty that would persist for over a century.

■ ■ ■

THE MOST SURPRISING AND haunting tunnel poem I know of is
Louis MacNeice's "Coda," which appears at the end of his final
book, *The Burning Perch*. Here it is in full:

> *Maybe we knew each other better*
> *When the night was young and unrepeated*
> *And the moon stood still over Jericho.*
>
> *So much for the past; in the present*
> *There are moments caught between heart-beats*
> *When maybe we know each other better.*
>
> *But what is that clinking in the darkness?*
> *Maybe we shall know each other better*
> *When the tunnels meet beneath the mountain.*

It's a cliché to call a poem mysterious, and yet in this case
that seems the perfect word. Too mysterious for some—writing
about MacNeice's collection in the *New Republic* in 1963, for
instance, Richard Elman complained, "There is a Coda in the
form of a love poem that falls flat because one never knows for
sure who is saying what to whom on what occasion."

It's true, one never knows who is speaking or why. Mac-
Neice's point is that this doesn't matter. "We"—whoever we are,
when- and wherever we are—want nothing more than simply to
"know each other better." This is a process, not an explanation.

Yes, perhaps in some distant time it was possible to see ourselves revealed in the moonlight, but now our best hope is to labor blindly in the darkness toward a meeting that, if it takes place at all, must occur deep within the earth. And that meeting won't allow us to know each other perfectly but only "better," which suggests that our tunnel leads only to more and deeper tunnels. In this sense, one might argue that the tunnel is really a cave.

■   ■   ■

By 1940 THE LONG-ABANDONED Stumphouse Mountain Tunnel was nothing more than a local curiosity, a place for families to explore briefly before eating sandwiches by the adjacent waterfall. But then a professor at nearby Clemson University (then Clemson Agricultural College) happened to visit. Clemson's dairy school was at that time experimenting with blue-cheese mold, and the professor realized that the damp, cool air of the tunnel might be ideal for curing Roquefort-style cheese. The Second World War nearly derailed the plan, but the school persevered and in 1953 succeeded in creating the first blue cheese ever produced in the South. That cheese is still manufactured by Clemson today, although it is now cured in specialized rooms designed to mimic the tunnel's conditions. If you run across some, if you couple it with pears or an apple slice, if you let its crumbled, creamy surface spread against your tongue and its tang fill your nose, you will find that it's like every other blue cheese: it tastes like nothing else.

VOLTA

THE STATE OF CONTEMPORARY

AMERICAN POETRY:

AN ALLEGORY

I.

If you approach along one of the usual paths, you'll notice what at first appear to be tumbled walls, broken chimneys, and a series of ruined fortresses or perhaps religious buildings. These are the fossilized remains of the previous inhabitants of the region, who were nearly the size of dinosaurs. The current inhabitants live and work in their forefathers' massive, abandoned bodies until those structures collapse into dust, a practice that anthropologists consider unique. And because each generation necessarily occupies less space than the one that preceded it (and that space must now be used as a dwelling), the inhabitants have been getting steadily smaller and smaller. Presumably this progression can't continue beyond a certain stage, but if so, that stage hasn't yet been reached. Indeed, some theorists have argued that the process will continue indefinitely, until everything vital in the country has either been reduced to minimum size and maximum density, like a dwarf star, or been drained away entirely, leaving the last inhabitant as weightless as a ghost.

II.

YOU MIGHT ALSO APPROACH from the sea and observe that the state consists entirely of an island roughly the size of Malta. You'll need to beach your boat, because there aren't any docks. You'll also need to bring food, because there aren't any restaurants. But there are taverns. And there is a wall. It stretches around the island and is scoured and battered whenever a big storm rolls in. The inhabitants keep their backs to the wall—and, by extension, to the sea—and face each other in a circle. Within that circle, there is warmth, light, and music. The inhabitants engage only in oblique discussion of the encroaching waters, but on certain nights a high, screaming wind cuts briefly through the conversation, and you can feel the inhabitants shiver.

III.

OR YOU PASS THROUGH a black and cobwebbed forest to find a city sparkling with clockwork. The inhabitants are inventors. Their first projects were simple tools designed to assist the memory (the abacus, for instance, and an assortment of color-coded blocks). Then they began attempting to reproduce the sounds and shapes of animals, most notably in the form of mechanical birds that could sing the time of day with shattering poignancy.

Eventually the inhabitants started tinkering with their own flesh, replacing limbs with pistons and vocal cords with nets of steel mesh. The progression will conclude until the inhabitants have separated themselves entirely from their bodily heritage, at which point they will be indistinguishable from the miles of machinery that surround them.

IV.

COMING FROM THE WEST, you notice a city facing the ocean and sitting almost exactly at the level of the incoming waves. The inhabitants have been placed on watchtowers so high above the city that they almost seem to exist in a separate territory. From this vantage point, the inhabitants believe they can see both the dangers imperiling the city from within and the dangers approaching from beyond its encircling dikes. But the inhabitants are so far away and have been in the same position for so long that it's unclear whether they could still cry out in warning, even if they wanted to. Should you put an ear to their lips, however, you might feel the stirring of what could be breath.

V.

IT'S NOT A COUNTRY, really, so much as a house. The city that surrounds it stretches endlessly in all directions and is filled with shouts, bright lights, and commodities of all sorts (the city is prospering, though in the past things have been otherwise, and the future is uncertain). The house in which the inhabitants live is in the oldest district. The area is no longer fashionable, though there are still a few desirable restaurants, and the rich occasionally visit as if to connect their present good fortune with history itself. The inhabitants spend their days making curiosities—alchemical mechanisms, snuff boxes, salvers, trinkets of bone and glass. Most objects vanish into an impenetrable basement upon completion. Occasionally one of the inhabitants goes mad, and the other inhabitants gather around, both to offer sympathy and to see if anything interesting might be learned from their fellow's anguished cries.

VI.

THE BROTHEL CATERS TO everyone, though its actual customers are few. Perhaps this is because each person in the brothel—professionals as well as occasional visitors—must wear a blindfold that can only be removed upon departure. In order to find what they desire, then, the inhabitants must rely entirely on senses other than sight. They gamble on the faint scent of apples; they follow an almost imperceptible taste of salt. Sometimes they correctly identify what they embrace. Many other times, though, they're caught in mistakes that would be embarrassing, disgusting, or shamefully pleasing if they were made aware of them. The situation becomes especially confused in the building's lower levels, which are entirely devoted to subtle games of control and influence. There it's possible never to know whom you have truly subjugated or to which master you've yielded your most secret self. On these levels, some people have suggested the brothel is not really a brothel at all.

VII.

THE UNIVERSITY ITSELF OCCUPIES large stretches of the countryside, but the place in question is a small corridor in the sub-basement of the hockey rink. The inhabitants of this corridor spend most of their afternoons teaching a handful of students how to mimic the cries of bird species that are slowly but surely going extinct. Occasionally one of the students will suggest that the arrangement is unsustainable. The student will propose that rather than imitating the birds' cries, they might instead attempt to reverse the process of extinction, thereby ensuring both the survival of the birds and the continuing employment of the inhabitants of the corridor. The inhabitants roll their eyes at this naïveté.

VIII.

THE CASTLE IS BUILT around a vast pit of clay. Every morning the inhabitants fashion the clay into vague likenesses of their friends and loved ones. When the likenesses are suitably developed, the inhabitants breathe on them, and each likeness becomes briefly filled with life, or something resembling life. As it opens its tiny clay mouth to speak its first word, the closest inhabitant rushes forward and captures the word in a glass jar.

The likeness is then tossed back into the pit. The jar is emptied into a pool of silver, which is in turn used to create the thousands of mirrors that line every corridor of the castle.

IX.

THE CARAVAN'S INHABITANTS SLEEP only lightly, if at all. They were great musicians once, and all of them had lovers of various sorts—some mournfully lovely, some domineering, some witty in the manner of old-fashioned romantic comedies. One night many years ago, the inhabitants camped beside a canyon, the bottom of which was lost entirely in shadow. As they slept, various beasts crept from the canyon into their camp and stole their lovers, dragging them far under the earth. Upon waking, the inhabitants were grief stricken but undeterred. They set up a temporary stage, used generators to power portable amplifiers, and began to play a song to soothe the beasts and call their lovers back to the surface. Alas, their lovers had all been eaten. The song—the greatest they had ever played—served only to summon forth the beasts, which have been pursuing the inhabitants ever since. Their nights are now longer, and their music has changed.

X.

SEARCHING FOR INFORMATION REGARDING the land's previous inhabitants, we came upon evidence of a group who had embarked on a similar search hundreds of years earlier.

The camp left behind by these long-ago investigators was a ruin, of course, but a few carved runes gave some indication of their discoveries, or lack thereof. Our rough translation is as follows:

From the beginning, we had things backwards:
The symbols that we thought suggested fire
Were plans for waterworks, drainage systems;
And years were wasted on "religious texts"
That were, in fact, just recipes for soup.
The closer we got, the farther away
The truth of all their relics came to seem,
As if our searching caused the thing we sought
To retreat, like a feather lifted high
In air pushed forward by a reaching hand.
And I [illegible, possibly a name]
Despair of understanding them at all,
Which means I may not understand myself,
Since my own past is just as lost to me.
Parts have gone ahead, parts have lingered on
Or swiftly receded, as if I were a land
Reshaped by unpredictable floods,
And the water, even now it seems, is rising.

There is more, but most of it is undecipherable at present. Still, the find is itself encouraging and expands our understanding of this group's culture. Our search begins again tomorrow.

ON POETS

LOUISE GLÜCK'S

METAMORPHOSES

P oetry has always been the handmaiden of mythology, and vice versa. Sometimes poets are in the business of collecting and tweaking existing myths, as with Ovid's *Metamorphoses* and the *Poetic Edda*. Other times poetry applies a mythological glamour to stories and characters from history, legend, or even other myths (the hero of *The Aeneid* is a minor character from *The Iliad*). Then there are poets who equate the idea of myth with the supposedly irrational essence of poetry itself. Here is Robert Graves in 1948: "No poet can hope to understand the nature of poetry unless he has had a vision of the Naked King crucified to the lopped oak, and watched the dancers, red-eyed from the acrid smoke of the sacrificial fires . . . with a monotonous chant of 'Kill! kill! kill!' and 'Blood! blood! blood!'" This might sound more like a strip-club picnic gone badly awry, but you get the idea.

The relationship between poetry and mythology is central

to Louise Glück's new *Poems 1962–2012*, if only because no poet of Glück's generation has relied more overtly on what Philip Larkin once called "the common myth kitty." A representative list of titles: "Gemini," "Aphrodite," "The Triumph of Achilles," "Legend," "A Fantasy," "A Fable," "Amazons," "Penelope's Song," "Telemachus' Dilemma," "Circe's Torment," "Eurydice," "Persephone the Wanderer," "Persephone the Wanderer" (again). This is not even to count her 1992 book *The Wild Iris*, which is basically an allegorical system based on garden plants. Myths, legends, and fairy tales are for Glück what heirloom tomatoes are for Alice Waters.

That's probably inevitable, given her sensibility. Glück has always (and self-consciously) favored abstraction over particularity—from the beginning she's written lines that are almost completely devoid of the kind of chatty reportage and pop-cultural name-dropping that have been common in American poetry since the death of Frank O'Hara. A Glück poem is dreamlike, chilly, enigmatic. It is still. It is spare. It is almost aggressively concentrated. It revolves around words like "dark," "pond," "soul," "body," and "earth." It is the kind of poem that involves frequent use of the expression "it is." It produces great effects with delicate shifts in tone, like an oceangoing bird that travels a hundred miles between wing flaps. Perhaps more than anything else, it relies on mood, suggestion, and atmosphere: Glück is a master, not of scenes, but of scene setting.

And those settings are usually dark. In her first collection—called, alas, *Firstborn* (1968)—we find a tortured array of thwarted lovers, widows, cripples, and angst-ridden families.

Even the robins are woebegone ("The mama withers on her eggs"). The debt to Sylvia Plath and Robert Lowell can be overwhelming in this early work, as in the first few lines of "The Lady in the Single":

> *Cloistered as the snail and conch*
> *In Edgartown where the Atlantic*
> *Rises to deposit junk*
>
> *On plush, extensive sand and the pedantic*
> *Meet for tea. . . .*

This may as well have "Lowell 1959" stamped on it. One sees the frightening outlines of what will become Glück's preoccupations, but they're awkwardly clothed in borrowed techniques, like ghosts muffled in L. L. Bean jackets.

But then in her second book, *The House on Marshland* (1975), Glück comes disturbingly into her own. Suddenly the choppy waters of the early poems become smooth, vast, and almost completely lightless. The temperament that emerges is relentlessly critical both of itself and of the world it creates, and that criticism is delivered in lines that are, as Helen Vendler once put it, "hieratic and unearthly." Here is the beginning of "Messengers":

> *You have only to wait, they will find you.*
> *The geese flying low over the marsh,*
> *glittering in black water.*
> *They find you.*

The voice here is strange in the word's original sense—
foreign—as if it were coming from an oracle who stopped worrying about humankind centuries ago. Having given us spooky
geese, Glück adds some deer ("How beautiful they are, / as
though their bodies did not impede them"). The poem ends:

> You have only to let it happen:
> that cry—release, release—like the moon
> wrenched out of earth and rising
> full in its circle of arrows
>
> until they come before you
> like dead things, saddled with flesh,
> and you above them, wounded and dominant.

The key word here is "dominant," which is Glück's way of
pointing out the covert will to power in the traditional romantic
nature poem (to see ourselves reflected in nature is to make nature
our servant). Above all, Glück's mature poetry is fixated on control.

This is true of all poets to an extent; the structures of poems are ways of organizing (that is, controlling) experience. But
it's one thing to want to control the way a poem looks, quite another to have dreamed up the beginning of "The Drowned
Children," which appeared in Glück's collection *Descending
Figure* (1980):

> You see, they have no judgment.
> So it is natural that they should drown,

first the ice taking them in
and then, all winter, their wool scarves
floating behind them as they sink
until at last they are quiet.
And the pond lifts them in its manifold dark arms.

"So it is natural": Obviously, it isn't natural at all for children to drown, or to the extent that it is natural it should make us wonder what we mean by the word—which is Glück's point. The impersonal forces that really do control our lives (time, space, our own unconscious desires) operate in a way that transcends the day-to-day demands of car payments and deadlines. They're not so much irrational as unrational, and they are implacable. That truth can be frightening, but as Glück's first few books demonstrate, it can also be unsettlingly beautiful, in the way that a shark can be beautiful, or a tidal wave.

The type of control that most interests Glück, however, is the struggle for mastery among and within people. Her poems about relationships—romantic and familial—are focused relentlessly on the whip hand. On sisters: "One is always the watcher, / one the dancer." On sex: "A woman exposed as rock / has this advantage: / she controls the harbor." On friendship: "Always in these friendships / one serves the other, one is less than the other." On mothers and daughters: "Suppose / you saw your mother / torn between two daughters: / what could you do / to save her but be / willing to destroy / yourself." It's an attitude all too easy to parody—not every disappointing weekend getaway is a ritual battle between archetypes—but in the strongest of Glück's earlier poems, one sees how monstrous desires penetrate and determine our supposedly ordinary behavior, inciting quiet violence that we don't even recognize as damage.

The depiction of those unconscious desires is one of the basic functions of myth. It explains why Glück—drawn as she is to questions of who is doing what to whom and why—returns repeatedly to characters who aren't people so much as embodiments of generalized anxieties, particularly anxieties about betrayal and desertion. (In "Gretel in Darkness," Gretel addresses Hansel: "Nights I turn to you to hold me / but you are not there.") The problem is that this strategy can result in poems stranded in their own extremity, like forgotten trail markers in the Arctic.

Glück is well aware of this potential difficulty. So as she entered middle age, she began to add more obvious personal references to her work; *Ararat* (1990) is centered on her father's death, *Meadowlands* (1996) on her divorce. She tinkered with colloquial language. She dabbled in being, you know, funny. ("I thought my life was over and my heart was broken. / Then I moved to Cambridge.") In taking this route, she followed a narrative well established in American poetry. Roughly, the idea is that a poet who is intense, closed, and obsessed when young gradually learns to appreciate and understand the world, giving rise to a personal, personable middle style that is richer than the furious early work.

It's not a story that should be applied to Glück. While the poetry of her middle period is almost never bad, it can be self-indulgent in its general approach. Where previously Glück invoked myth in ways that preserved its essential strangeness (which is also its truth), she now began to invoke it in ways that felt more obviously like psychological diagnosis. Mythology, psychology, and poetry are related but different ways of thinking about how we exist in the world, and while they often overlap to one another's mutual benefit, it can be deadly to let one determine the other. Or as Carl Jung put it, "If a work of art is explained in the same way as a neurosis, then either the work of art is a neurosis or a neurosis is a work of art." In Glück's earlier work, we get lines like these from "The Garden" in 1980:

> *The garden admires you.*
> *For your sake it smears itself with green pigment,*
> *the ecstatic reds of the roses,*
> *so that you will come to it with your lovers.*

But that astringency gives way to lines like these from "Vita Nova" in 1999:

> *In the splitting-up dream*
> *we were fighting over who would keep*
> *the dog,*
> *Blizzard. You tell me*
> *what that name means. He was*
> *a cross between*
> *something big and fluffy*
> *and a dachshund.*

"In the splitting-up dream": Now, Miss Glück, vee may perhaps to begin. Yes?

If that were the end of the story, it wouldn't be a bad thing.
After all, no poet is required to keep the fire kindled for decades.
If she can write five or ten or a dozen very good poems over a career, then she has succeeded—and Glück has managed that feat
easily. But there is another element to this particular myth.
Glück's most recent book, *A Village Life* (2009), is one of her best,
and it is good in a way that recalls her earlier work without imitating it. The poems are centered on an unnamed, imaginary village
and spoken in the voices of various inhabitants (including a memorable earthworm). The darkness and air of unreality are typical
Glück, but the atmosphere is something new. It has the sad hope-
fulness of the seasons: death, birth, death, rebirth. More than
anything, it has other people. Not other people whom we realize
the real Glück probably knows, but people as imagined—which
is to say, people who represent a deepening of Glück's sensibility.
Here is a farmer speaking at the end of "A Village Life":

> In the window, the moon is hanging over the earth,
> meaningless but full of messages.
> It's dead, it's always been dead,
> but it pretends to be something else,
> burning like a star, and convincingly, so that you feel
>   sometimes
> it could actually make something grow on earth.
>
> If there's an image of the soul, I think that's what it is.

I move through the dark as though it were natural to me,
as though I were already a factor in it.
Tranquil and still, the day dawns.
On market day, I go to the market with my lettuces.

The lettuce is a small thing, and so is the market. But they are not nothing. And the creation of "not nothing"—that is the power given even to the loneliest gods.

THE OBSCURITY
OF MICHAEL O'BRIEN

N o contemporary poet is famous, but some are less unfa-
mous than others. That's because the poetry world, like
most areas of American life, has its own peculiar celebrity
system—and if the rewards of that system rarely involve gift
suites filled with swag from Jean Patou, they remain tempting
enough to keep grown writers hustling. The problem is, poetic
stardom is an unpredictable business. Good writing doesn't
guarantee a reputation; bad writing doesn't guarantee oblivion;
nor can grace, money, or nimble careerism entirely explain why
poet X reads to overflowing auditoriums, whereas poet Y reads
to his cats. Maybe it's simply the case that, as William Munny
remarked in *Unforgiven*, "Deserve's got nothing to do with it."

Which brings us to Michael O'Brien, whose new collection,
Sleeping and Waking, makes one wish the laws of poetic celebrity were less chaotic. O'Brien, who was born in 1939, began his
career as a participant in the Eventorium, a coterie of New York

artists with a surrealist bent. Unlike other groups with more ambition (or better promotional skills), this collective never became a major feature in the landscape of contemporary American poetry, and O'Brien's early work is now extremely difficult to find. Not that it's easy to get your hands on his more recent writing. Aside from the present volume, none of O'Brien's individual collections is still in print. His 1986 book *The Ruin*, an assortment of translations, is currently being sold on eBay by a book trader that claims to have "the only copy on the web!" An excellent volume of selected poems, called *Sills*, was published in 2000, but there are so few copies available that one recently listed for $59.95 on Amazon. As a writer, O'Brien seems to have opted for solitary dedication; unfortunately that admirable choice may have made him invisible even to those who are looking for him.

That should change. *Sleeping and Waking* is a quietly startling collection that ought to earn O'Brien, not only poetry-world notoriety, but actual readers. They'll have to be attentive ones, though. O'Brien is primarily an observer rather than a debater, which means that the poems here are heavy on isolated images, dream logic, bits of overheard conversation (typically urban conversation), and memories, with larger themes emerging through juxtapositions and repetitions. Indeed, many poems consist of nothing but juxtapositions and repetitions. "Another Autumn," for instance, is a series of one-line sketches—"a feathering of the ink whereby characters lose definition" is followed by "overlapping windowscreens, one pattern interfering with another," which is in turn followed by "sideways, all the politeness, all that irony, trying for a draw" (an echo of a line from "A Pillow-Book," a much earlier O'Brien poem). Reading the best work here is like watching watercolors blur across wet paper, gradually mingling to produce soft yet definite shapes. It's the sort of writing that's more interesting to sink into than to parse.

That shouldn't, however, be taken to suggest that *Sleeping and Waking* lacks organization or wit. On the contrary, O'Brien is an assured technician who excels at any line length (including the prose poem), but whose favorite structure is the relatively short, steeply enjambed free verse line first perfected by William Carlos Williams. Notice, for example, how he uses line breaks to balance the conclusion to "Once":

> *work against correspondence, the*
> *world is not a*
> *book, everything is*
> *not something else, you*
> *could look it up.*

The poet plays his desire to find correspondences—metaphors, likenesses—against the knowledge that such correspondences must always fall short in some sense (because reality is reality, and can't be altered by the poet's imagination). It's a familiar theme. But O'Brien renews it by allowing the competition between desire and knowledge to emerge as part of the poem's structure. Take the phrase "the world is not a book, everything is not something else." By breaking between "everything is" and "not," the poet sets up an implicit rival claim: "the world is not a book, everything is." And of course, in order to learn that "the world is not a book," we're instructed to "look it up." It's become a cliché of poetry criticism to say that a poem "enacts" one of its subjects, but here the word seems justified. This is smart, tight work.

Perhaps the highest praise one could give O'Brien, though, is that he knows when to quit. That may seem like an odd compliment—after all, the problem with most contemporary poems isn't that they go too far but that they never go anywhere at all. In the type of poetry O'Brien writes, however, leaving well enough alone is a sign of confidence and good judgment. Consider the end of "Hush":

> *tiny spider in the*
> *teaspoon, no, the*
> *huge chandelier*
> *reflected there*

As in many of his poems, the idea is to capture perception just before it yields to analysis—a kind of musical rest on the page. O'Brien is strongly influenced by Asian writing (titles here include "After Lu Yu" and "After Kiyohara Motosuke"), and one of the benefits of that influence is his willingness to let small moments speak for themselves. To be sure, this can sometimes result in lines that don't do much ("Cloud touches / mountain so lightly, / folded into the folds, / on its slow way"). But by suggesting that the poet is open to whatever perception strikes him,

these slighter gestures prepare us for the surprisingly unre-
strained emotion of lines like these:

> *At a*
> *party my*
> *father suddenly*
> *appears, young,*
> *vigorous, I'm*
> *so glad to*
> *see him it*
> *wakes me up.*

While O'Brien's technical skills should be crisp enough to
please the iciest avant-gardist, he has one virtue that more cerebral poets often lack: he isn't afraid to make a plain statement. In
other hands, that virtue can become a self-satisfied vice, but here
it lends a necessary sharpness to an otherwise fluid and dreamlike collection.

Of course, as fine as *Sleeping and Waking* is, it may still join
the rest of O'Brien's work in the peculiar limbo inhabited by the
writing of so many strong but unrecognized poets. After all, as
Donald Justice once said, "There may well be analyzable causes
behind the oblivion some good writers suffer, but the causes,
whatever they are, remain elusive." Still, if the causes of oblivion
are unknowable, the causes of recognition are equally obscure—
which means that luck can always turn. Or as O'Brien himself
puts it in a very different context, "Like a defective purgatory no
one remembers the point of, or how to turn it off. Like being

hazed by one's needs. By human practice. Which can change."
A change in the way we've looked—or not looked—at this poet
might do more than simply alter his position in the star system
of the poetry world; it might help us change the way we think
about ourselves.

TOO CLOSE TO TOUCH:

THOM GUNN'S *SELECTED POEMS*

"All poets, if they are any good," Charles Simic has said, "tend to stand apart from their literary age." The key phrase here is "if they are any good"; average poets don't just stand within their age, they compose it. But we sometimes talk as if poets are exceptions, not simply when they write well, but because they write at all. According to this way of thinking, the art form demands such devotion to one's individuality that every poet, no matter how lowly, is a kind of outsider—a cheese who stands alone, if you will. This perception frequently finds its way into depictions of poets in popular culture; it also emerges in the vehemence with which poets themselves regularly declare their opposition to labels, categories, schools, allegiances, booster clubs, carpools, intramural softball teams, and so on. Yet when everyone is busy standing apart, how is it possible to stand out? What does real independence look like?

Possibly something like the work of Thom Gunn, whose

new *Selected Poems* is edited by August Kleinzahler. Gunn, who died in 2004, began his career as a hot young poet in England (he published his first book, *Fighting Terms*, with Faber & Faber when he was only twenty-five) and was generally associated with the taut, plainspoken aesthetic favored by writers like Philip Larkin and Donald Davie. In 1954 he left England for San Francisco, where he eventually settled with his partner after studying with Yvor Winters at Stanford. Gunn embraced the city's bohemian lifestyle—Edmund White called him "the last of the commune dwellers . . . serious and intellectual by day and druggy and sexual by night"—and he grew increasingly interested in syllabics and free verse even as he continued to hone the metrical forms that distinguished his early career. He's possibly the only poet to have written a halfway decent quintain about LSD, and he's certainly one of the few to profess genuine admiration for both Winters (the archformalist) and Allen Ginsberg (the arch . . . well, Allen Ginsberg). This is, even for the poetry world, a pretty odd background.

It's also the kind of background that leads to misleading career narratives. Like most people, poets rarely undergo multiple metamorphoses in their lives and art over a short period. In time, they might shift their style; they might take up different subject matter; they might buy a duplex in Miami. But generally speaking their existence is reasonably consistent, and they stick fairly close to what they know. Gunn, however, not only moved from England to America; he exchanged the rarified air of Cambridge for the hothouse of 1960s-era San Francisco, became openly gay, started dabbling in drugs, began writing about the

urban underbelly, and set about tinkering with the verse techniques that had made him (relatively) famous—all in the space
of about ten years. Critics often attribute changes in a poet's
style to changes in his life; this much change in both arenas
threw some readers into what could be described as a tizzy of
questionable causation. British reviewers who opposed Gunn's
technical shifts blamed California, just as American critics
would, slightly later on, begin connecting his adventurous lifestyle with his more "relaxed" versification. (You can still see this
particular dynamic at work today whenever critics contrast
Gunn's libido with his tight metrics—as if no one had ever written quatrains about getting laid before.) In any case, all the talk
about Gunn's life and style, and style and life, almost makes one
wish he had stayed in England; at least then no one could say he
wrote seven-syllable lines because of Jefferson Airplane.

Kleinzahler believes Gunn's development was steadier, and
in some ways, more conventional. He's right. Gunn began to
come into his own with the publication of *My Sad Captains* in
1961, when he was thirty-two, and his work steadily strengthened for the next four decades. In his best, most characteristic
writing, Gunn is what you might call a poet of friction: he's interested in the ways surfaces push off against or into each other.
Consider his description of surfing in "From the Wave":

> *The mindless heave of which they rode*
> *A fluid shelf*
> *Breaks as they leave, falls and, slowed,*
> *Loses itself.*

Clear, the sheathed bodies slick as seals
  Loosen and tingle;
And by the board the bare foot feels
  The suck of shingle.

There are many ways to write about surfing—one could focus on the danger, the grace, the speed, and so forth. But it's typical of Gunn that while he gives us a sense of all these elements, he's drawn to instances of contact: the point at which "the bare foot feels / The suck of shingle"; the moment in which "marbling bodies have become / Half wave, half men, / Grafted it seems by feet of foam." Feel and touch and pressure are constants throughout this selection, whether it's the longing of a hawk for "the feel . . . / Of catcher and of caught / Upon your wrist," the swimmer who remembers "the pull and risk / Of the Pacific's touch . . . / Its cold live sinews pulling at each limb," or simply the "secure firm dry embrace" of longtime domestic affection.

Even in the AIDS-related elegies that dominate his most famous book, *The Man with Night Sweats*, Gunn is drawn to comparisons involving substance brought to bear on substance. "Still Life," a poem about a terminal patient, concludes with the image of "the tube his mouth enclosed / In an astonished O." "The Missing" imagines the vast web of friendships, now vanishing, as a "Supple entwinement through the living mass / Which for all that I knew might have no end, / Image of an unlimited embrace." But the poem that gives *The Man with Night Sweats* its title is perhaps Gunn's most arresting use of this sort of metaphor. It begins with a man waking at night ("I wake up

cold, I who / Prospered through dreams of heat") and recognizing the rising weakness in his once-powerful body. It concludes:

> *I have to change the bed,*
> *But catch myself instead*
>
> *Stopped upright where I am*
> *Hugging my body to me*
> *As if to shield it from*
> *The pains that will go through me,*
>
> *As if hands were enough*
> *To hold an avalanche off.*

The delicate suggestion of alienation, or at least separation,
between self and body ("Hugging my body to me") presages the
even greater disruption that occurs in the final couplet. We
think of the earth as being our foundation: we're "on solid
ground." The image of an avalanche is especially disturbing,
then, because it suggests that what had supported our bodies is
now bent on destroying them. The touch has become a blow;
the heat of friction has become a conflagration. Here Gunn is
(consciously or not) rewriting the great American poem of unity
between body and earth, Robert Frost's "To Earthward." That
poem ends: "When stiff and sore and scarred / I take away my
hand / From leaning on it hard / In grass and sand, // The hurt
is not enough: / I long for weight and strength / To feel the earth
as rough / To all my length." Oh no, says Gunn, you don't.

One can quibble with some of the choices made in this volume. Kleinzahler's version of Gunn is a little more austere than some might like, even when the poems themselves are bent on advertising their countercultural bona fides. It's puzzling, for instance, that space was made for a druggy yet prim couplet about, yes, Jefferson Airplane ("The music comes and goes on the wind, / Comes and goes on the brain") but not for any of Gunn's epigrams; for instance, the superb "Barren Leaves," which reads in its entirety: "Spontaneous overflows of powerful feeling: / Wet dreams, wet dreams, in libraries congealing." Gunn was a very funny poet, and it would have been good to see more of that. But, of course, his total output ran well over five hundred pages, almost all of which are well worth reading, and any selection was bound to have holes critics would cry over. It's to the credit of this remarkable writer that those absences seem unimportant beside what is so rousingly present.

TOMAS TRANSTRÖMER

AND THE ART OF TRANSLATION

If you're a poet outside the Anglophone world, and you manage to win the Nobel Prize, two things are likely to happen. First, your ascendancy will be questioned by fiction critics in a major English-language news publication. Second, there will be a fair amount of pushing and shoving among your translators (if you have any), as publishers attempt to capitalize on your fifteen minutes of free media attention.

And, lo, for the Swedish poet Tomas Tranströmer, it has come to pass. The questioning came from, among others, Philip Hensher for the *Telegraph* (in Britain) and Hephzibah Anderson for Bloomberg News, both of whom implied that real writers—Philip Roth, for instance—had been bypassed to flatter a country largely inhabited by melancholic reindeer. And when Tranströmer hasn't been doubted by fiction critics, he's been clutched at by publishing houses. Since his Nobel moment in October, three different Tranströmer books have been released (or reissued): *The Deleted World: Poems* (Farrar, Straus and Giroux), with translations by the Scottish poet Robin Robertson; *Tomas Transtrۀmer: Selected Poems* (Ecco/HarperCollins), edited by Robert Hass; and *For the Living and the Dead: Poems and a Memoir* (Ecco/HarperCollins), edited by Daniel Halpern. These books join two major collections already in print: *The Half-Finished Heaven: The Best Poems of Tomas Transtۀmer*, from Graywolf Press, translated by Robert Bly, and *The Great Enigma: New Collected Poems*, from New Directions, translated by Robin Fulton. So a little complaining, a glut of books: pretty typical.

But what's unusual about Transtrۀmer is that the most interesting debates over English versions of his work actually took place before his Nobel victory. In this case, the argument went to the heart of the translator's function and occurred mostly in the *Times Literary Supplement*. The disputants were Fulton, one of Transtrۀmer's longest-serving translators, and Robertson, who has described his own efforts as "imitations." Fulton accused Robertson (who doesn't speak Swedish) of borrowing from his more faithful versions while inserting superfluous bits of Robertson's own creation—in essence, creating poems that are neither accurate translations nor interesting departures. Fulton rolled his eyes at "the strange current fashion whereby a 'translation' is liable to be praised in inverse proportion to the 'translator's' knowledge of the original language." Robertson's supporters countered that Fulton was just annoyed because Robertson was more concerned with the spirit of the poems than with getting every little *köttbulle* exactly right.

To understand this dispute, it's necessary to have a sense of the poetry itself. Tranströmer prefers still, pared-down arrangements that rely more on image and tone than, say, peculiarities of diction or references to local culture. The voice is typically calm yet weary, as if the lines were meant to be read after midnight, in an office from which everyone else had gone home. And his gift for metaphor is remarkable, as in the start of "Open and Closed Spaces" (in Fulton's translation):

> *A man feels the world with his work like a glove.*
> *He rests for a while at midday having laid aside*
> * the gloves on the shelf.*
> *They suddenly grow, spread,*
> *and black out the whole house from inside.*

The first comparison is surprising enough—work is a glove? With which we feel the world? But notice how quickly yet smoothly Tranströmer extends the metaphor into even stranger territory; the gloves expand from the refuge of the house (which is implicitly the private self) to obscure everything we know and are. The poem becomes a meditation on what constitutes a prison, what could be considered a release ("'Amnesty,' runs the whisper in the grass") and whether these states might lie closer together than we realize. It ends:

> *Further north you can see from a summit the*
> * endless blue carpet of pine forest*
> *where the cloud shadows*

are standing still.
No, are flying.

The clouds appear motionless but are actually flying—just as our lives move, or fail to move, in ways we only dimly understand. Open spaces may become closed, but the reverse is true as well.

Tranströmer, trained as a psychologist, has always been interested in the ways our personalities obscure as much as they reveal. "Two truths approach each other," he writes in "Preludes" (translation by May Swenson), "One comes from within,/one comes from without—and where they meet you have the chance/to catch a look at yourself." In this context, his heavy reliance on metaphor isn't surprising. A metaphor insists on the similarity of its tenor and vehicle but also declares their fundamental difference: after all, the metaphor itself would be unnecessary if its components were identical. These countervailing purposes become, in Tranströmer's hands, a way of holding together what he can and can't say. As he puts it in "April and Silence" (Fulton): "I am carried in my shadow/like a violin/in its black case." He balances these often startling juxtapositions with simple diction and generally straightforward syntax, making the complexity of his poetry a matter of depth rather than surface. His poems are small, cool fields dissolving into dreams at their borders.

This is exactly the sort of writing that tends to do well in translation, at least in theory. The plainer a poem looks—the less it relies on extremities of form, diction, or syntax—the more we assume that even a translator with no knowledge of the original language will be able to produce a reasonable match for what the poem feels like in its first incarnation.

The problem is, simple can be complicated. It's impossible to say how much Robertson did or didn't rely on Fulton's translations in preparing *The Deleted World*, but it's not too hard (if you can corral a Swedish friend, as I did) to figure out where he deviates from the originals. The changes generally make Tranströmer less strange and more typically poetic. Consider "Autumnal Archipelago (Storm)," which in Robertson's version begins like so:

> *Suddenly the walker comes upon the*
>   *ancient oak: a huge*
> *rooted elk whose hardwood antlers, wide*
>   *as this horizon, guard the stone-green*
> *walls of the sea.*

And here is Fulton's more literal take:

> *Here the walker suddenly meets the giant*
> *oak tree, like a petrified elk whose crown is*
> *furlongs wide before the September ocean's*
>   *murky green fortress.*

Robertson forgoes the poem's sapphic stanza form, which seems reasonable, but he also turns the passage's deliciously bizarre doubled metaphor (an oak tree is like an elk turned to stone) into a less jarring formulation. Similarly, in "From March 1979," Robertson translates the line "Det vilda har inga ord" into "Wilderness has no words" when a more accurate version would be, "The wild has no words" (Fulton says, "The untamed . . ."). "Wilderness" is a bunch of trees; "the wild" is another thing entirely. But perhaps the least successful adjustment is in "Calling Home":

> Our phonecall spilled out into the dark
> and glittered between the countryside
>   and the town
> like the mess of a knife-fight.

There's no fight, with knives or otherwise, in the original— Tranströmer's speaker "slept uneasily" after the call home, but the cause of his unease is unresolved. Again, the poem seems simplified.

That said, some of Robertson's alterations do a fine job of conveying a poem's spirit. Rather than using the literal "shriveled" to describe a sail, he says it's "grey with mildew." Rather than telling us that "dead bodies" are smuggled into "a silent world," he says "the dead" are so transported. In general, while one can quibble about Robertson's book, *The Deleted World* is pleasurable whether or not it's a good translation of Tranströmer.

Is that enough? In some ways, certainly—we read poetry for entertainment, not nutritional value. But translating a poem is like covering a song. We can savor the liberties someone is

taking with, say, "Gin and Juice" in a way we couldn't understand similar variations on songs written by martians. And
Tranströmer, however popular he is among poets, remains
largely unknown to readers eager to see work from the new Nobel laureate. In this instance, even a sincere imitation probably
isn't the most helpful form of flattery.

ROUGH GEMS: THE UNCOLLECTED
WORK OF ELIZABETH BISHOP

You are living in a world created by Elizabeth Bishop. Granted, our culture owes its shape to plenty of other forces—Hollywood, Microsoft, Rachael Ray—but nothing matches the impact of a great artist, and in the second half of the twentieth century, no American artist in any medium was greater than Bishop (1911–79). That she worked in one of our country's least popular fields, poetry, doesn't matter. That she was a woman doesn't matter. That she was gay doesn't matter. That she was an alcoholic, an expatriate, and essentially an orphan—none of this matters. What matters is that she left behind a body of work that teaches us, as Italo Calvino once said of literature generally, "a method subtle and flexible enough to be the same thing as an absence of any method whatever." The publication of *Edgar Allan Poe & the Juke-Box*, which gathers for the first time Bishop's unpublished material, isn't just a significant event in our poetry; it's part of an ongoing alteration in the scale of American life.

Just don't expect that change to be announced with a fanfare. In a tribute to Bishop, James Merrill famously noted her "lifelong impersonations of an ordinary woman," and the observation applies to her writing as much as to her comportment. From the beginning, Bishop's work was descriptive rather than assertive, conversational rather than rhetorical, and discreet rather than confessional (it was also hard to come by: in her lifetime she published only about ninety poems). This was surprising for two reasons. First, the approach was completely unlike the modes favored by her more flamboyant peers—Robert Lowell, John Berryman—as well as the guts-spilling styles they helped inspire. Second, if you believe art mirrors life, reticence is the opposite of what you'd anticipate from Bishop, whose biography contains enough torment to satisfy Saint Sebastian. An abbreviated list: her father died when she was a baby; her mother vanished into an insane asylum when Bishop was five; her college boyfriend committed suicide when she refused to marry him and sent her a parting postcard that said, "Go to hell, Elizabeth"; and the great love of her life, Lota de Macedo Soares, with whom she spent many years in Brazil, fatally overdosed in Bishop's apartment. From a writer with a history like that, we might expect announcements like Lowell's "I hear / my ill-spirit sob in each blood cell." We don't expect to be told, "I caught a tremendous fish."

This curious restraint has been admired by many critics (over the course of twenty years, Bishop won the Pulitzer Prize,

the National Book Award, and the National Book Critics Circle
Award), but it also explains why she often has been identified
with words like "quiet," "charming," "scrupulous" and, above
all, "modest"—all of them perfectly useful adjectives, but none
likely to tip the reader off to the harrowing nature of her life or
(more important) the colossal ambition of her poems. Even her
admirers sometimes struggle to forgive her for seeming so remarkably unremarkable. Dana Gioia, a longtime Bishop advocate and chairman of the National Endowment for the Arts, gets
only four paragraphs into an essay on her reputation's dramatic
rise in the poetry world after her death before asking, almost
apologetically, "Is Elizabeth Bishop overrated?" "Perhaps a bit,"
he answers, which presumably is what you say when you've gotten in the habit of thinking about poetry so much that you forget
Bishop's poems are less well-known to many people than the
lyrics to "Total Eclipse of the Heart."

So why do we feel compelled to elevate Bishop while simultaneously worrying that we're raising her too high? In large part,
the answer has to do with the difference between difficulty and
subtlety. Difficulty is a beloved concept in the poetry world, because it's the crux of an old but cherished argument: Are poems
too obscure? Or not obscure enough? The debate is a canned
one, of course, but it lets all parties make their favorite points,
and everyone is therefore happy to argue over difficulty at the
drop of a hat. The reality, though, is that most readers and writers aren't actually made nervous by difficulty, at least as the term
is usually meant. For one thing, difficulty is straightforward—
you either figure out what's difficult or you don't. You might fail,

but you aren't going to be misled. (In this sense, and in its implicit endorsement of hard work, difficulty is a concept that has long been central to our shared identity as Americans.) Subtlety is different, though. Subtlety wants to be missed by all but the chosen few; it is aloof, withholding, and aristocratic—sometimes manipulative and always disguised. It has less to do with theory and technique, which can be learned mechanically, than with style and sensibility, which require intuition. It wants to be looked at but not seen. It's unnerving.

It's also exactly what distinguishes Bishop's greatest poetry, which is why it's so hard to be entirely comfortable with this writer or to know where she belongs. To begin, there is the peculiar Bishop voice, which is often called "faux-naïf," but is probably closer to faux normal (the imitation isn't of innocence but stability). On one hand, she can seem perfectly straightforward—no poet, for instance, starts a poem more matter-of-factly: "In Worcester, Massachusetts, / I went with Aunt Consuelo / to keep her dentist's appointment." And, of course, no poet is as enamored of local color: "The ghosts of glaciers drift / among those folds and folds of fir: spruce and hackmatack— / dull, dead, deep pea-cock colors, / each riser distinguished from the next / by an irregular nervous saw-tooth edge." Yet no one else moves as easily or abruptly into the most uncanny registers of our literature: "The iceberg cuts its facets from within"; "Everything only connected by 'and' and 'and'"; "More delicate than the historians' are the map-makers' colors." None of this is difficult, but it's astonishingly subtle and strange. The more one reads a Bishop poem, the greater the sense of

huge forces being held barely but precisely in check—like currents pressing heavily on the glass walls of some delicate under-
sea installation. It doesn't seem as if the glass will break, but if it
were to do so, we'd find ourselves engulfed by what Frost (her
truest predecessor) called "black and utter chaos."

Edgar Allan Poe & the Juke-Box allows us to see the cracks
that could form on those crystalline surfaces. It's no criticism of
this collection to say the virtues of Bishop's finished poetry—
style and poise chief among them—are often missing from the
writing gathered here. These are, after all, pieces that Bishop
herself chose not to publish but found valuable for some reason;
as this volume's editor, Alice Quinn, the *New Yorker*'s poetry
editor, noted in a recent interview, "A big part of the pleasure
and understanding to be gained is in knowing what was on her
mind during those years and in discovering new phrasing of
hers, new avenues of vision." In addition to drafts of poems—
some accompanied by photos of the manuscript pages in question, all following Bishop's often handwritten versions as closely
as possible—Quinn has gathered several prose pieces, including an intriguing series of notes that begins, "Writing poetry is
an unnatural act." Essentially, this is a book for two groups of
people: Bishop fans (most of the poetry world, that is), and the
increasingly tiny group who still think this poet was an unambitious and slightly chilly minor writer. The former will be grateful for the insight into her meticulous process; the latter will
have to acknowledge the enormous patience and skill that allowed her to hold the volcanic feeling on exhibit here in the
poised vessels of her finished poetry. Lest you think that's

overstating the emotional content of these drafts, consider the presence of such decidedly un-Bishopian lines as, "I have suffered from abnormal thirst— / I swear it's true—and by the age / of twenty or twenty-one I had begun / to drink, & drink— I can't get enough."

That shouldn't, however, be taken to mean that the poems here are all unformed, lesser efforts. If some of this work is mostly of interest because of what it tells us about Bishop's published writing, other pieces can stand alongside anything the *New Yorker* got its hands on back in the 1960s. "Vague Poem" plays on a confusion between rockroses and rose rocks; it concludes:

> *Rose-rock, unformed, flesh beginning, crystal by crystal,*
> *clear pink breasts and darker, crystalline nipples,*
> *rose-rock, rose-quartz, roses, roses, roses,*
> *exacting roses from the body,*
> *and the even darker, accurate, rose of sex—*

This openly erotic approach is more successful than much of her published love poetry, which is considerably less forthcoming. Equally strong are several of the poems intended for a sequence called "Bone Key" and parts of the later poem "Keaton," which has one of Bishop's finest, saddest openings—"I will be good; I will be good." Quinn's notes throughout are superb. In glossing "Vague Poem," for example, she meticulously connects a particular phrase to a speech given by Bishop in 1976, discusses the poet's interest in crystallography, and includes another, earlier, erotic fragment that recalls the more finished poem she is annotating. This is the devoted editing this material needed and deserved.

A few days after her death in 1979, Elizabeth Bishop's obituary in the *New York Times* noted that she "enjoyed extraordinary esteem among critics and fellow poets" but was "less widely known than contemporaries such as Robert Lowell." One can only imagine how Lowell and Bishop, lifelong friends, would have felt about the comparison. In any case, though, things have changed. The world of contemporary poetry can be a fractious place, but one thing almost everyone agrees on is the significance of Elizabeth Bishop—and that's as it should be. Our greatest poets aren't monuments to be looked at but grammars to be absorbed; however long it takes, we speak through them and they through us. "When you write my epitaph," Bishop once wrote to Lowell, "you must say I was the loneliest person who ever lived." Lonely? Maybe once, but not anymore, and never again.

THE LETTERS OF TED HUGHES

There are two ways to talk about the new *Letters of Ted Hughes*, edited by Christopher Reid. The first is to approach Hughes's correspondence as an illuminating aesthetic record, the clearest insight we're likely to get into the mind of a poet viewed by some critics as one of the major writers of the twentieth century. The second way is to discuss, well, "it." "It," of course, is what Hughes called "the Fantasia," the swirling, decades-long hoo-ha brought about by his relationship with Sylvia Plath: their brief, difficult marriage; their separation due to Hughes's affair with Assia Wevill; and Plath's suicide shortly thereafter. "It" ultimately involved a series of bitter clashes over Plath's legacy, the occasional illicit removal of the surname Hughes from her tombstone (by aggrieved *Bell Jar* fans), a series of disputed biographies, at least one lawsuit, endless critical appraisals, reappraisals, and re-reappraisals, a lame song by Ryan Adams ("I wish I had a Sylvia Plath," Adams croons, apparently unaware that they don't come in six-packs), and the inevitable film featuring Gwyneth Paltrow flopping around with Daniel Craig. "It" is a big deal.

But should it be? "When gossip grows old," the Polish writer Stanisław Lec said, "it becomes myth." In the case of Ted Hughes and Sylvia Plath, the myth made by gossip has long obscured the art made by a couple of poets. That's a pity. It's a pity not only because many people might enjoy the poetry if they were to read it on its own merits, rather than for the customary vicarious frisson, but also because many people might not enjoy it. They might instead find themselves wondering why so much time has been spent on two writers whose most notable shared feature was the ability to write a poem dripping with blood, moons, and psychic violence about anything from soccer to provincial beekeeping clubs. They might wonder whether the supposed primal intensity of the poetry isn't lessened by the fact that there's an awful lot of it: more than three hundred pages in Plath's *Collected Poems* (and she died at thirty); more than thirteen hundred pages in Hughes's (with the complete poems yet to come). They might even begin to think that what Plath and Hughes both stand for is a particular kind of poetic and psychological simplicity, according to which the best way to convey fraught concepts is to use words like "writhed" and "cancerous" and "Nazi." They might question whether this is actually the revelation it is sometimes claimed to be. Or they might not. But at least they would be making an actual judgment based on an actual encounter with poetry.

To judge from the evidence gathered here, Hughes would

have been grateful for less "sensational involvement" and more reading. He lived for nearly seven decades and wrote many letters, and by "many" I mean around 2,500 pages worth, according to Reid's estimate in his introduction. (Fortunately, Reid has cut that down to 750, which is longer than the *Selected Letters of Robert Frost*, but—in fairness—shorter than *The Lord of the Rings*.) Hughes is a good letter writer, which is to say his letters are immediately interesting and accessible to third parties to whom they aren't addressed. In part, this may be because Hughes anticipated they might be read by those very parties—as he observes to Assia Wevill, "I'm always expecting my notes to get intercepted so I don't write a fraction of what I would." Be that as it may, Hughes can turn out a memorable description (biographies of Plath are "a perpetual smoldering in the cellar for us. There's always one or two smoking away"), and his offhand observations about poetry can be startlingly perceptive ("Surrealism . . . is basically analytical"). There are correspondences here with a number of well-known writers—Seamus Heaney, Robert Lowell, Yehuda Amichai—and the notes by Reid are uniformly helpful and occasionally amusing. Glossing a letter to T. S. Eliot in which Hughes wishes the older writer a pleasant April, Reid dryly observes, "Whether the author of *The Waste Land* was enjoying April is not recorded."

If there's one letter that sums up the personality that emerges in this collection, it's a note Hughes sent to Philip Larkin on November 21, 1985. Larkin and Hughes had been rivals for most of their lives, a fact of which both poets were acutely aware. In private, Larkin gave Hughes such compliments as,

"He's all right when not reading!" Hughes returned the favor by complaining that various newspapers "have prostrated themselves and finally deified" Larkin. Yet as Larkin lay dying, Hughes reached out with a letter of extraordinary tenderness and decency that is also possibly the most boneheaded piece of correspondence ever addressed to the mordant, brittle, doubting Larkin. Here's what Hughes wrote: "Ever since I heard you'd been into hospital I've been wanting to communicate something which for some reason I've assumed you'd reject outright. . . . I simply wanted to let you know somehow of the existence of a very strange and remarkable fellow down here, quite widely known for what seem to be miraculous healing powers. . . . He's called Cornish. . . . He explains his 'power' as some sort of energy that flows from him and galvanizes the patient's own auto-immune system." Bear in mind that these sentences are addressed to the author of a poem called "Faith Healing," which is not, to put it mildly, an endorsement of faith healing. The whole episode is so earnestly miscalculated as to achieve a kind of grandeur.

Which isn't a bad way to look at much of Hughes's writing. Hughes was, for better or worse, devoted to elaborate symbolic structures. Yeats had *A Vision*; Robert Graves had *The White Goddess*; Hughes had his personal hodgepodge of mysticism, astrology, and Jungian psychology. And like many true believers, he was willing to offer the wisdom of that hodgepodge to whoever he figured might need it. Sure, most people would recognize the absurdity of suggesting magical healing to Philip Larkin, but to Hughes it would have made perfect sense, because in his mind such healing was closely tied to poetry it-self. As he remarks in a draft of a letter to an Anglican bishop, "I regard poets such as myself as a sort of country healer, where the Church is Orthodox Medicine"; and in a later note about Eliot, "If one were to regard his poetry as a performance of 'healing power' . . . I don't think one can assume that when he ceased to write poetry, he ceased to be a 'healer.'" Seen in this light, Hughes's letter to Larkin may have been tone-deaf, but it was also kindly meant.

On the other side of that kindness, however, lay the irrita-bility of a born crank. In 1992, Derwent May, the European arts editor for the *Times* of London, attempted to soften a pan of Hughes's idiosyncratic book on Shakespeare by publishing his own, kinder piece alongside. Those efforts earned May a letter in which Hughes explained that "King Lear was the Llud who was Bran" and "Apollo, Asclepius and Bran were Crow Gods," and "Edgar in Llyr's myth is Gwyn," and "Gwyn, as a British Hero, bequeathed all his legends to Arthur," and "My Hawk is the sleeping, deathless spirit of Arthur/Edgar/Gwyn/Horus—the sacrificed and reborn self of the great god Ra," and, finally, inevitably, "I don't just jot these things down, you know."

Still, it's hard not to have sympathy for Hughes. However taxing his personality may have been for others, his own life was never easy, and he seems to have moved through it with more stoicism, good humor, and humility than most writers manage. For him, little mattered but poetry. As he writes: "I hang on tooth and nail to my own view of what I do—which is a view from the inside. It is fatally easy to acquire, through other people, a view of one's own work from the outside. As when a child is admired, in its hearing, for something it does naturally. Ever after—that something is corrupted with self-consciousness." His work and life now exist in a place well beyond such self-consciousness, a place no less mythic than the realm populated by figures like Apollo, Asclepius, and Bran. Who were, you know, Crow Gods.

THE DREAM LOGIC OF

MATTHEA HARVEY

"We poets in our youth begin in gladness," said Words-worth, who might have felt otherwise had he spent his own youth as an adjunct assistant professor of creative writing. If he'd done so, as many younger writers do nowadays, he'd probably have thought twice about pairing "gladness" with a job that often involves fifty thousand dollars in student loans and no health insurance. To be fair, it's never been easy to be a young poet, and teaching creative writing is certainly safer than working as a roofer. Yet because most are neither wealthy (like the young James Merrill) nor constantly in jeopardy (like Villon), writers in their early careers today face a peculiar and sometimes unenviable set of circumstances. On one hand, the proliferation of MFA programs gives a poet the chance to make a sort of living from his art; on the other hand, the insularity of that world can tax both an artist's social skills and his resistance to fashion. Given these difficulties, it's tempting to replace Wordsworth's salute to youthful vitality with the twenty-nine-year-old Bon Scott's less optimistic observation: "If you wanna be a star of stage and screen / Look out, it's rough and mean."

The good news, however, is that America's younger poets are generating more than their share of our country's best writing. At thirty-five, Matthea Harvey is a case in point. She is in many ways a typical American poet in early career: She teaches workshops, helps edit a journal, keeps a busy reading schedule, pops up at artists' colonies, publishes widely, and has had to learn the basic steps of the po-biz hustle (her website is polished, her *Wikipedia* entry primed for expansion). And Harvey's technique is a variation on the trendiest contemporary style, which relies heavily on disconnected phrases, abrupt syntactical shifts, attention-begging titles ("The Gem Is on Page Sixty-Four"), quirky diction ("orangery," "aigrettes"), flickering italics, oddball openings ("The scent of pig is faint tonight"), and a tone ranging from daffy to plangent—basically, two scoops of John Ashbery and a sprinkling of Gertrude Stein. It's not hard to write acceptable poetry in this mode, which is one of the reasons so many people make use of it. After all, poets need jobs, and for those, they need books—and for those, well, they need poems.

But if it's relatively easy to write passable poetry in the style du jour, it's never easy to write good poetry in any style, which is what makes Harvey's new collection, *Modern Life*, such a pleasure. In part, *Modern Life* continues the path she's followed for two books, and it has all the attractions one would expect from that approach (and some of the flaws as well). But the best thing about Harvey's new work is that it reaches for subjects that don't lend themselves to her usual bag of tricks. She's willing to risk genuine failure, and her reward—our reward—is that richest and rarest thing, genuine poetry.

To appreciate what's different about this collection, though, it's first necessary to understand what a Harvey poem usually looks like. At her best, Harvey is a soft-touch poet who has Stevie Smith's knack for writing throwaway lines that in the end seem less like Post-it notes than ransom letters. This sly, mannered quality is coupled with an almost Victorian sense of whimsy ("More Sketches for a Beautiful Hat") and balanced by a true technician's interest in the nuts and bolts of writing. For instance, she'll call a poem "Pity the Bathtub Its Forced Embrace of the Human Form," and begin one of its syntax-bending sections:

> Pity the bathtub its forced embrace of the human
> Form may define external appearance but there is room
> For improvement within try a soap dish that allows for
> Slippage is inevitable

As an essay on form—poetic and otherwise—it's a satisfying performance: light and quick rather than ponderous and self-occupied. If you're going to write like this, though, your commitment had better match your cleverness, or the poem becomes little more than an obsessive exercise in lacework. When Harvey is at her precious worst ("Is it your / hermeneut's helmet not letting me / filter through?"), you can practically see the honeycomb stitching.

Modern Life isn't completely free of this problem. You'll still find coy productions like "A Theory of Generations," which consists in its entirety of three repetitions of the line "You're it." And you'll also find poems that are good in the way one expects a Harvey poem to be good—like a sweetly disturbing prose poem that begins, "The ham flowers have veins and are rimmed in rind, each petal a little meat sunset." But what makes *Modern Life* more than just another neatly accomplished collection from a neatly accomplished poet are two long, strange, nervous sequences: "The Future of Terror" and "Terror of the Future." These are among the most arresting poems yet written about the current American political atmosphere, and they're all the more surprising coming from a writer whose sensibility seems so resistant to our usual ideas about political poetry. But, then, our usual ideas are often not our best ones.

"The Future of Terror" and "Terror of the Future" are abecedarian poems, which is to say that they follow a particular scheme through the alphabet. There's a longer explanation for their arrangement—which Harvey unnecessarily provides—but the formal strictures themselves are infinitely less interesting than what's been done within those strictures. (One suspects that the reason Harvey likes to talk about the safe subject of form so much is that she's a bit unsettled by her own project.)

The sequences aren't exactly stories, but they follow a kind of dream logic in which "we" and "I" do various things in the first sequence, with a "you" emerging more fully in the second. The end of the opening poem in "The Future of Terror" is representative:

> *The navigator's needle swung strangely,*
> *oscillating between the oilwells*
> *and ask again later. We tried to pull ourselves*
> *together by practicing quarterback sneaks*
> *along the pylons, but the race to the ravine*
> *was starting to feel as real as the R.I.P.'s*
> *and roses carved into rock. Suddenly the sight*
> *of a schoolbag could send us scrambling.*

There have been many poems written about September 11 and its aftermath, but most fall short because their subject isn't really a subject—it's a change in context, a mood of uncertainty. This atmosphere is oddly suited to a writer like Harvey, whose preoccupation with play and formal reversals is the lighter, kinder side of the muteness that proceeds from horror. It's easy to be frustrated with this poet when she seems to be avoiding the point, but when the point is pointlessness—a kind of omnipresent dread—Harvey's poetry becomes a glass through which we can perceive, darkly, an even greater darkness.

Considering the apprehensions that propel *Modern Life*, it might be inappropriate to say that this collection should make us optimistic about the future of American poetry—or the future of anything, for that matter. But if we limit ourselves to the present—which is, after all, the only thing we can truly account for—we should be grateful to Harvey for reminding us, as the best poets do, that being here together is enough.

JACK GILBERT'S

DAILY DEVOTIONS

It is impossible to picture certain poets buying Cheetos at a Sunoco. Granted, this is true of a particular sort of person in any occupation—for example, it's hard to imagine Mitt Romney with iridescent orange dust all over his hands, unless he had accidentally purchased Halloween. But there is a kind of poet for whom involvement in the tackier, saltier elements of everyday life and popular culture seems not only unlikely but almost inappropriate. Robinson Jeffers, for instance, wrote lines like "I'd sooner, except the penalties, kill a man as a hawk," and praised "the massive / Mysticism of stone" and "the implacable arrogance" of birds of prey, while enjoying watching orcas maul sea lions because "there was nothing human involved; no lies, no smirk and no malice." One struggles to envision him at a Bennigan's happy hour.

This kind of poet is relatively rare nowadays. (More common is the writer who invokes popular culture while remaining carefully distanced from it, who titles poems and/or books something like "The Rambo Variations," who buttresses Walter Benjamin with Jay Z.) The scarcity of poets like Jeffers is in many ways not such a bad thing. After all, the dailiness of life can be as vividly poetic as death or birth or sex, and a poet who seems disconnected from that reality risks becoming disconnected from a certain kind of reader. And poetry, so the conventional wisdom goes, is already about as disconnected as an art form can get.

Still, what counts as the dailiness of life depends upon the type of life we lead—so it's perhaps helpful that some poets resist the idea that day-to-day existence is best described in terms of consumer culture. Jack Gilbert is one of those writers. Gilbert is now eighty-seven, and his new *Collected Poems* is a monument to an aesthetic off the grid. Born in Pittsburgh, he moved to San Francisco in the late fifties, where he took part in Jack Spicer's poetry workshops and met Allen Ginsberg, who read early versions of "Howl" to him. Gilbert won the Yale Younger Poets competition in 1962, and a few years later he left for Europe, where he would spend a good bit of the next twenty-odd years, living at times in conditions of near poverty. His entire body of work consists of only five books, and the collected volume comes in at only 380 pages. (By comparison, this is probably 1,000 pages less than the collected work of John Ashbery, who is about the same age.) Gilbert doesn't do many events, almost never appears at conferences, and probably has spent more time with Greek fishermen than with college sophomores.

As you might expect, his writing is somewhat unfashionable by the standards of the contemporary poetry world. Gilbert regularly deploys words like "light," "dark," "love," "heart," "soul," "spirit," and "moon" in a way that, while not naive, tends to lack any leavening irony ("People complain about too many moons in my poetry," he says, adding another one). He writes openly and plainly about grief, love, marriage, betrayal, lust, and more lust, often with a little rural Mediterranean color ("Goats occasionally, and the sound of roosters"). While Gilbert can work in form—his first book contains a villanelle, some haiku, and a partial sestina—he prefers simple, orderly free-verse constructions that take up on average about one-half to three-quarters of a page. The work tends to be a bit decorous in phrasing (he "cannot" more than half as much as he "can't") and more focused on physical needs and wants than the trappings of personality. Lines like "But Apollo is not reasonable about desire" are typical. Nouns like "sorrow" and "body" are common; ones like "mopiness" and "noggin" are not.

Gilbert sounds, in other words, like a man who's spent a lot of time on a Greek island doing nothing but cleaning squid, having affairs, and thinking about poetry and purity. If the work of some poets seems eager to play tour guide, to show you every knickknack in the flea market while keeping up a constant stream of patter, a good Gilbert poem is content simply to stare at you—not hostile, not friendly, just very focused. It's a stark approach that can work well with equally stark subject matter. Consider "Michiko Dead," one of many lovely poems about the death of his first wife at age thirty-six. The poem begins, "He manages like somebody carrying a box / that is too heavy" and continues the conceit as it concludes:

> *He moves his thumbs slightly*
> *when the fingers begin to tire, and it makes*
> *different muscles take over. Afterward,*
> *he carries it on his shoulder, until the blood*
> *drains out of the arm that is stretched up*
> *to steady the box and the arm goes numb. But now*
> *the man can hold underneath again, so that*
> *he can go on without ever putting the box down.*

Grief is survivable ("he can go on") but only at the price of making it perpetual ("without ever putting the box down"). The poem is as plain as can be, yet Gilbert manages to capture all the evolving complexity of mourning, the sad reality that when one method of coping becomes exhausted, "different muscles take over" that will themselves quickly tire.

The closer Gilbert sticks to neutral observation, the better his poems tend to be. He's particularly comfortable with the ambiguities of romance (maybe a little too comfortable), as in "Trying to Be Married":

> *Watching my wife out in the full moon,*
> *the sea bright behind her across the field*
> *and through the trees. Eight years*

and her love for me quieted away.
How fine she is. How hard we struggle.

Gilbert delicately balances their "struggle" to stay together with the struggle they have with each other. The poem resolves into uncertainty, and he knows well enough to leave it alone. He exercises similar restraint in the strange "Textures":

We had walked three miles through the night
When I had to piss. She stopped just beyond.
I aimed at the stone wall of a vineyard,
But the wind took it and she made a sound.
I apologized. "It's all right," she said out
Of the dark, her voice different. "I liked it."

Notice how much the poem depends on the use of the word "different," rather than, say, "aroused" or "excited" or "intrigued." What we are like in "the dark"—of sex, of physicality—is more than anything else simply "different." This, Gilbert implies, is what frightens and compels us. It's an elegant point delivered with understated accuracy.

Such subtlety is not, alas, always the rule. Like a lot of poets who are more interested in the spirit of the art than in its technical felicities, Gilbert sometimes inflates lines into life lessons. As in: "Grief makes the heart / apparent as much as sudden happiness can," or "The way my heart carols sometimes, / and other times yearns," or" A wonderful sad dance that comes after."

Gassy balloons like these drag the worst of Gilbert's poetry completely off the ground. A similar problem extends to the women in these poems, of which there are scores, all of them exactly alike and frequently doing something Passionate or True or Simple. (To be fair, any poet whose work inclines toward myth is going to have a habit of turning people into archetypes.) Nor is the sense of sameness relieved by formal variety, as Gilbert works a few basic techniques nearly to death. For instance, he relies heavily on gerund phrases followed by periods as a drama-heightening method. In fifteen pages we have: "Going over and over afterward / what we should have done / instead of what we did." "Trying to escape the mildness of our violent world." "Making together a consequence of America." "Carrying Michiko dead in my arms." "Trying to see if something comes next." "Wondering whether he has stalled." Noticing this formula. Noticing it a little too much. In general, reading Gilbert at his worst can be like running into a hermit determined to tell you all about his devotion to solitude and the women beautiful and lonely as stars whom he totally slept with.

And yet if it's easy to poke fun at Gilbert's least interesting work, this is precisely what makes his strongest writing memorable. He isn't afraid of embarrassment. He doesn't hedge his bets. He believes that poetry is worthy of devotion, that it ought not be subordinated to the things that clutter up day-to-day life. He isn't right, and he sets up a division that is unnecessary. But neither is he completely wrong. Poets have always been tempted to live poetry, not merely to write it. If the work of poets like

Gilbert and Jeffers tends to demonstrate that this ambition is impossible, there are still good poems to be found in the demonstration of that impossibility. To take Gilbert slightly out of context: "The silver is worn down to the brass underneath / and is the better for it." The better, unlike the perfect, being no enemy to the good.

THE NEGLECTED MASTER

Modern poetry is long on Lucite but short on cash. As Philip Larkin once put it, a good poet has no trouble amassing "medals and prizes and honorary-this-and-thats . . . but if you turned round and said, Right, if I'm so good, give me an index-linked permanent income equal to what I can get for being an undistinguished university administrator—well, reason would remount its throne pretty quickly." Larkin was British, but his remark applies just as well to American poetry, which often has been a game for the amply trust-funded (Stein, Merrill), with occasional participation from the upper middle class (Bishop) and only rare appearances by actual po' folks (James Wright). Larkin's observation also helps explain why "medals and prizes and honorary this-and-thats" can be as important in the poetry world as the currency they so closely resemble. After all, when what you're mostly hoping to earn is prestige, the coin of the realm is the gold-star sticker.

And the thing about stickers is, they're awfully easy to print. One of the main points of James F. English's recent study of cultural awards, *The Economy of Prestige*, is that prizes have been proliferating rapidly for at least a hundred years and probably won't stop doing so anytime soon. To this a poet can only say: no kidding. Maybe you've written a short poem that addresses "a philosophical or epistemological concern"? The Cecil Hemley Memorial Award from the Poetry Society of America may be in the cards. How about a few lines inspired by "a very famous White Leghorn hen who was raised by the Oregon State Agricultural Experiment Station"? Look no further than the Lady MacDuff Poetry Contest. Nor is it a coincidence that both these prizes are memorial awards—as English astutely notes, prizes are often given "in memoriam" because we intuitively connect cultural awards with concepts like timelessness and immortality.

So there may soon be a blue ribbon for almost every kind of poetic achievement, and each such trophy will claim to stand for something that transcends day-to-day life, with all its humdrum compromises, ATM withdrawals, and funerals. We may be poor, but we'll be permanently prized. The surest sign that this state of affairs is already taking shape is (naturally) an award— one that takes the memorial function and simultaneously amplifies and reverses it. This is what you might call the Prize for Not Getting Enough Prizes. There are several awards that play on this theme, but the most interesting recent variation is the product of two institutions that have old-fashioned capital to go along with the cultural kind: the Library of America (recipient of grants from, well, everybody) and the Poetry Foundation (which has $150 million from Eli Lilly in its coffers). The accolade they've come up with is the Neglected Masters Award, and its first recipient is the New York poet Samuel Menashe, whose *New and Selected Poems* is being published by the Library as part of the prize's mandate.

The first thing to be said about all this is that calling someone a "neglected master" makes for one hell of a left-handed compliment. Beyond that, however, bestowing an award for neglected mastery is a gesture so fraught with contradictions, ambiguities, and obscure hopes and fears that it risks confusion at best, incoherence at worst. First, there's that strangely self-refuting title—presumably Menashe can no longer be considered neglected after getting recognized for his unjustly ignored brilliance, can he? Then there's the notion that the appropriate cure for neglect is an award with the word "neglected" in its name. Then there's the implicit assumption that mastery is something we can identify with certainty in our own lifetimes (after all, if we have neglected masters, we must have some un-neglected masters). Related to this is the poetry world's obsession with and fear of its own marginality, which in this case results in the hopeful application of the word "neglected" to a single older poet from the West Village, when one easily could argue that the entire art form—even the lord of the prize, John Ashbery—is about as neglected as neglected gets. But above all else is the assumption that the awards system is an appropriate and inescapable measure of artistic worth. When we give a prize for neglected mastery, we aren't just celebrating a good poet, we're conspicuously correcting a system error—and we care only about the mistakes of systems that we think have some claim to legitimacy. Is that really what we believe about poetry prizes?

Before answering that question, it's worth remembering that the one tangible result of the Neglected Masters Award is a new book by Samuel Menashe. It's only fair to ask: does this collection help justify the muddled honorific that gave it life? It does. Menashe, who is now eighty, has struggled with American publishers for decades, but he's been celebrated by British and Irish poets like Austin Clarke, Donald Davie, and Stephen Spender (the editor of this volume is Oxford professor of poetry and would-be Bob Dylan sideman Christopher Ricks). Menashe's difficulties in his home country probably have a lot to do with the fact that, as an American poet, he appears to have done almost everything wrong. He didn't teach creative writing, didn't ally himself with his more sociable peers, didn't serve on many committees, and didn't finagle his way into many anthologies. He appears mostly just to have just . . . written poetry.

Fortunately, he happens to have done it well. Menashe is a curious and meticulous writer—the poems here are no longer than a page, most have very short lines, they're either unpunctuated or very carefully and lightly punctuated, and they rely on tricky rhyme and assonance schemes to carry observations that Ricks describes as "apophthegmatic" and a nonprofessor might call "proverbial." Basically, each poem reads like it's been hand-blown, filled with an exactly measured dose of wisdom and then polished nine thousand times by the world's most precisely

folded chamois. Here's "The Niche," which is a kind of statement of Menashean principles:

> *The niche narrows*
> *Hones one thin*
> *Until his bones*
> *Disclose him*

Like many Menashe poems, this one gets better the more
you think about it. The idea that the self is unveiled by a process
of reduction is balanced by the suggestion that the "niche"
itself—one's lot in life, one's choices as an artist—may be creating the kind of self that can be so revealed. Or to put it another
way: is it the man that's found in the niche or the niche that
makes the man? (It's also worth noting the buried joke on the
phrase "the clothes make the man." Here the bones "disclose"—
dis-clothe—the true self.) The poem is a considerable technical
achievement; as Donald Davie notes, Menashe sets up two
chains of assonance (the short *i* in "niche," the long *o* in "nar-
rows") and then follows them through each line to their union
in the keystone word "disclose." This kind of thing is a lot
harder to do than it looks.

And Menashe does it over and over. He's a wry but essentially optimistic poet, and his best writing demonstrates that the
stylistic limitations we choose quickly cease to be limitations,
even when we identify them as such ("A pot poured out / Ful-
fills its spout"). Among the strongest poems here are "At Cross
Purposes," "Descent," "Sleep," "Beachhead" (a great war poem),

and "At a Standstill"—any one of which will be as appealing to a reader not deeply acquainted with American poetry as it will to a fellow poet familiar with the austere Dickinsonian school to which Menashe belongs. However it comes to us, this is a book well worth reading.

Does it matter, then, whether the author of that book is a neglected master, as duly sanctioned by the prize system, an Oxford professor of poetry, and two organizations with lots of money? Sadly or not, yes. With the fading of transcendent ideals in certain areas of American life comes the inevitable fading of the dream of unsullied, undying art—and the nostalgic desire for prizes that remind us of that dream, if nothing else. But just because dreams are involved doesn't mean consequences aren't real: we're a more mystical and nostalgic culture than is usually thought, and the poetry world has every right to sell itself on that basis. It's worth wondering, though, as we give away another medallion for Best Thing Having to Do with Poetry, what kind of heaven we may be buying for ourselves and at what very earthly cost.

PUBLIC POETRY: FOUR TAKES

All poetry is public, in the sense that every poem implies an audience. But some publics are more public than others. Most contemporary poets, for example, address a public that consists only of close friends, professional acquaintances, and a few handy abstractions like the Ideal Reader and Posterity. This kind of public is very different from (and much smaller and more homogenous than) the one that buys novels by Zadie Smith or Jonathan Franzen. And, of course, both of these audiences pale beside the public that we usually think of as "the public"—the ocean of humanity that votes in elections, watches the Super Bowl, and generally makes America what it is, for better and worse. Poetry has famously little contact with this last and largest public. Indeed, the only such public appearance by a poet in recent memory was Elizabeth Alexander's reading at the inauguration of President Obama, which earned a predictably ambivalent reaction from segments of poetry's own public.

But if poets don't often find themselves reading before a million citizens on the National Mall, that doesn't mean they don't address issues of national concern. The question is, which public gets to hear those public thoughts—and exactly how public are they, anyway?

Skin, Inc.
by Thomas Sayers Ellis

THOMAS SAYERS ELLIS'S *SKIN, Inc.* follows up his 2004 collection, *The Maverick Room*, and focuses on the always fraught issue of race in America, particularly race in American literature, and even more particularly, race in American poetry. The book is roughly 170 pages and is divided into seven sections, some dominated by eponymous long poems ("The Pronoun-Vowel Reparations Song," for instance), others organized around a theme ("Gone Pop" consists of fifteen poems about Michael Jackson). The work here is conspicuously public in the largest sense, which is to say that Ellis talks about issues of obvious societal concern in a manner that smart general readers might follow and possibly even admire or criticize. He is blunt, rude, sometimes intentionally clumsy, and determined to get some awkward things said, fair or not. It's an admirable and sadly unusual thing for a contemporary poet to attempt.

Nor is it easy to pull off. As Ellis realizes, speaking broadly isn't a matter of writing simply or straightforwardly; on the contrary, there's an appealing slyness to Ellis's best poetry that recalls the cagey work of Gwendolyn Brooks, who remains one of the touchstone poets of the modern era. Indeed, in the strongest poems in *Skin, Inc.* Ellis proves himself a true heir to Brooks's uncanny talent for addressing multiple audiences while still remaining faithful to her own ambiguities and ambivalent feelings. Most poets faced with the challenge of such audiences produce poem-by-committee blandness (q.v., September 11, poetry thereof). Ellis's approach, however, is utterly distinctive, even as he happily tosses everything but the kitchen sink onto the page. The diction here ranges from "discourse" to "mo betta" to "eeeeeeeeeeeyow"; forms run the gamut from the villanelle ("A Few Excuses") to visual poetry ("The Pronoun-Vowel Reparations Song"); and as if that weren't enough, Ellis throws in photographs and footnotes. The overall effect is of a table sagging with the day's labor of a manic chef, and individual results can sometimes be similarly excessive (the visual poem is better as an eye chart). But the best work is enriched by its sense of superabundance, as in the beginning of "Or":

> *Or Oreo, or*
> *worse. Or ordinary.*
> *Or your choice*
> *of category*
>
> *or*
> *Color*

or any color
other than Colored
or Colored Only.
Or "Of Color"

        or
          Other.

Ellis has an excellent ear, and he uses it here to convey the uncertainty and possibility that surrounds any discussion of race (as Ellis is well aware, the conjunction "or" can be both prison and key). His knack for incorporating different registers and ranges of speech is equally evident in poems like "My Meter Is Percussive" and in his superb elegy for James Brown, "Mr. Dynamite Splits." But the strongest poem is "The Identity Repairman," which takes up the labels—for example, "Negro" and "Colored"—that have attached over time to African Americans. Here are its final sections:

BLACK

My heart is a fist.
I fix Blackness.
My fist is a heart.
I beat Whiteness.

AFRICAN AMERICAN

Before I was born,
I absorbed struggle.
Just looking
at history hurts.

So the heart is a fist (as in Black Power) that "fixes"—repairs—Blackness. But "to fix" also means "to hold in place" and "to neuter," allowing Ellis to quietly suggest both the strength and the limitations of the label. Similarly, when the fist becomes a heart that "beat[s] Whiteness," the victory is necessarily incomplete, because it requires the perpetuation of the thing beaten: the idea of whiteness is circulated like blood (the heart beats it) even as it is overcome. In work like this, Ellis is writing some of the finest truly public poetry of our time.

But there is, it has to be said, another, less interesting side to *Skin, Inc.* This is the side that still clings to an exalted idea of the public that we call the poetry world, and especially the poetry world as filtered through the lens of Cambridge, Massachusetts (Ellis went to Harvard). It's helpful here to pause and think again about the idea of a poem's public presence. When Ellis writes as he does in "The Identity Repairman," he's writing for almost anyone who's ever thought about what it means to talk about him- or herself "as" something. That audience is large, heterogeneous, and interesting. And when he's writing about poetry—not the poetry world, but poetry itself—that audience, too, is heterogeneous and interesting, if not necessarily large. But who's the audience for lines like this from "The Judges of Craft"?

Someone in charge decides.
Someone in charge
     designs.

A someone considered worthy of width,
wider than content,
country,
continent.

I have disappointing news, but there's a big silver lining. We discussed your poems at length and with admiration and excitement, but in the end we didn't find one in *this* batch that we felt would be a great debut for you in the magazine. It's just that so many of them are about writing, and we try to shy away from poems explicitly addressing the subject of writing—much less the politics of the writing scene. But you are definitely on the screen here, and I'm only (and deeply) sorry I took so long.

Yes, there is actually a poem in this book that includes the text of various rejection letters that Ellis apparently has received from poetry journals. Imagine a gifted and widely acclaimed operatic tenor pausing midsong to deliver a rant about the way *Opera News* once failed to mention him in an article, and you'll have some idea of the jarring note this performance strikes. Along the same lines, Ellis pauses elsewhere in *Skin, Inc.* to compare John Ashbery's rhythm and imagery unfavorably to that of "bling-bling," and to snipe at "the Grolier," a poetry bookstore in Harvard Square where he apparently worked as a college student.

The problem is not that these criticisms are undeserved. Maybe the editors who sent Ellis rejection notes are indeed insensitive. Maybe Ashbery does pale in comparison with Lil Wayne. Maybe the bookstore was a lousy place. The problem is that these criticisms seem unambitious when compared with the provocations in Ellis's better work. Who, after all, even knows what "the Grolier" is? Contrary to Ellis's suggestion, one odd local bookshop isn't symbolic of American poetry, much less American literature, and considerably much less American society. At most, the store is representative of a provincial subculture in the American poetry world, and on the list of things that are of great cultural import, that probably puts it about even with wherever Boston-area Renaissance faire participants go to get their tunics hemmed. A writer this good ought not spend his time peeling potatoes this small.

That said, the motivation here isn't hard to fathom, or to sympathize with. There's a lingering insecurity behind the swagger in some of these poems, and because Ellis is a tough-minded poet, he's reluctant to admit (much less surrender) to that uncertainty. So he stands his ground; he pushes back. The instinct is entirely to his credit, but when the thing that makes you feel belittled is itself tiny, then the consequences of such a response can be unfortunate. And there is almost nothing tinier than the poetry world, just as there is almost nothing bigger, stranger, and more disturbing than the bloody country that contains it. It's clear throughout *Skin, Inc.* that Ellis is equal to this latter, larger challenge; in his next book maybe he'll make it the sole focus of his considerable attention. If so, we will all be, if not repaired, at least made slightly better.

The Cloud Corporation
by Timothy Donnelly

TIMOTHY DONNELLY, LIKE THOMAS Sayers Ellis, is a talented writer who has recently released a second collection that isn't short. But for the most part, the similarities end there. Donnelly's new book, *The Cloud Corporation*, is a nearly immaculate exercise in haute academic style, from its aggressively quirky titles ("Team of Fake Deities Arranged on an Orange Plate") to its deliberately affected tone and pose ("Roll back the stone from the sepulcher's mouth!") to its frequently Jamesian syntax (sentences here regularly wind through six or seven lines). On top of that, we have diction borrowed equally from business-speak ("optimize my output") and the vernacular ("I was totally into it"); the deployment of bizarre phrasing generated by collage ("a consistent sweat paragraph"); a mood of pessimism, anxiety, and unhappiness ("We revolt ourselves; we disgust and annoy us"); general distaste for finance and/or capitalism ("To His Debt"); and, finally, a fundamental reliance on abstraction ("the sky again // the temple of the mind perceiving it"). If you were trying to concoct a recipe involving every flavor in the cupboard of the hip contemporary poem, you would come up with *The Cloud Corporation*. It is the epitome of Our Moment.

And it is, in many respects, a strong statement on the vitality of that moment. That may seem an odd way to put things, given that Donnelly spends roughly 135 of the book's 140 pages being depressed in some way or another. He is depressed by conspicuous consumption ("the circuitry that suffers me to crave // what I know I'll never need, or what I need but have / in abundance already . . ."). He is depressed by empire building and militarism ("that photograph / of women and children shot down by an American / battalion . . ."). But mostly he's depressed by the fact that he spends a lot of time inside his own head ("thoughts / lilt back to the terms of this existence, its fundamental // . . . insignificance"). This could all easily end up as sub-Stevensian moping, a sort of "Auroras of Ugh." But Donnelly is an astonishing technician who is capable of finding nearly infinite shades in the gray of his malaise. Consider the beginning of "Antepenultimate Conflict with Self":

The times the thought of being pulled apart from
you comes as a relief have now come to outnumber
those it startles me like light from a hurricane
lamp left burning unattended dangerously near
the curtains of the theater we both attend and are.

To unpack: the thought of being separated from his own self now relieves him more often than it threatens him with a sense of impending dissolution (and of course, who is he if not himself). Also, the thought of dissolution is worrying like the prospect of a hurricane lamp threatening a theater (metaphor 1) that is both attended by the poet and his self (metaphor 2), and composed of the poet and his self (metaphor 3). The key to this stanza is its speed, which Donnelly intends to mimic the crazy tilt of the ideas he's assembling. The lines, with their heavy breaks ("hurricane / lamp") and densely packed, interrelated metaphors, come out almost as an exhausted gasp or gulp (it's not surprising when Donnelly later defines a unit called the "snailsdeath" as being "roughly / equivalent to the pause between swallows in a human / throat . . ."). And if Donnelly's technical skill is impressive, his humor can be winning. "The world tries hard to bore me to death," he notes at the beginning of one poem, "but not hard enough." You can be as mopey as you like when you write this well.

What makes the book more than simply an example of highly polished competence, however, is its peculiar combination of whimsicality and desperation. "Despair" isn't a word you'd expect Donnelly to be fond of; it's all too often a euphemism for naive self-regard, and Donnelly is anything but naive. But notice how artfully it's deployed in the opening of "Fun for the Shut-in":

> *Demonstrate to yourself a resistance to feeling*
> *unqualified despair by attempting something like*
> *perfect despair embellished with hand gestures.*

Is this funny? Well, yes. But it also puts Donnelly at risk; it breaks up the pattern of smoothly unfolding aestheticism. Even

more interesting is the conclusion of "The New Hymns," which
is both a rejection of certain kinds of poetry and a statement of
principle:

> *I don't want to have to*
> *locate divinity in a loaf of bread, in a sparkler,*
> *or in the rainlike sound the wind makes through*
>
> *mulberry trees, not tonight. Listen to them carry on*
> *about gentleness when it's inconceivable*
> *that any kind or amount of it will ever be able to*
>
> *balance the scales. I have been held down*
> *by the throat and terrified, numb enough to know.*
> *The temperature at which no bird can thrive—*
>
> *a lifelong feeling that I feel now, remembering*
> *down the highway, half-hypnotized in the*
> *backseat feeling what I feel now, and moderate*
>
> *happiness has nothing to do with it: I want to press*
> *my face against the cold black window until*
> *there is a deity whose only purpose is to stop this.*

There have been many versions of Frost's "Acquainted with
the Night" written over the decades by many poets, but Donnelly is more than up—or down—for the task.

Strong as this collection is, however, there are things to

question about it and, more broadly, the sort of writing it represents. And this is a good occasion to do so, both because Donnelly
is a gifted writer (who therefore can take the criticism) and because
The Cloud Corporation already has been widely and rightly praised.
Here is what a skeptic might say: This is a collection that is frequently fixated on the sort of vague melancholy and technical
bravura that captivates certain audiences in the poetry world but
leaves other readers cold or, worse, bored. This is a collection that
takes up subjects of great public import—the political economy,
the environment—yet talks about them in ways that don't risk
judgment from any public without a subscription to *Fence*. And if
Ellis sometimes lapses into bluster, Donnelly has a habit of suffo-
cating poems with exquisite, cheerless noodling. As in:

> *I dreamt in complex packaging that posed no less a threat*
> *at the factory warehouse than up among my cupboards*
> *or dropped in the superabundant trash bins at airports.*

> *Found it simple and good to forget that threat by letting*
> *perception of such objects occlude true knowledge of them.*
> *Any worry washed in umbra. Like being in the moment*
> *only endlessly. I hear the naked hands of strangers make*

> *My dumplings but experience suggests what makes*
>   *them mine*
> *is money. I open the door and I extend good money*
> *into ancient night. . . .*

Sure, there are things to praise in writing like this. But it's also coy and pleased with itself (nor does it help much that the above poem goes on for five pages). It almost makes you want to go order lasagna at an Olive Garden—made, no doubt, by "the naked hands of strangers"—just to spite the poem's disdain for the world in its sloppy, awful, unfair actuality. Or how about this:

> Meanwhile we wanted the sentence to continue
> fading as we thought another would begin
> only after the first had finished and the last
> vibrations seemed not to extend from the sentence
> anymore but the fact that we had heard it
> fading there together. . . .

There's plenty of good work in this book, to be sure, and any critic should welcome the opportunity to talk about that work in front of any audience anywhere. But there are other poems that, like the lines above, are harder to talk about, not because they're too complex, or because the audience for poetry is too ignorant, or because our cultural moment won't allow it, or because of capitalism or Sarah Palin or food courts. No, it's harder to talk about some of these poems because they just don't say much. They're the equivalent of playing scales, and fresh paint on the guitar doesn't change that fact. For all Donnelly's many strengths, this is a potential weakness that his rapidly forming legion of imitators ignores at its peril.

One with Others
by C. D. Wright

FEW BOOKS HAVE NOBLER intentions than C. D. Wright's *One with Others*. The collection attempts to capture events occurring in Wright's native Arkansas around the time of a protest march in 1969 led by a Memphis activist called Sweet Willie Wine; it also serves as a memorial to Wright's friend Margaret Kaelin McHugh, who is referred to by her nickname, V. V, a white woman, apparently participated in the march and suffered the scorn of her community for it. (As Wright puts it, "While she was in jail her husband bought airtime and denounced her. When she was released she was served with papers for divorce and custody.") Though the bulk of the book focuses on V's town in the late sixties, Wright occasionally returns to the present day, and in particular to the apartment in Hell's Kitchen where V died.

This is, by any measure, extraordinary material. Wright's approach to it is the one that has become her signature: She creates an enormous (150-page) collage of voices, historical notes, fragments from "Dear Abby" (allegedly), lists, asides, quotations, and discussions of copperheads, cookie prices, temperatures—you name it. The idea is that the picture that emerges gradually from this assortment will be all the stronger for lacking narration, that its repetitions and occasional bursts of clarity will enable us to understand a person, an area, and a time better than if we were simply told what happened. In this sense, the book is similar to Wright's *Deepstep Come Shining*, which details a tour across Georgia and the Carolinas, and *One Big Self*, her book on Louisiana prisons. And, of course, the roots of the strategy extend back to Williams's *Paterson* and (as Joel Brouwer observed in an excellent essay on Wright) Muriel Rukeyser's "The Book of the Dead."

This approach is unfortunately less successful here. To be sure, there are many passages in *One with Others* that are equally lyrical, funny, enraging, and tender. For example:

THE BROTHER TO WHOM A CERTAIN INJUSTICE
WAS DONE [who lives in Reno]: One night after the
conviction, the police let me go in the middle of the night.
Just like that. I showed up on Mother's porch. The police
told me to get out of town before dawn. So the family
pitched in and bought me a one-way ticket to San Francisco
and I went. Believe you me, I went.

How did you feel when you first saw those golden gates.
You got me there.

People wore purple pants.
Come again.
In California, people wore purple pants.

The excerpt, presumably taken from an interview, shows Wright at her most perceptive. A man who's been unjustly imprisoned, exiled, taken from his family, doesn't think, upon reaching potential safety, of a capitalized abstraction. No, he notices that Californians wear purple pants. It's a human, genuine response, and Wright knows well enough to leave it alone.

But there are several interrelated problems that prevent 150 pages of excerpts like the above (plus many considerably less interesting ones) from cohering into a satisfying whole. First, the structure of the book is itself problematic. Wright's methods work best in short pieces, in which her electric leaps are startling enough to carry a poem on their own. Here, however, the pressure of the story overwhelms the sprawling collage framework—you find yourself saying, as you encounter another grocery list, "This might be fascinating, but could I hear more about the riot at the school?" It's not that Wright's disjunctive approach is too confusing but rather that the actual facts are at least as moving and disturbing as the pirouettes Wright makes around and above them. Consider Wright's fullest description of the imprisonment of high school kids at the local swimming pool, an appalling episode that she references several times:

> After the pool was drained for the season, they arrested the kids who marched to the white school. Who stood and sang "Like a Tree Planted by the Water." They took them to the jailhouses in school buses. They took them to the drained pool in sealed 18-wheelers. The sheriff told them they were to be taken to the woods and there shot. Then the sheriff told them they were to be taken to the pool and there drowned.

Here is the same incident as described by a historian named
Randy Finley:

> On September 16 [1965], police arrested nearly 200 stu-
> dents and SNCC workers for disturbing the peace. The
> arrests overwhelmed the St. Francis County jail, forcing
> authorities to hold many protestors at the swimming
> pool, the civic center, or the dog pound. The jail includ-
> ed the "Bullroom," a filthy, dark cell teeming with lice
> and chiggers. Toilets overflowed. Meals consisted of
> peanut butter sandwiches. As parents and SNCC lead-
> ers scurried to come up with $25,000 bail, city officials
> reportedly told parents that charges would be dropped
> if they signed documents promising to keep their chil-
> dren away from SNCC's Freedom Center and out of
> future demonstrations. On September 20, the school
> board broke off discussions with local black lead-
> ers. The next night, police broke into the Freedom
> Center at 1:30 A.M. to harass workers. By September
> 22, the town "crawled with state troopers."

This incident doesn't need, as Wright puts it, "the
borrowed-tuxedo lining of fiction." In fact, that's arguably the
last thing it needs.

In Wright's more mysterious poems, one feels there is a story
not being told, and the withholding is appealing, almost erotic.
Here, however, one knows there is a story not being told, and the
withholding is simply frustrating. The parceling out of information

makes the book needlessly confusing and obscures rather than reveals its central characters. For example, Wright mentions that the march itself consisted of "six Negroes walking to Little Rock and [a] white woman driving a station wagon," and she rightly (and amusingly) mocks the officials of a town along the route who summon up a massive police presence to face this tiny, courageous group. But why was the march so small? Wright doesn't say. Perhaps part of the explanation is that Sweet Willie Wine appears to have called the march on his own, without the support of the NAACP and against the wishes of the two local activists, Cato Brooks and J. F. Cooley, who had been working as leaders of the black community in V's town. (Wright actually mentions Cooley in the poem—he's the teacher whose dismissal caused a riot at the all-black high school—but she never uses his name, and he and Brooks are otherwise strangely absent from the book.)

This kind of omission matters. Not because it demonstrates that Sweet Willie Wine's march may not have been the symbolic triumph that Wright implies it was—on the contrary, it was surely an act of bravery and moral force. The omission matters, rather, because it causes the poem to lose complexity. One of the obvious questions the poem raises is why V chose to participate in the march in the first place. In many ways, it's the puzzle around which the entire work revolves. Here's Wright's take:

V, what spurred you to get involved.

It was when they put the kids in the swimming pool. My babysitter's granddaughter. They put her in the pool.

Fair enough. Then one thinks: But the babysitter herself didn't go on the march. Nor did the babysitter's daughter. Nor did the overwhelming majority of the African American population of the town (which apparently was 50 percent black at the time). So why did V? The answer, whatever it may be, is almost certainly to the credit of Wright's friend. But the answer has to be something other than simply that V was an amazing person with great integrity who knew right from wrong.

Yet that's more or less what Wright leaves the reader with. Lines about V tend to look like this:

She was guilty of no fear, no meanness and when if
once-in-a-knocked-up-again moon she felt a twinge of
desire for a certain silk blouse, she was sure to touch the
wearer, to touch the other on the sleeve that she not be
afflicted by any such shallow tendencies.

She was not an eccentric. She was an original. She was
congenitally incapable of conforming.

Yeats she knew well enough to wield as a weapon.

Something else, LIE, was not in her vocabulary. The pure
inflammatory truth she could take it, and Gentle Reader,
she knew how to inflict it.

All of this was likely true. But it's also flat and banal; one gets no sense of V beyond the feeling that she was a tart, brave, hard-drinking bookworm—which makes her sound like a sit-com character. The difficulty here, at bottom, is that as a poet Wright is inclined toward compassion and preservation; her de-sire is to hold close and to keep safe. These are fine qualities for any writer to possess, but they're dangerous when applied to an elegy (which is, by its nature, already bent on preservation). And they're even more problematic if the elegy in question is going to be tied to the history of the civil rights movement, which raises grand questions of good and evil. The death of a friend and the greatest sickness of our country: these are two subjects that over-whelm compassion, that turn it toward sentimental memorializ-ing. And the result in *One with Others*, sadly, is a lovely cartoon.

Tourist in Hell
by Eleanor Wilner

ELEANOR WILNER DOESN'T LIKE war or violence, which is un-derstandable, since most people don't—at least, not when they're on the receiving end of it. Her new book, *Tourist in Hell*, opens with two sections focused on bloodshed from the histori-cal ("Back Then, We Called It 'The War'") to the symbolic ("History as Crescent Moon") to the contemporary ("Cold Dawn of the Day When Bush Was Elected for a Second Term"), with another two sections on slightly less bruised material clos-ing out the book. Wilner's preferred form is a clean free-verse line that exists in the shadow of pentameter, and her diction ranges from the assertively everyday ("the soul is not so clean & white / as Kleenex") to the self-consciously poetic (a shriek is "heart-scalding," alas). The beginning of the very good "Magnificat" gives a sense of the stately tone she often adopts:

> *When he had suckled there, he began*
> *to grow: first, he was an infant in her arms,*
> *but soon, drinking and drinking at the sweet*
> *milk she could not keep from filling her,*
> *from pouring into his ravenous mouth,*
> *and filling again, miraculous pitcher, mercy*
> *feeding its own extinction . . . soon he was*
> *huge, towering above her, the landscape,*
> *his shadow stealing the color from the fields.*

It's Yeats's rough beast, slouching hither again. Wilner is a cerebral poet by nature, and the more her work relies on symbolic arguments (as here), the better it tends to be.

This is regrettably not the case with many of the antiwar and antiviolence poems in *Tourist in Hell*, the majority of which are run-of-the-mill contemporary public poetry—which is to say, they're intended to speak on a subject of great public importance to an audience composed almost entirely of poets. There's much bearing witness without much worrying over who the witness gets borne to. This isn't to suggest that Wilner's poems are especially oblique or esoteric; on the contrary, it's usually fairly clear what she's getting at. The problem is simply that she appears to find violence as incomprehensible as the behavior of lions or martians. As she writes in the second stanza of "Back Then, We Called It 'The War'":

> For though when as a child, I watched the news unreel
> at the movies: the smoke and guns, the stirring symphonic
>   music
> rousing the blood, the black-and-white legions marching
> on film, the flare of anti-aircraft guns, the little planes
>   turning
> in a slow spiral as they went down in flames, the heavy-
>   bellied
> bombers opening their doors, and the bombs falling,
> and where each one fell, a rising pillar of fire; and though
> the voice of the announcer was manly and confident,
>   the news
> always good, we were winning, we were certainly
>   winning, and
> everyone was so proud, and collected cans, and went
>   without
> nylons and chewing gum and butter, and clustered around
>   radios
> speaking in hushed tones as if in a holy place:
> nevertheless I did not understand.

Wilner plainly believes that her failure to understand war (World War II, no less) is virtuous. It's not. As a poet, you don't have to countenance our violent tendencies—you can, in fact, argue vehemently against them. But you do have to understand them. Otherwise, you find yourself ending poems with sentimental scenes involving "a little girl / who will never understand, who / nevertheless / is picking up stone after stone, / trying to piece it together again." More likely, that little girl is picking up stones in order to peg them at her brother. Kids are mean.

Fortunately, *Tourist in Hell* ends with stronger material, and it's hard not to applaud Wilner's intelligence in poems like "The Minotaur" (a rare example of perfectly executed shaped verse) and "Restored to Blue" (which riffs on the inadvertent marring of a work of art during the process of restoration). But the best poem here is "Encounter in the Local Pub," which begins:

> *As he looked up from his glass, its quickly melting ice,*
> *Into the glowing bisected demonic eyes of the goat,*
> *He sensed that something fundamental had shifted,*
>
> *Or was done. As if, after a long life of enchantment, he*
> *Had awakened, like Bottom, wearing the ears of an ass,*
> *And the only light was a lanthorn, an ersatz moon.*

No, the goat is not explained. The bizarre encounter continues with the man's realization that he can no longer be confident in "every Large Meaning" and is now at the mercy of "the hole at the heart of things." Wilner concludes:

> *The goat,*
> *he noticed, had a rank smell, feral. Unnerved,*

he looks away, watches the last of his ice
as it melts, the way some godlike eye might see
the mighty glaciers in a slow dissolve back into the sea.

He notes how incommensurate the simile, a last
attempt to dignify his shaking gaze, and reaches
for the bill; he's damned if the goat will pay.

The poem is strange, funny, and troubling in equal measure (and it's technically elegant—notice the clever play above on "ice" [eyes], "godlike eye," "see," and "sea"). If it's not clear from this collection that Wilner is a reliable tourist in hell, she brings with her a more than welcome perception of the darkness in the dailiness of life. Which is where, after all, most publics are at home.

THE TROUBLE WITH POETRY

"I wonder how you are going to feel
when you find out
that I wrote this instead of you"

is how the first poem begins
in the new book by Billy Collins
called The Trouble with Poetry.

It is a typical Collins beginning—
a good-natured wave
across the echoing gulf that stretches

between writer and reader,
as if to suggest
that the poem itself exists

in that uncertain, cloud-filled gap,
and that we, as readers,
are very nearly poets ourselves,

even if we are unlikely
to receive recognition as such
in the form of a generous grant

from the Guggenheim Foundation,
which is not to say
that we would turn one down, mind you.

Anyway, it is a tribute
to the former poet laureate
that he is able to make us believe,

despite our anxious response to poetry,
that we are participating
in each Billy Collins poem,

and that the humorous touches—
like calling a book of poetry
The Trouble with Poetry—

are a kind of knowing salute,
one writer to another.
It is a technical achievement

all too easy to underestimate,
and it involves a special sensitivity
to the nature of reading, of hearing,

which is perhaps the reason
that so many Billy Collins poems
are about the process of poetry,

as when in his recent poem "Workshop"
he makes the poem itself
a history of its own unfolding,

a strategy that appears again here
in slightly altered form
as the opening to "The Introduction":

"I don't think this next poem
needs any introduction—
it's best to let the work speak for itself."

A suave parody
of the nervous preambles
one hears at so many poetry readings,

and exactly the kind of beginning
that allows us to chuckle gently
as a convention is tweaked,

almost as we chuckle gently
in anticipation when we realize
that the book review we've been reading

is about to turn the corner,
and begin placing a writer's shortcomings
alongside his virtues,

by observing, for instance,
that Billy Collins too often relies
on the same blandly ironic tone

and the same conversational free verse,
loosely organized in tercets
or the occasional quatrain
when an extra line jogs onto the page,

or that his poems often begin well
and then spiral down
into unsurprising imagery

like exhausted birds
unable to imagine anything
beyond the fact of exhaustion,

or that, most important,
he is often humorous
without actually being funny,

a difference that depends largely
on a writer's willingness
to let his violent, comic sensibility

turn its knives on the reader,
on the poem,
and on poetry itself,

which may seem like an odd complaint,
given Collins's reputation
for teasing our stuffy poetic traditions.

But the teasing that this writer does
is harmless, really, and contrary
to what some critics have suggested,

the problem with his work
is not that it is disrespectful,
but that it is not disrespectful enough;

it never cracks wise
to the teacher's face,
but meekly returns to its desk,

lending itself with disappointing ease
to the stale imagery
of teachers, desks, and wisecracking.

In the end, what we need
from a comic poet with Collins's talent
is not a friendly wave

from writer to reader,
or a literary joke, or a mild chuckle;
what we need is to be drawn

high into the poem's imaginary air
and allowed to fall
on rocks real enough to hurt.

JAMES FRANCO, POET

I f you were alive in 1985 and happened to buy Eddie Murphy's album *How Could It Be* (featuring the hit single "Party All the Time"), then you may have asked yourself—in addition to wondering what shape of Band-Aid is best suited to the human ear—why it is that artists who are vastly successful in one genre feel the need to dabble in another. Because they do, a lot. Sometimes it's just the case that they happen to be very good at more than one thing (by all accounts, Steve Martin is a genuinely excellent banjo player). But often there seems to be something else going on.

Nor is this a recent phenomenon. In his 1855 poem "One Word More," Robert Browning suggested that creative sensibilities are drawn to "art alien to the artist's" because branching out lets a person "be the man and leave the artist, / Gain the man's joy, miss the artist's sorrow." He meant that the more we master the techniques of our native art, the more our art becomes an expression of those techniques rather than a portal on our individuality. The more fluent we become, the more we become armored in that fluency. The issue is further complicated because arts differ in more than their formal elements; they also occupy different areas of the culture. So what happens when the genre switch is not merely between forms but between practices that stand in relation to each other as, say, professional football stands in relation to professional badminton?

Directing Herbert White: Poems is a new book by James Franco, the Oscar-nominated actor, former Oscars host, and all-around celebrity. That he would put out a book of poems with a respected press isn't groundbreaking—Billy Corgan of the Smashing Pumpkins published a collection, *Blinking with Fists*, with Faber & Faber in 2004, an act for which we will all surely pay when great Cthulhu rises. But what's different about Franco's book is that it doesn't obviously represent a cash grab by the publisher or an ego trip by the artist. The blurbs accompanying this collection are from actual poets—Tony Hoagland, Frank Bidart—as opposed to the expected gaggle of hanger-arounders. And Graywolf, while one of the best publishers of American poetry, is probably not in a position to pay Franco an enormous advance or put him in front of the *Oprah* audience. This book is intended for real poetry readers, all five of them, as well as Franco's Twitter followers, all 2.2 million.

But is it, you may be wondering, good? No. Though neither is it entirely bad. *Directing Herbert White* is the sort of collection assembled by reasonably talented MFA students in hundreds of MFA programs stretching from sea to shining sea.

This is perhaps not surprising, since Franco actually has an MFA in poetry. I'm obliged here to note that this writer is no stranger to the educational system, having apparently attended graduate programs at Yale, Columbia, New York University, Brooklyn College, Warren Wilson College, the Rhode Island School of Design, Le Cordon Bleu, Quantico, Hogwarts (Ravenclaw), Embry-Riddle Aeronautical University, and the Jedi Academy.

But for all his inclination to wander—a Google search for "James Franco" and "dilettante" returns some twenty thousand hits—his interest in poetry is genuine. *Directing Herbert White* is divided into seven sections (two of them riff on Smiths songs), and the poems are uniformly written in the kind of flat, prosy free verse that has dominated American poetry for ages (typical line: "New Orleans Square is my favorite part of Disneyland"), with stanzas that aren't so much stanzas as elongated paragraphs. Franco takes his title from a Bidart poem that he turned into a short film in 2010, but this book's preoccupations exist far from the usual terrain of contemporary poetry: "Lindsay" is the Lohan; there are elegies for people more famous than anyone you've ever met; and the movie business is discussed with convincing first-person authority ("It's fun to react. It may be less/Intrusive, doing long takes. . . .").

As with most first-book poets, the farther Franco gets from himself, the better his work tends to be. The best poems here are six "film sonnets," in which you can sense the cagey intelligence that emerges in his acting. Here is the beginning of "Film Sonnet 2," which is about Fellini's *8½* :

Marcello is fatigued. A passive-aggressive genius,
A man wrapped in himself: art, mistress, and wife.
He goes to the spa, why? At the spa, people in white
Walk about the plaza, there is a fountain, everyone is rich.

The poem ends:

Fellini's getting old, inspiration dries up, but here,
This despair is nice because it is the sorrow of an artist.
An important artist has important despair, and everything
He does can go on the screen: sex, religion, fear.
A confession of pain and proclivities.

"This despair is nice": The tone is neatly judged. Franco writes similarly well in poems like "Hello" and "Editing," and you find yourself wishing this sensibility pervaded the book.

It doesn't, unfortunately. Franco has a decent ear for speech but a bad sense of the poetic line ("And my nose was a blob"). He's prone to phrases that collapse under scrutiny ("Webbed by a nexus of stone walkways"). Some of the writing is almost aggressively lazy: "There is one of two things that happen," one poem begins, practically begging for an editor to excise "There is" and "that" (and to change "happen" to "happens"). Many poems rocket past sincerity and plunge straight into sentimentality; others demonstrate a self-disgust more interesting to the author than to the reader.

So Franco is never going to be Wallace Stevens—or Cathy

Park Hong or A. E. Stallings or Devin Johnston, for that matter.
But most writers won't be. His work is a fair representation of a
certain strand in contemporary poetry, and there's no shame in
that. God knows he can write circles around Billy Corgan. To
say this, though, is to ignore the larger issue, which is the grand-
piano-in-a-bathtub impact of Franco's celebrity in an art form
notably short on figures recognizable to anyone who doesn't
subscribe to *Ploughshares*. This book wouldn't be published by
Graywolf (I hope) if James Franco weren't James Franco. James
Franco wouldn't be doing events with Frank Bidart if he weren't
James Franco. For that matter, James Franco wouldn't be getting
reviewed right now if he weren't James Franco. In fact, if James
Franco were just another MFA student struggling to catch the
attention of the two part-time employees of Origami Arthropod
Press, he'd probably be reading this piece and fuming about all
the attention being given, yet again, to James Franco.

It's easy to sympathize, even if one suspects some of the
complainers are no better at writing poems than Franco is. Yet
the annoyance this collection will inspire is rooted in a deeper
anxiety: the attention commanded by James Franco's poetry has
everything to do with James Franco and almost nothing to do
with poetry. And that cultural wealth is not transferable. Attention withheld from Franco's poems will not instantly devolve
upon some worthy but obscure poet; it will go to another actor
or singer or commercial nonfiction writer or memoirist—or
even to James Franco in his novel-writing incarnation. Poetry
is the weak sister of its sibling arts, alternately ignored and

swaddled like a nineteenth-century invalid, and that will change only by means of a long, tedious, and possibly futile effort at persuasion. Perhaps it's a blessing to have James Franco on one's side in that struggle, until he leaves for Westminster Choir College.

HOW FAR
CAN YOU PRESS A POET?

How far can you press a poet?
To the last limit and he'll not show it
And one step further and he's dead
And his death is upon your head.

For most poets, craziness is a virtue, silliness a mortal risk. After all, true craziness is a serious thing, and if there's one thing that unites the contemporary poetry world, it's the desire to be taken more seriously than, say, the world of PEZ-dispenser collecting. This attitude isn't entirely new, of course: English-language poetry has been busily defending itself since Sir Philip Sidney enjoined the art's Puritan assailants "no more to scorne the sacred misteries of Poesie" over four hundred years ago. Yet something different—something plaintive—has crept into the usual rallying cries over the past century. Seldom these days do poets and critics get to fight the good fight against accusations of indolence or blasphemy; instead they tend to find themselves addressing an infinitely less gratifying question best phrased as the title of an influential essay by the critic Dana Gioia: "Can

Poetry Matter?" This state of affairs isn't necessarily a bad thing (sometimes a little self-doubt can do an art form a world of good), but it can make life difficult if you're the sort of writer who likes to draw cartoons of cats, dress up in schoolgirl's clothes, and begin poems "The Cock of the North / Has forgotten his worth / And come down South / In a month of drouth." At the very least, this kind of behavior is going to make your fellow poets, many of whom are trying to be taken seriously, inclined to forget you exist.

Which brings us to Stevie Smith, the cartoon-drawing, schoolgirl-dress-wearing, near-doggerel-spouting British poet who died in 1971 at age sixty-nine. It's probably fair to say that of all poets generally considered to be "serious," Stevie Smith ranks among the silliest, both personally and poetically. As to the former, this was largely a matter of presentation—in addition to her eccentric wardrobe, Smith was known for warbling her poems during readings in a manner that Seamus Heaney once characterized as a cross between "an embarrassed party-piece by a child . . . and a deliberate faux-naif rendition by a virtuoso." As for the poetry itself, well, Stevie Smith is a willfully ridiculous writer—or, as some have preferred, "eccentric" (Heaney), "completely original" (Philip Larkin), and "a rare bird" (Clive James)—which means, more or less, that nobody has a clue as to how to describe her. You could talk about the peculiar rhythm of lines like "All the waters of the river Deben / Go over my head to the last wave even." You could mention the clowning, idiosyncratic rhyming ("Under wrong trees / Walked the zombies"), which makes many of her poems sound like badly translated ballads. You might pause over the patently ludicrous asides ("May we inquire the name of the Person from Porlock? / Why, Porson, didn't you know?") with which she interrupts poems that examine creative exhaustion and the longing for death. You could dwell on her bizarre habit of including throw-away jottings, not to mention amateurish cartoons, beside her most accomplished pieces. You could discuss her obsessive mor-bidity ("I cannot help but like Oblivion better"), her piercing humor ("This Englishwoman is so refined / She has no bosom and no behind"), or her fearful tenderness ("I can call up old ghosts, and they will come, / But my art limps,—I cannot send them home"). You could do all of this and more. But something would still be missing.

In fact, the best description of a Stevie Smith poem is not a description of a Stevie Smith poem at all, but rather an account of one of her public readings by the art historian Norman Bryson that appears in Frances Spalding's enjoyable *Stevie Smith: A Biography*. Here's what Bryson witnessed:

> The performance was unnerving because it was so ex-cessive. . . . The meaning of the words was set aside in the performance. And the motives for this were entire-ly unrevealed: this seemed almost the main point. It was as though what was being dramatized was a state of being so pent up, so much without outlet, that emo-tions couldn't have, any longer, appropriate objects. . . .

Nothing in the world could focus them or make them cohere, or earn them or deserve them.

This is almost (but not quite) a description of pure song, and it is almost (but not quite) a description of pure silliness. What Bryson's account captures is the way in which Smith's poetry seems both ferociously concentrated and utterly arbitrary—as if the poet were a figure skater who, over the course of her seemingly purposeless meanderings around the rink, somehow managed to cut into the ice the figure of a hanged man. To read through Smith's *Collected Poems* is to be amused, amazed, confused, and disconcerted; most of all, though, it is to wonder how something so alarming could seem so natural.

But how, exactly, does she create this unique effect? What does it look like on the page? It's often the case that a poet's best-known poem is neither typical nor particularly good, but not where Smith is concerned. The perennial Stevie Smith anthology piece is "Not Waving but Drowning":

Nobody heard him, the dead man,
But still he lay moaning:
I was much further out then you thought
And not waving but drowning.

Poor chap, he always loved larking
And now he's dead
It must have been too cold for him his heart gave way,
They said.

Oh, no no no, it was too cold always
(Still the dead one lay moaning)
I was much too far out all my life
And not waving but drowning.

Is this sad? Funny? Both? Neither? The nominal subject—a plea for help mistaken for a salutation—practically embodies the dominant theme of twentieth-century lyric poetry; that is, the agony of the insulated, isolated self, which keeps straining and failing to metamorphose into language. But Smith pushes things to the border of parody—the "dead one" is somehow "still moaning" (and moaning an unpoetic "Oh, no no no" at that), his life is flippantly eulogized by the phrase "he always loved larking" (larking?), and the simultaneously fussy and tub-thumping rhyme on "They said" in the second stanza puts a weirdly comic spin on the spectacle of a man's heart giving way. One reaches for the word "tragicomic," but it doesn't seem adequate; as in many Smith poems, we seem to be getting too much information and not enough.

This, for Smith, often seems to be the point: as she writes in "The Donkey," "No hedged track lay before this donkey longer / But the sweet prairies of anarchy." Smith encourages this sense of incongruity by changing registers within and across poems with calamitous speed; her voice often seems to be arriving belatedly and inappropriately at images her mind's eye has already passed over. Consider, for example, "Do Take Muriel Out," which, like many Smith poems, begins in a childlike singsong ("Do take Muriel out / She is looking so glum") but then ends in an altogether different key:

Do take Muriel out
Although your name is Death
She will not complain
When you dance her over the blasted heath.

This poem would be unusual enough on its own; it's even more peculiar when you notice that the final, apocalyptic stanza is followed a few pages later by an unrepentantly trivial homage to Smith's office cat. In each Smith collection, the pattern seems to be this lack of pattern. No sooner has the poet rhymed "pinkie" and "thinky" in one poem than she serenely announces in another:

Would that the hours of time as a word unsaid
Turning had turned again to the hourless night,
Would that the seas lay heavy upon the dead,
The lightless dead in the grave of a world new drowned.

No pinkies here, thanks (though there's probably some Swinburne). The weightiness of Smith's "serious" lines only intensifies the absurdity of her "silly" poems; the result is that the poetry on the whole can seem half-cocked. That, at any rate, is what Seamus Heaney seemed to argue in a review of Smith's *Collected Poems* that appeared about five years after her death. Heaney suggested that Smith's tendency to wander (or "wobble," as he put it) between the profound and the nonsensical revealed a fundamental flaw in Smith's poetry: her "literary resources are not adequate to [her] somber recognitions." Though he admired certain poems, Heaney ultimately found in Smith's poems "a retreat from resonance, as if the spirit of A. A. Milne successfully vied with the spirit of Emily Dickinson."

So arise, Tigger, and get thee gone. In phrasing his concerns in this way, Heaney seems to have had in mind an old theory of literary emotion best expressed by T. S. Eliot in his essay on *Hamlet*. This is the idea that in a good poem emotions match up with their contexts in more or less the way that certain elements, when combined, always form the same compounds. As Eliot tells us,

> The only way of expressing emotion in the form of art is by finding an "objective correlative"; in other words, a set of objects, a situation, a chain of events which shall be the formula of that particular emotion. . . . The artistic "inevitability" lies in this complete adequacy of the external to the emotion.

If a poet wants to express, say, a "somber recognition," she should develop an "objective correlative" for somberness and build it into the poem; otherwise, we don't know whether we're supposed to be sad or annoyed or just confused. Like Heaney, Eliot is suggesting that poems can be divided into what we're meant to feel and what the poet means to say and, furthermore, that those two things should correspond in some way that makes reasonable sense. According to this theory, Smith's quirks can be explained as deficiencies—not only does her work rarely stand still long enough to be much of a correlative for anything, but as noted above, her poems are always accompanied by her cartoons. And while nobody knows exactly what a "somber recognition" looks like, the odds are good that it doesn't resemble a scribble of a tap-dancing cat. Does this mean that Heaney is right? Is Smith's poetry ultimately unsatisfying because it "wobbles"? Because it's silly?

Before drawing any conclusions, it's helpful to remember that Eliot used his objective correlative theory to claim that *Hamlet* was "most certainly an artistic failure." Perhaps hoping for a comparable failure, our better poets have tended to ignore Eliot's advice and create effects, not through correspondence, but through a compelling lack of correspondence. Consider John Ashbery's "Pleasure Boats":

> *Wash it again*
> *and yet again.*
> *The equation drifts.*
> *Wallowing in penguins,*
> *she was wallowing in penguins.*
> *With fiendish cleverness,*
> *the foreground was closing in.*
> *The four-leaf clover loses.*

Whatever this poem may do or not do, it certainly isn't playing by the rules Eliot described. More assertively avant-garde

poets go even further—in Christian Bök's book *Eunoia*, to pick
one of many examples, the poet allows himself only one vowel
per chapter, leading to lines like "He engenders newness wherever we need fresh terms." To seem properly objective, an objective correlative would probably need to buy more vowels than
that. If the poetry world has room for things like *Eunoia*, you'd
think it would have no trouble whatsoever with Stevie Smith.
And, indeed, when an author's customary critical label begins to
peel, it's always tempting to argue for the opposite description—
to insist, for example, that a writer previously thought of as anti-
romantic was "really" a romantic all along. In Smith's case, the
temptation is to say that her frivolousness is really sophistication, that she's a calculated lounger along the lines of Frank
O'Hara or a studied rebel like Allen Ginsberg—at heart an
avant-garde poet.

The problem, though, is that Smith doesn't really fit into
any of the avant-garde traditions (an oxymoron, but a fair one)
any better than she does into Heaney's more conventional for-
mulations. She's too earnest about God ("O Lord God please
come / And require the soul of thy Scorpion"), too pleased to be
English ("Time and the moment is not yet England's daunt"),
and far too committed to the traditional subjects and themes of
lyric poetry (hardly a page of her collected works goes by without making a point about love, death, or justice). Most of all,
though, she's just too ridiculous. That may sound odd, considering that the heirs of Gertrude Stein have long made outrageous
wordplay a central part of their practice. But "practice" here is

the key word: for contemporary experimental writers, the ridiculous is generally part of a method, a system intended to "make new" or to "subvert" or to "reexamine"; it is a ridiculousness that is underwritten by theories, argued over in journals, and justified with footnotes. It's a ridiculousness that isn't silly.

For Stevie Smith, however, ridiculousness means:

Aloft,
In the loft,
Sits Croft;
He is soft.

Or if that seems too willful to be truly silly, how about:

Oh my darling Goosey-Gander
Why do you always wish to wander
Evermore, evermore?

What makes Smith distinctive—as opposed to coy or clever or conventionally unconventional—is that her silliness is silliness. It exposes her; it makes her seem vulnerable. And that's exactly why it seems to work.

In this sense, Smith's poetry complicates an old question about technique: to what extent can we separate being something (like an artist) from doing something (like writing sonnets)? Most people would agree that great art transcends technique—which is related to saying that you can learn to write pretty good iambic pentameter, but you can't learn to be Elizabeth Bishop. But no one would say that technique is irrelevant to great art. For one thing, accepting a writer's distinctive style requires an act of faith from readers, and we usually like to know that someone can shoot a bow and arrow before we put blindfolds over our eyes and apples on our heads. Yet with her absurd titles like "Hippy-Mo," her public singing, and her doodles, Smith not only declines to demonstrate recognizable mastery, she refuses to give us any justification for her failure to do so. (Stein, by contrast, had the literary-political savvy to proclaim her genius to anyone within earshot.) The same quality that makes Smith's poems convincing—their naturalness—can make them seem slight, as if Smith's technical achievement consists of little more than, well, being Stevie Smith. Can she be great if she's just being herself?

WITH THIS QUESTION IN mind, it's useful to take a closer look at how one of Smith's characteristic "wobbles" affects one of her better poems, "Thoughts about the Person from Porlock." The person from Porlock is the anonymous figure who supposedly interrupted Coleridge as he was writing "Kubla Khan," and whose visit (according to Coleridge) caused the poet to lose the fragments of his vision "like the images on the surface of a stream," leaving him unable to finish the poem. The anecdote is often taken as a metaphor for the eternal incompleteness of art, the fleeting nature of inspiration, the tragedy of . . . You get the idea. Smith is skeptical of all this:

Coleridge received the Person from Porlock
And ever after called him a curse,
Then why did he hurry to let him in?
He could have hid in the house.

It was not right of Coleridge in fact it was wrong
(But often we all do wrong)
As the truth is I think he was already stuck
With Kubla Khan.

The wit is sharp, but the tone is slightly unstable, even for Smith—the oddest thing is the repetition of "wrong," which appears again in the first section's closing couplet, "It was not right, it was wrong / But often we all do wrong." What's so wrong about making an excuse? Smith doesn't answer that question for us immediately, instead "wobbling" into what seems to be patent nonsense:

May we inquire the name of the Person
*   from Porlock?*
Why, Porson, didn't you know?
He lived at the bottom of Porlock Hill
So had a long way to go,

He wasn't much in the social sense
Though his grandmother was a Warlock,
One of the Rutlandshire ones I fancy
And nothing to do with Porlock,

And he lived at the bottom of the hill as I said
And had a cat named Flo,
And had a cat named Flo.

Smith once described this section as a parody of academic inquiry, but if so, it's an amazingly unconvincing one. Since Smith proves in other poems to be a deft satirist (read one way, "Not Waving but Drowning" is a wicked rewriting of Eliot's "Prufrock"), it probably makes more sense to interpret her remark as an attempt to justify in more conventional terms what she knew might strike many readers as a flight of pure foolishness. But foolishness, like love, is a many-splendored thing— and here it's curiously strained and repetitive. The third stanza (if you could call it that) seems to be winding down, as Smith repeats herself ("as I said"), and then repeats herself again ("And had . . . / And had . . .")—the effect is like a slowing nervous twitch. Is there some reason for this, or is the poem just badly written?

Smith gives us a hint about the answer to that question in the next section:

I long for the Person from Porlock
To bring my thoughts to an end,
I am becoming impatient to see him
I think of him as a friend,

. . . .

I am hungry to be interrupted
For ever and ever amen

O Person from Porlock come quickly
And bring my thoughts to an end.

"I am finished, finished," Smith has Coleridge cry as the poem begins, and now we understand that his cry is hers—the agony involved in finishing a masterpiece has become the agony of simply living life. Like Emily Dickinson, Smith is forever taking long walks in the moonlight with Death, who as she puts it here, "comes like a benison." Generally these references are too stylized to take entirely seriously (as Clive James memorably observed, Smith had "an ostentatiously suicidal Weltschmerz that for most of her long adult life made it seem unlikely she would get through another day without trying to end it all under a bus"). But here the pressure seems genuine. Not because Smith seems to be more "serious" or "adequate," but because her repetitions ("a cat named Flo") and hiccups ("as I said") seem increasingly inadequate as the poem progresses—less like flights of fancy than worried muttering.

These mutters become clearly audible as, in her conclusion, Smith turns away from Death and toward the subject that has underwritten the poem from the beginning:

These thoughts are depressing I know. They are depressing,
I wish I was more cheerful, it is more pleasant,
Also it is a duty, we should smile as well as submitting
To the purpose of One Above who is experimenting
With various mixtures of human character which goes best,

All is interesting for him it is exciting, but not for us.
There I go again. Smile, smile, and get some work to do
Then you will be practically unconscious without positively
having to go.

Philip Larkin said that Smith's poetry "speaks with the authority of sadness," but what it more frequently speaks with is the license of despair. And Smith's despair isn't the wild despair of grief or defeat, but the hushed despair of drudgery and isolation, of a quicksilver mind ground down again and again in repetitions that stack up like unfinished chores: "we all do wrong," "There I go again," "as I said," "And had a cat named Flo," "bring my thoughts to an end . . . Bring my thoughts to an end . . ." Smith matches her plate-juggling absurdity—her wobble—against this pressure, and absurdity loses out in the mechanical flatness of the final line, "Then you will be practically unconscious without absolutely having to go." Recall Bryson's description of Smith's public reading: "It was as though what was being dramatized was a state of being so pent up, so much without outlet, that emotions couldn't have, any longer, appropriate objects." This is a fair sketch of idiosyncrasy run amok, but it's also a compelling portrait of mental and spiritual extremity. Though biographical details generally tell us much less about writers than we suppose, it's worth noting that Smith entered secretarial school around the age of eighteen and spent much of her life in a clerical job that was dull at best, crushing at worst ("Dark was the day for Childe Rolandine the artist / When she went to work as a secretary-typist"). It should come as no surprise that one of Smith's most passionate admirers was the equally beleaguered, if differently situated, Sylvia Plath.

But where does this leave the question of Smith's technique? Is there a method to her melancholy? The best answer is no, not exactly, not unless we're willing to say that the lack of technique is itself a technique—which is both tautological and uncharitable to Smith, given that her great accomplishment in poems like "Thoughts about the Person from Porlock" is to change our perception of what constitutes a poetic accomplishment in the first place. In his appreciative, if slightly puzzled, review of Smith's work, Larkin concludes that her "successes are not full-scale, four-square poems that can be anthologized and anatomized, but occasional phrases or refrains that one finds hanging about one's mind." Larkin was clearly on to something, but his critique inadvertently undercuts itself by substituting one form of anthologizing for another—instead of poems, now we're to single out "occasional phrases." Better, maybe, to single nothing out, to say instead that Smith is not so much a poet of poems as a poet of sensibility. And as such, she needs to be read whole.

All poets write poems with varying degrees of polish, and for most poets, the unfinished poems are exactly that: not finished. In Smith's work, though, poems aren't a series of objects; they're movements in an atmosphere—and to ask why Smith can't be more serious is like asking why the wind can't be squarer. As Larkin intuited, she can't be selected into perfection because she doesn't appear in pieces. That observation is true of poetry in general, of course, but it isn't true of all poets to the

same degree. In particular, it isn't true of poets like Heaney or
Eliot, whose bodies of work are acts of self-conscious authority,
and whose poems bear the master's seal on each enjambment.
Smith, on the other hand, demands total devotion rather than
sampling; she will either have the reader who will listen to her in
all her falling-down absurdity, or she'll scorn readers altogether
and vanish across the gray sands. This desperate posture forces
her poetry to the very edge of speech, where a poem could just
as easily have been a cartoon or a snatch of song or a flick of the
wrist, and what emerges from the chill of this leveling aesthetic
transcends conventional notions of ambition.

This is why poets determined to show us their mastery
struggle to match this writer in the extreme terrain she favors.
Consider these stanzas from Robert Lowell, a poet much praised
for both his ambition and his ability to translate intense emotion:

> *One dark night,*
> *my Tudor Ford climbed the hill's skull,*
> *I watched for love-cars. Lights turned down,*
> *they lay together, hull to hull,*
> *where the graveyard shelves on the town. . . .*
> *My mind's not right.*
> *A car radio bleats,*
> *"Love, O careless Love. . . ." I hear*
> *my ill-spirit sob in each blood cell,*
> *as if my hand were at its throat. . . .*
> *I myself am Hell,*
> *nobody's here—*

Now set Lowell's lines, with their careful, Miltonic echoes ("I myself am Hell") and self-conscious poetic flourishes ("my ill-spirit"), against Smith's "Dirge":

From a friend's friend I taste friendship,
From a friend's friend love,
My spirit in confusion,
Long years I strove,
But now I know that never
Nearer shall I move,
Than a friend's friend to friendship,
To love than a friend's love.

Into the dark night
Resignedly I go,
I am not so afraid of the dark night
As the friends I do not know,
I do not fear the night above,
As I fear the friends below.

Lowell's lines are more complex, more erudite, and more obviously ambitious. They are also profoundly less effective. "There's more enterprise / In walking naked," Yeats tells us, and Smith has stripped herself of nearly all defenses, including her identity as a poet, if not as a writer of poetry. Left bare is the essence of the lyric.

Smith pays a price for this exposure, of course; the same arbitrariness that gives her poems their anarchic intensity also denies her the comforts of "adequate" language. An art of pure chance creates a temporary shelter, not a home, and Smith is a writer whose understanding of loneliness is greater even than that of Wallace Stevens. Her isolation could only have been exacerbated by the critical underestimation her poetry has often received, an underestimation of which Smith herself was well aware. Her late poem "The Poet Hin" addresses the issue with equal portions of self-mockery and self-defense:

> I am much condescended to, said the poet Hin,
> By my inferiors. And, said the poet Hin,
> On my tombstone I will have inscribed:
> "He was much condescended to by his inferiors."
> Then, said the poet Hin,
> I shall be properly remembered.

Having made light of her ambitions for herself ("You know the correct use of *shall* and *will*. / That, Hin, is something we may think about."), Smith quietly asserts her ambitions for her poems:

> Yet not light always is the pain
> That roots in levity. Or without fruit wholly
> As from this levity's
> Flowering pang of melancholy
> May grow what is weighty,
> May come beauty.

Levity is light, of course, but it's also cold and scattered, changeable and cutting. Considering the time that Stevie Smith spent cultivating this unforgiving territory in solitude, the least that serious poets and serious readers can do is give thanks for the great harvest with which she returned.

ON ROBERT HASS

The publication of a volume of selected poems is an appropriate occasion to appraise a poet's career, and an equally appropriate occasion to wonder why we use the word "career" in connection with poetry at all. After all, many readers would agree with Randall Jarrell's definition of a poet as someone "who manages, in a lifetime of standing out in thunderstorms, to be struck by lightning five or six times." This assumes that writing poetry is mostly a matter of waiting and hoping, which in turn raises questions about how confident we can be in discussing (to say nothing of criticizing) a poet's development. As long as the writer in question makes a valiant effort to prepare himself for revelation—as long as he greets every raindrop by waving a putter like Bishop Pickering in *Caddyshack*—is it really his fault if the lightning striketh not?

Robert Hass's book *The Apple Trees at Olema: New and*

Selected Poems is a milestone in what is generally regarded as one of the more successful careers (that word again) in contemporary American poetry. Hass won the Yale Younger Poets competition with his first book, *Field Guide*, in 1972; since then he's picked up a MacArthur "genius" fellowship, two National Book Critics Circle Awards (one for poetry, one for criticism), the National Book Award and the Pulitzer prize. He served as the United States poet laureate from 1995 to 1997, has been a chancellor of the Academy of American Poets, and has translated haiku selections from Bashō, Buson, and Issa, as well as numerous books by his former Berkeley colleague the Nobel laureate Czesław Miłosz. As poetic résumés go, Hass's is about as gold-plated as it gets.

And indeed the best work here is terrific. Hass is frequently referred to as a "West Coast poet," which makes sense to the extent that his work involves Californian flora, fauna, and locales, but is more problematic as an indication of temperament (believe it or not, New York also contains mellow poets fixated on organic chard). His writing is densely literary and cultured in a laid-back, faculty-lounge sort of way; one isn't surprised to find a poem beginning, "On the morning of the Käthe Kollwitz exhibit," or to discover a five-page sequence about grad school romance ("Like Landor's line— / she was meandering gold, pellucid gold"). Most poems here involve long, loping free-verse lines and occasional haiku-like fragments. In Hass's hands, both approaches resist closure and convey a slightly earnest sensuality that often involves plain old physical desire (there are a lot of women here, and they're regularly being "made love to"), but also emerges in lovely, exacting natural descriptions: "In the pools / anemones, cream-colored, little womb-mouths."

Hass's greatest strength as a poet, however, is his equanimity, a quality that sets him apart from peers who rely on a sense of imbalance. That imbalance can register as pressure (that is, the language of the poem may seem inadequate to the task it's asked to perform), or it can involve deliberate disjunctions in voice, tone, syntax, and so forth. Reading a good Hass poem, however, is like watching a painter whose brushstrokes are so reassuringly steady that you hardly notice how much complex and unsettling depth has been added to the canvas. Consider, for instance, the beginning of "Songs to Survive the Summer," from Hass's second book, *Praise*:

> *These are the dog days,*
> *unvaried*
> *except by accident,*
>
> *mist rising from soaked lawns,*
> *gone world, everything*
> *rises and dissolves in air,*
>
> *whatever it is would*
> *clear the air*
> *dissolves in air and the knot*

of day unties
invisibly like a shoelace.
The gray-eyed child

who said to my child: "Let's play
in my yard. It's OK,
my mother's dead."

That final, potentially melodramatic line is brought off with
a poised efficiency that seems inevitable and characteristic.
As Louise Glück has observed, Hass uses a kind of constantly
expanding empathy to bind together elements that would ordinarily disrupt a poem. In work like "Santa Lucia," "Against Bot-
ticelli," and "The Nineteenth Century as a Song," you feel that
Hass has imagined his way into every aspect of each scene he
presents.

The thing is, each of those poems is at least thirty years old.
It's not that Hass hasn't written anything worthwhile in the in-
tervening decades; a poem like "Pears" is worthwhile by any
reasonable measure. But his finest work (thus far, anyway) was
written early—which returns us again to the problem of a poetic
"career." What does it say that this volume of selected poems
lacks the sort of consistent development for which people usually get gold watches? Or, to make the issue a little more modest:
what is true of Hass's stronger, earlier poetry that isn't true of his
more recent writing?

One way to approach this question is to think about the
nature of poetic empathy. Empathy involves the intimate

understanding of other points of view, but it doesn't necessarily imply pity or kindness. As the poet Katy Lederer writes in her memoir, *Poker Face: A Girlhood among Gamblers*, the key to being a good poker player is managing to "empathize with your opponents while remaining devoid of all compassion." Hass's strongest writing demonstrates exactly this sort of dry-eyed approach. "Heroic Simile," which opens his second book, begins:

> *When the swordsman fell in Kurosawa's* Seven Samurai
> *in the gray rain,*
> *in Cinemascope and the Tokugawa dynasty,*
> *he fell straight as a pine, he fell*
> *as Ajax fell in Homer*
> *in chanted dactyls and the tree was so huge*
> *the woodsman returned for two days*
> *to that lucky place before he was done with the sawing*
> *and on the third day he brought his uncle.*

Hass then moves rapidly through a series of scenarios for the imaginary woodsman and his uncle that begins to fray as the speaker realizes he must keep inventing elements to keep the scene going: "I have imagined no pack animal. . . . They are waiting for me to do something." The poem concludes, simply, "There are limits to imagination." "Heroic Simile" is, then, a poem of imaginative empathy intended to show that however much we may understand the world outside ourselves, we must always return, as Hass puts it, to "separate fidelities." It's not a consoling thought, perhaps, but it's a true one.

Hass's later work, however, has been reluctant to embrace this kind of truth. Sometimes empathy bleeds over into self-regard ("What is to be done with our species?"); other times it congeals into a buttery sentimentality ("I want to end this poem singing"). Both outcomes are the result of wanting boundaries to blur, rather than recognizing them as necessary restrictions. "Meditation at Lagunitas," which directly follows "Heroic Simile" and is Hass's most famous poem, begins in the same dry mode as its predecessor: "All the new thinking is about loss./In this it resembles all the old thinking." But the poem ends in an altogether damper place:

> *There are moments when the body is as numinous*
> *as words, days that are the good flesh continuing.*
> *Such tenderness, those afternoons and evenings,*
> *saying* blackberry, blackberry, blackberry.

One might say that the problem with Hass's career is that as he's gotten older, his poems have been more willing to say "*blackberry, blackberry, blackberry*" than to declare, "There are limits to imagination." Still, it's a rare thing for a poet to write genuinely powerful poems, to be struck those all-important five or six times. We can only be grateful to someone who has worked so hard to be rendered incandescent by the lightning and then welcomed it when it hit.

CHRISTOPHER GILBERT'S

IMPROVISATIONS

O ne of the few career advantages a poet has over a tax attorney—the only one, maybe—is that the poet's work has a greater chance of being remembered. Or so, at least, the thinking has traditionally gone. The sonnet, for instance, is practically built on the idea of poetry's unfading presence, from Petrarch's assertion that "our art is that / Which makes men immortal through fame" to Shakespeare's claim that "Not marble, nor the gilded monuments / Of princes shall outlive this powerful rhyme." Similar rhetoric tends to appear whenever a critic is doling out high praise, whether it's Randall Jarrell announcing in 1947 that some of Robert Lowell's poems "will be read as long as men remember English," or Jason Guriel writing in *Poetry* magazine in 2010, pretending to review Kay Ryan from a distant future in which she's become an inescapable literary influence. Poetry, we suppose, is like papyrus: it may be delicate, but it lasts and lasts.

But what if it doesn't? Or, rather, what happens *when* it doesn't? Because the fact is that most poetry won't be read even five years after it's published, let alone twenty, and definitely not a hundred. Most poets won't find their work growing more and more noticed; they will find it growing less and less noticed, until it vanishes entirely from everything but a few water-stained notebooks in a cardboard box in the basement.

Is it brave or crazy to devote oneself to poetry in these circumstances? Perhaps a little of both. "Persistence in the face of such certitude of oblivion," Donald Justice once wrote, "is in its small way heroic, or so my romantic spirit commands me to believe." And if it is, by some lights, heroic to continue plugging along on one's own poetry in an increasingly hopeless struggle against obscurity, then surely it's an act of great charity to spend time trying to lift somebody else's writing out of the very oblivion one is hoping to avoid. Yet that's been a recent theme in the American poetry world. It emerges indirectly in prizes (the Poetry Foundation's Neglected Masters Award; the Poetry Society of America's Robert H. Winner prize for "a poet who has not had substantial recognition"), and it frequently finds its way into criticism (Garrett Caples's *Retrievals* is devoted to underrecognized writers, many of them poets).

But mostly it shows up in books by actual poets—books that wouldn't exist if not for the faithful attention of some other writer. The poet Weldon Kees, who vanished in 1955, leaving his car abandoned on the Golden Gate Bridge, is perhaps the most well-known example of this sort of reclamation; his *Collected Poems*, published by Bison Books, is the product of many years of labor by various poets, including Donald Justice. And the admirable Unsung Masters series from Pleiades Press has republished selected work from the intriguing but largely unknown American writers Dunstan Thompson and Russell Atkins.

The most recent beneficiary of this recovery effort is Christopher Gilbert, whose only book, *Across the Mutual Landscape*, originally appeared in 1983. That collection has now been reissued, along with an unpublished manuscript titled "Chris Gilbert: An Improvisation," by Graywolf Press as part of a series called Re/View, which is meant to offer "all-but-lost masterworks of American poetry to a new generation of readers." Gilbert was born in Alabama in 1949 but grew up largely in Michigan, where his parents worked for General Motors. After receiving a masters degree in psychology from Clark University in Worcester, Massachusetts, in 1975, he worked for many years as a practicing psychotherapist before taking a teaching position at Bristol Community College in Fall River, Massachusetts, in 1993. He died in 2007 from a kidney disease with which he'd struggled for two decades.

It would be a stretch to say that Gilbert was an unknown twenty-five years ago—he studied with Robert Hayden and collected the usual array of poetry-world trinkets—but his writing has indeed fallen by the wayside since then. In part, that's to be expected. Gilbert's first collection is, as Alan Williamson put it in a review for the *New York Times* in 1985, a "very fine, very promising first book." But like most good first books, it often takes on the borrowed finery (or not so finery) of several different period styles. There's a little "deep image" mysticism in the manner of James Wright: "I close my eyes / and am flowered deeper in myself." There's a touch of manly sentimentality from the school of Galway Kinnell: "We are not making love but / all night long we hug each other."

Yet there is also something different, something that emerges in Gilbert's deliberately corkscrewed syntax ("It is gotten winter") and occasionally startling descriptions ("Januaried movements"; "our attention is blue-insistent"). Consider these lines from "Kodac and Chris Walking the Mutual Landscape," which are about Gilbert walking his dog, and which begin by echoing the poem's opening, "Let's be simultaneous":

> *Simultaneous as the weather's feeling,*
> *Finding another place for residence—*
> *No neighbor's yard is a boundary.*
> *Don't you got this earth in you?*
> *And I'll be damned if it divides*
> *Into yards of different kinds.*
> *Your heart is a boat's blue sail*
> *So I'll be damned if it don't feel*
> *Your step is the perfect weight.*

Gilbert is playing a variation on an old theme—the distinction between our own troubled, human consciousness, with its hall-of-mirrors self-searching, and the comparative ease with which animals appear to inhabit the world. But this theme is advanced through, or possibly under, a cascade of dense, cheerfully peculiar effects. The lines seem to shift sideways, almost resolving into tetrameter couplets ("And I'll be damned if it divides / Into yards of different kinds"), as if they're moving toward a variant on the blues stanza—presumably with "I'll be damned" as the refrain—that the poem never quite reaches. Meanwhile, the diction wobbles elsewhere from "piss" to "monoecious," and the metaphors don't so much clarify the picture as wrap it in gauze ("Your heart is a boat's blue sail," and later, "stars materialize as pools of milk"). It's as if Gilbert can't decide whether he's feeling one thing or many things or anything at all, and then can't decide how he feels about that feeling.

That might sound like a criticism (Williamson faults him for "a kind of secondhand existentialism or Zen"). But Gilbert thinks about thinking in a manner that's both impressively complex and subtly tender, and this gift dominates the best poems in the previously unpublished work titled "Chris Gilbert: An Improvisation." The self, both conscious and un-, has been a preoccupation for American poets for over three decades now (and the source of much navel-gazing). So it's remarkable to see Gilbert pour new water into this dry vessel in the manuscript's titular poem, which situates the poet in the hospital room in which he has just received a kidney transplant. The hematology team, he says, will come asking if he is the transplant patient, and "my family, who will be / visiting and who will have helped me into whatever / state of mind I am will clear the air for me to declare / I am." The poem concludes:

The ID bracelet
I've been wearing since I got here will say for me,
"I am." The scar the surgeon left as a signature
on my belly's right side will say, "I am." I am
I feel a gathering possibility passing from temporary
articulation to articulation the way the horizon
arises in the sun as a series of evident illuminations
while the earth spins clockwise toward futurity.
When the time comes I'll rise and say, "I am."
I'll gather all my questions, step into their midst
and say, "I am." I am I am.

"I am I am." Whether Christopher Gilbert's poetry—or any poet's poetry—will outlive the gilded monuments of princes is impossible to know. But one of the hidden strengths of art is that there is always the possibility that what had seemed like a final breath may simply be the long pause before a new inhalation.

MATTHEW ZAPRUDER

AND RACHEL WETZSTEON

According to conventional wisdom, younger poets are engaged in "finding their voices"—a process often described in terms that make it seem like a cross between having an epiphany and an aneurysm. For instance, here's Thom Gunn, in his elegy for Robert Duncan, detailing the emergence of Duncan's distinctive talent:

> When in his twenties a poetry's full strength
> Burst into voice as an unstopping flood,
> He let the divine prompting (come at length)
> Rushingly bear him any way it would.

Gunn is having a little fun in this portrait, true, but the idea he's playing with here is an oddly pervasive one. Many readers think of a poet's distinctive style as being found, rather than, for instance, built. They suppose it arrives as "an unstopping flood," rather than in dribs and drabs and half measures. They believe it's a matter of, yes, inspiration.

And in some ways, it is. But it also isn't. The achievement of a style is like the composition of an individual poem writ large: it's a delicate balance of confidence and guesswork, as the writer simultaneously relies on what's worked in the past, bets on what might work right now, and tries to leave a little room for things that might work in the future. It's like baking a pie with a recipe in one hand and a wish list in the other. Some poets manage the feat in their first books (Bishop), others take a couple of outings to get things right (Larkin), and still others pass through multiple styles over the courses of long careers (Yeats, Auden). The process is fascinatingly byzantine, but it's not really a matter of "divine prompting"; rather, a poet arrives at a style through the same combination of staggering labor and jolts of luck that most complex activities depend on.

This makes the eventual attainment no less impressive. Two recent books, Matthew Zapruder's *Come On All You Ghosts* and Rachel Wetzsteon's *Silver Roses*, help demonstrate the point. Zapruder, who is forty-three and an editor at Wave Books, has been a fixture in the poetry world since the publication of his first collection, *American Linden*, in 2002. From the beginning, he's worked in the tradition that extends from Auden through John Ashbery, Frank O'Hara, and (particularly) James Schuyler—a mode that will be overwhelmingly familiar to anyone who's spent much time with literary journals since the mid-1990s. The contemporary incarnation of this style is broad and loose, but generally speaking it values gesture over statement;

favors mixed diction and shifting tones; eschews traditional form; often involves dreams, collage, and touches of surrealism; and inclines toward moods of whimsy, melancholy, or mild happiness rather than fury, ecstasy, or despair. It's no surprise to see titles like "Warning: Sad"; or to find opening lines like "Often I have an idea and say it immediately"; or conclusions like "I came up to tell you // I have never seen / such beautiful scissors." At its best, this approach can be delicately moving; at its worst it can be precious and sentimental: the indie rock of the indiest art.

The work in *Come On All You Ghosts*, however, is the strongest of Zapruder's career. Many of the poems in this collection have a stillness and confidence that he hasn't managed with such consistency in the past. Consider the beginning of "Pocket":

> *I like the word pocket. It sounds a little safely*
> *dangerous. Like knowing you once*
> *bought a headlamp in case the lights go out*
> *in a catastrophe. You will put it on your head*
> *and your hands will still be free. . . .*

It's a standard Zapruder opening—charming, daffy, smartly put together (notice the internal rhyming of "dangerous" with "knowing you once," and "catastrophe" with "still be free"). And it's followed by some standard Zapruder meandering ("Look out scientists! Today the unemployment rate / is 9.4%. . . ."). But the poem's conclusion shifts into a different register:

And now I am looking away
and thinking for the last time about my pocket.
But this time I am thinking about its darkness.
Like the bottom of the sea. But without
the blind fluorescent creatures floating
in a circle around the black box which along
with tremendous thunder and huge shards
of metal from an airplane sank down and settled
here where it rests, cheerfully beeping.

The poem plays, consciously or not, on Bishop's famous conclusion to "The Bight": "All the untidy activity continues / awful
but cheerful." And it has an accordingly greater sense of risk:
what Zapruder is coming up against here is the knowledge, not
just of death and loss, but of the banality ("cheerfully beeping")
of both. Few artists are fazed by the possibility of seeming cryp-
tic, but the list of poets willing to dare banality is short. Yet that
risk must sometimes be run in order to capture experiences that
are simultaneously conventional and brutal, like the loss of a
parent (which Zapruder handles gracefully in "They" and "Sch-
winn") or the paradoxes of desire (deftly sketched in "Franken-
stein Love"). There are, of course, a few poems in *Come On All
You Ghosts* that don't come off ("Letter to a Lover" is adorable,
which is to say, annoying), and the book's admirably ambitious
eponymous closing sequence is sometimes a little too ardent for its
own good. But these are exactly the chances Zapruder should be
taking, as he moves from channeling a tradition into shaping it.

Rachel Wetzsteon killed herself at age forty-two, in

December of 2009. Like Zapruder, Wetzsteon was a well-known figure in the poetry world—she was the poetry editor for the *New Republic* and a past winner of the National Poetry Series, among various other medals and gold-star stickers. And like Zapruder, her style owes a great deal to Auden, in particular to the side of Auden fascinated with the desires and fears of childhood. But where Zapruder's finest writing has a child's steady, accepting gaze, Wetzsteon's work draws on childhood's extremity, its joys and rages. She is sustained, not by Auden's warmth, but by his wit and speed. In this she follows yet another strand in American poetry, the debonair school that has James Merrill as a presiding figure and whose practitioners like their poems formal, urban, scrupulously intelligent, and chockablock with art (Wetzsteon's title, *Silver Roses*, is a reference to Strauss's opera *Der Rosenkavalier*).

This collection, compiled prior to her death, is uneven, but its best work consolidates the gains Wetzsteon made in her signature book, *Sakura Park*. Wetzsteon is the kind of poet who invariably gets called a "flaneuse"—even by herself, in "Halt!"—probably because she writes about Manhattan in a Dorothy Parker sort of way—that is, if Dorothy Parker had gone to Yale. As you might expect, she's a deft hand at verse that is, if not light, certainly lightish, as in "Freely from Wyatt":

> *I have become the forlorn type who buys*
> *Almond biscotti for a long night in,*
> *Glumly recapturing a sense of sin*
> *Through stomach-aches. It hath been otherwise.*

This is fine and droll, but her strongest writing takes on richer tones: its sorrow isn't gray but black, and its pleasure is sun yellow. Here is "Gold Leaves":

> *Someone ought to write about (I thought*
> *and therefore do) stage three of alchemy:*
> *not inauspicious metal turned into*
> *a gilded page, but that same page turned back*
> *to basics when you step outside for air*
> *and feel a radiance that was not there*
> *the day before, your sidewalks lined with gold.*

The challenge for Wetzsteon, always, is to let wit enhance the poem, rather than retreating into wit before the poem really starts. It's a challenge she backs away from in some of the lesser poems in *Silver Roses* (a sequence pairing seventeenth-century poets with classic Hollywood directors is the poetic equivalent of a chef who makes puns on your dish's name, rather than actual food). But in work like "New Journal," "Ruins," "Algonquin Afterthoughts" (the kind of light verse that isn't so light), and "The Menaced Objects Series" (an elegant play on Edward Gorey), Wetzsteon was writing at the top of her incandescent style. It's far more than a pity that the room has gone dark.

THE RAW AND THE COOKED:

FRANK STANFORD AND

DEVIN JOHNSTON

"Two poetries are now competing," said Robert Lowell in 1960, "a cooked and a raw." The "cooked," as Lowell saw it, was the university poetry of the midcentury period, which was often served on platters borrowed from Auden and sprinkled with croutons chipped from Eliot's *Four Quartets*. This was "a poetry of pedantry" meant to be "digested in a graduate seminar." "Raw" writing, on the other hand, involved "blood-dripping gobbets of unseasoned experience" offered up (again, as Lowell saw it) by the Beat poets for their coffeehouse constituency. This was crude stuff, "a poetry of scandal."

Poets—people, for that matter—have always been drawn to binaries, and Lowell's distinction echoes dozens of earlier pairings, spanning hundreds of years. But two things are especially interesting about the "cooked" versus "raw" formulation, echoes of which occur in discussions of poetry to this day. The first is that both terms are negative: "cooked" poems aren't that appetizing, but "raw" doesn't sound so tasty either. The comparison therefore seems to call for a better, middle way: half-cooked, or maybe just raw enough. Certainly that's what Lowell had in mind, and he imagined his own poetry as fitting that bill quite nicely, thanks.

The second, more curious aspect of the juxtaposition is that it mirrors the schema that the anthropologist Claude Lévi-Strauss used to describe the way societies conceive of the transformation of the products of nature (raw) into manifestations of culture (cooked). But poetry is always and inevitably cultural, whether it's being written in a garret or declaimed from a stage. So where poems are concerned, there is really only the "cooked" and the "cooked differently"—and as is the case with any meal, the question of satisfaction involves not merely the style of the dish but the sensibility of the diners.

This can be an easy thing to forget when looking at a book like *What About This: Collected Poems of Frank Stanford*. If ever there was a "raw" poetry, this surely is it. Stanford, a native Arkansan, killed himself at age twenty-nine, in 1978, but his fire has been tended for years by an assortment of fellow poets, most notably C. D. Wright, and he is sometimes talked about as one of the great lost figures of his generation. His story follows an archetypal pattern in the popular conception of artists: a handsome young writer from the backwoods (though Stanford's family was quite well-off) who has an overwhelming devotion to his art (supposedly Stanford often wrote all day) achieves precocious recognition (he was well-known in the Arkansas literary community by his midtwenties) and makes contact with national luminaries (Allen Ginsberg was an admirer) amid scenes of poetic wildness (one of Stanford's old friends recalls parties involving shotguns and chainsaws) only to meet an early death. Put some leather pants on him, and he could've been Jim Morrison.

Stanford's poems are not subtle. In his introduction, the poet Dean Young describes them as "authentically raw, even brutal. . . . Many of these poems seem as if they were written with a burned stick. In blood, in river mud." Indeed, Stanford leans on the clichés of the Southern Gothic genre until he is nearly horizontal. Much fishin' is done. Knives and rivers and hog blood are plentiful. The moon must be exhausted from all the appearances it makes. His diction is roughly four parts vernacular ("chickenshits") to one part purplish ("Death," capitalized, gets a real workout), to one part yes-I-have-done-my-homework ("caryatid"). Lines may be long ("Field Hands on Plantation Night") or short ("The Bass"), and you're almost startled when he assembles them in, say, quatrains ("Rooms") rather than just stitching them together helter-skelter. At his best, Stanford musters an admirably off-kilter intensity:

> The man's tongue laid down beside him when he slept.
> The man did not know it.
> He thought his tongue was safe and quiet
> In the pillow of his mouth.
> The man thought his tongue was his wife.

Then again, some of the writing is no better for being (presumably) intentionally bad:

> *When I stand in the moonlight of the clitoris*
> *I am like a canticle*
> *The light years of the hermit's*
> *ear in a conch.*

It's believed that Stanford wrote much of his epic poem *The Battlefield Where the Moon Says I Love You*—excerpts of which are scattered throughout this seven-hundred-page volume—in high school. This seems entirely possible. Here is a not untypical line: "They exist in the natural musk of the farmgirl seer." Here is another: "I have inhaled the fumes of the chicken feathers of death myself."

To an extent, however, focusing on the quality of these observations is beside the point: the goal for a poet like Stanford is to create an atmosphere of feverish surrealism in which categories like good and bad buckle under the mysterious force of the creative drive itself. He does not believe, as he puts it, in "the techniques of a self-conscious poetics." It's an almost touchingly literary project, because it assumes that writing could somehow become equivalent to the experience it describes—as if, by turning the flame down low enough, one could transform steak into a living cow.

This is very nearly the opposite of the assumption that animates Devin Johnston's *Far-Fetched*. Johnston, who teaches at Saint Louis University in Missouri, is one of the most ambitiously painstaking craftsmen currently working in contemporary American poetry. (He is also, like Stanford, a native Southerner, though of a very different stripe.) Johnston's poems are not merely cooked; they are tenderized, trimmed, aged, gently marinated, and then braised until the finished product practically shouts, "Care has been taken in this preparation!" although Johnston is such an instinctively restrained poet that the shout is more of a charged whisper.

Far-Fetched is Johnston's fifth collection, and it continues a project that has only gotten more impressive over the past decade. The outlines of that project may be difficult to perceive, however, because a Johnston poem often requires the reader to look for emotional content in the meticulousness of a poem's construction, rather than in, say, the title. (It is impossible to imagine him ever calling a poem, as Stanford does, "Would You Like to Lie Down with the Light On and Cry.") This is work in which the often spare, impersonal presentation is discreetly enriched by slant rhymes, couplets, the occasional fifty-cent word ("hachures," "auriculars") and delicately consummated metaphors ("Clouds purl / in a conch whorl") Consider the complexity of even an apparently straightforward poem like "Bright Thorn":

> Excrucior,
> *the crux of it:*
> *torn between*
> *two states of mind,*
> *the axes of*

a new life
and of the one
you left behind.
Time and time
again, you learn
nothing but pain
from pain.
Behind the school
each bright thorn
collects
a bead of rain.

"Nothing but pain / from pain": This seems plain enough; it's a poem about the spiritual extremity we feel during life's great transformations. Which is true enough. But *excrucior* is the key word from Catullus 85 (roughly, and emphasis mine, "I hate and love. Maybe you wonder why I do this? / I don't know, but I feel it, and *I am in agony* [*excrucior*].") Johnston also deliberately calls out the root of *excrucior*, the word "crux," which means "cross," and he gives us a closing image of thorns in the rain. So Catullus's great poem of romantic self-torture is combined with the Christian emblems of suffering and rebirth, giving us a kind of doubled portrait of the turmoil that accompanies deep changes.

This seems plenty cooked, and we haven't even gotten to the poem's connection to Percy Shelley's "Ode to the West Wind" ("I fall upon the thorns of life! I bleed!"). But perhaps we might try another metaphor. A poem doesn't nourish, after all, so much as persuade—we're interested, captivated, captured. Johnston, borrowing from some old texts on fishing, including Gervase Markham's *The Pleasures of Princes* from 1614, writes:

> At no time let your shadow
> Lye upon the water
> Or cause a stone to clap on stone.
> Be stil, and smoothly draw your flye
> To and fro in a kind of daunce
> As if it were alive.

"As if it were alive": the point is not that the poem is cooked or raw, made or found, but that when we look at it, we believe we see its wings move, its bright body shifting.

THE COLLECTED POEMS

OF LOUIS MACNEICE

M ajor poets, like trick-or-treaters, tend to arrive in pairs or
small groups (whether this is a matter of fate or academic convenience may be debated). And yet from roughly 1930
to 1950, British and Irish poetry seemed to fall under the sway
of a single writer, W. H. Auden. Auden was hardly a solitary
figure, of course—his compatriots famously included Louis
MacNeice, Stephen Spender, and Cecil Day-Lewis (father of
Daniel), and the four writers were once thought to be so inti-
mately related that the poet Roy Campbell referred to them as
"MacSpaunday." But it wasn't a relationship of equals: the Mac-
Spaunday poets were usually considered notable, not because of
how closely they resembled one another, but because of how
much all of them looked like Auden.

That has begun to change for Louis MacNeice, whose reputation has been steadily rising for twenty years in Britain and
Ireland, in part because of vigorous support from Irish writers

like Edna Longley, Paul Muldoon, and Derek Mahon. His *Collected Poems* has finally been published in the United States, where readers will now have a chance to approach this underestimated writer on his own terms.

MacNeice was born in Belfast in 1907, the son of a school teacher inclined to melancholy and an Anglican clergyman who was himself not brimming over with joie de vivre ("I could hear his voice below in the study," MacNeice writes of a boyhood memory of his father, "intoning away, communing with God.") Shortly thereafter, the family moved to the ancient town of Carrickfergus, where MacNeice's mother descended into a depression that resulted in a scene straight out of childhood nightmares. "My mother became steadily more ill," MacNeice says in his memoir, "and at last she went away; the last I can remember of her at home was her walking up and down the bottom path of the garden . . . talking to my sister and weeping." She would die in a nursing home within the year. MacNeice was six.

Though he would go on to distinguish himself at Oxford, meet and befriend many of the great literary figures of his day, and travel the world as a journalist for the BBC, there is always a sense in which the isolated boy described in the conclusion to "Autobiography" has a hand on the pen of the grown-up Louis MacNeice:

When I woke they did not care;
Nobody, nobody was there.

Come back early or never come.

When my silent terror cried,
Nobody, nobody replied.

Come back early or never come.

I got up; the chilly sun
Saw me walk away alone.
Come back early or never come

He is one of the twentieth century's great poets of loneliness. And yet this aspect of MacNeice can be easy to overlook,
in part because he seems (as is frequently said of Auden) entirely
comfortable with the rhythms and clutter of the modern world:
"Cubical scent-bottles artificial legs arctic foxes and electric
mops." We think of solitary, alienated poets as writing about
ragged claws scuttling across the floors of silent seas; we don't
usually think of them as being interested in "electric mops."

Nor do we think of them as being fluent. Yet MacNeice is
effortlessly, almost ridiculously articulate—he seems capable
(again like Auden) of writing about nearly anything, and in
nearly any form. The six hundred pages here include tiny poems
(the nine-line "Upon This Beach"), book-length poems (*Autumn Journal*, which helped make his reputation), book-length
poems in terza rima (*Autumn Sequel*, which nearly undid it),
virtuoso deployment of nearly all forms of rhyme ("London
Rain" rhymes a word with itself in every stanza), and a vocabulary that suavely extends from "Tom or Dick or Harry" and

"trams" to "ochred" and "archaize." Surely a poet of loneliness should do a little more stammering.

Or should he? The difference between loneliness and mere solitariness, after all, is that the lonely sensibility wants to be otherwise. There is a reaching out that never quite touches. In MacNeice's best work, the ingeniousness and inevitable failure of that reaching indicates the depth of the longing. He is a superb love poet, for instance, yet his love poems often foreground their own ephemerality, like ice sculptures in the summertime. Consider "Meeting Point," which is about the fiction writer Eleanor Clark, one of MacNeice's many, many paramours. Here is how the poem begins:

> Time was away and somewhere else,
> There were two glasses and two chairs
> And two people with the one pulse
> (Somebody stopped the moving stairs)
> Time was away and somewhere else.
>
> And they were neither up nor down;
> The stream's music did not stop
> Flowing through heather, limpid brown,
> Although they sat in a coffee shop
> And they were neither up nor down.

After five more stanzas of Cole Porterish elegance, the poem ends:

Time was away and she was here
And life no longer what it was,
The bell was silent in the air
And all the room one glow because
Time was away and she was here.

But of course, time is never "away"; it is by nature constantly present. The poem is about the illusion of permanent connection in passing happiness, but it is no less lovely for that.

And that loveliness is in part a function of repetition and refrain, two overlapping tactics MacNeice used for opposed purposes throughout his career. In warmer poems like "Meeting Point" or "The Sunlight on the Garden" they provide a formal symbol for continuity or synthesis: they are the hopeful side of loneliness. But in many other poems the act of repeating is an indication of futility. Consider "Reflections," which opens with a scene of tripled repetition:

The mirror above my fireplace reflects the reflected
Room in my window; I look in the mirror at night
And see two rooms, the first where left is right
And the second, beyond the reflected window, corrected
But there I am standing back to my back.

The reflections multiply and extend in an astounding display of technical wizardry until the very act of writing becomes impossible:

I can see beyond and through the reflections the street
   lamps
At home outdoors where my indoors rooms lie stranded,
Where a taxi will perhaps drive in through the bookcase
Whose books are not for reading and past the fire
Which gives no warmth and pull up by my desk
At which I cannot write since I am not lefthanded.

In the brilliantly frightening poems of MacNeice's last collection, the repetitions that give shape to his loneliness begin to take on the blacker outlines of despair: lovers introduced in a "grave glade" find themselves in a "green grave"; childlike refrains like "tra-la" and "Touch me not forget me not" indicate horror, not whimsy. But perhaps the most striking use of repetition occurs in his final poem, "Coda":

Maybe we knew each other better
When the night was young and unrepeated
And the moon stood still over Jericho.

So much for the past; in the present
There are moments caught between heart-beats
When maybe we know each other better.

But what is that clinking in the darkness?
Maybe we shall know each other better
When the tunnels meet beneath the mountain.

What we most want, MacNeice suggests, is simply "to know each other better," but that possibility depends on laboring blindly through darkness. With the publication of *Collected Poems*, MacNeice's own excavation is now complete; readers who meet him halfway will find a passage that opens and opens and opens.

VERSIONS OF ZBIGNIEW HERBERT

I t's easy to say which nation has the fastest trains (France) or
the largest number of prime ministers who've probably been
eaten by sharks (Australia), but it's impossible to know which
country has the best writers, let alone the best poetry. Even so,
if cash money were on the line, you'd find few critics willing to
bet against Poland. Since 1950, the Poles have two Nobel Prize–
winning poets, thirty-four pages in *The Vintage Book of Contemporary World Poetry* (seven better than France, a country
with 25 million more people), and enough top-flight artists to
populate dozens of American creative writing departments,
probably improving many of them in the process. The
nineteenth-century Polish poet Cyprian Norwid said he wanted
to see "Polish symbols loom / in warm expanding series which
reveal / Once and for all the Poland that is real"—for decades
now, those symbols and that reality have been hard to ignore.

Of course, for most of us, discovering "the Poland that is

real" means reading works translated from Polish. The most sig-
nificant such translation this year—possibly in many years—is
Zbigniew Herbert's *Collected Poems*, which was published by
Ecco in April to (almost) universal acclaim. The book is significant for two reasons. First, Herbert himself is significant—like
Frost and Auden, he's a poet whose failure to win the Nobel
Prize says more about the prize committee than the writer.
Second, his poetry is relatively difficult to find. Although most
of Herbert's collections have been translated by John and Bog-
dana Carpenter, many of those books are now out of print. For
the casual reader, then, this *Collected Poems* is the likeliest path
to this poet's achievement.

That achievement is well worth the journey. Along with Ta-
deusz Różewicz, Wisława Szymborska, and Czesław Miłosz,
Herbert is one of the principal figures in postwar Polish
poetry—and, by extension, in European letters generally. Born
in 1924, he was active in the Polish resistance during the
German occupation, then became an admirably uncooperative
citizen of the subsequent Soviet puppet state. (According to a
recent article in the *Süddeutsche Zeitung*, whenever Herbert was
asked by the secret police to write up reports on foreign trips, he
would fill them "with interpretations of the poems of the Nobel
Prize laureate Czesław Miłosz . . . as well as long-winded
cultural-philosophical observations.")

The quiet but determined insubordination that marked his
public life is echoed in his poetry, which is lucid, low pitched,
and saturated with irony. A typical Herbert poem uses spare
diction and a meticulously orchestrated syntax to investigate

ethics as much as aesthetics—indeed, a Herbert poem often points out the blurred border between these two categories. As he puts it in "The Power of Taste,"

> *It did not take any great courage*
> *our refusal dissent and persistence*
> *we had a scrap of necessary courage*
> *but essentially it was a matter of taste*

Herbert is sometimes described as a poet of precision and reserve—as if he were interchangeable with the subject of his much-quoted poem "Pebble": "The pebble / is a perfect creature // equal to itself / mindful of its limits . . . its ardour and coldness / are just and full of dignity." There's some truth to this, but the compression in this poet's writing can also produce considerable heat. Unlike many poets who focus on morality, Herbert has a powerful sense of right and wrong without a corresponding belief in a system that would make right action more likely. The difficulty of this position gives his work a peculiar, knotted intensity and leads to the stoicism evident in poems like "Mr. Cogito's Monster," in which Herbert's alter ego, Mr. Cogito, challenges a monster each day that "lacks all dimension" and exists only as "the flickering of nothingness" (recalling the Nazi and Soviet occupations). Cogito's quest is hopeless yet necessary: a vivid symbol of Herbert's ethical irony.

Our ability to appreciate such effects, however, depends on the skill with which they're translated—and this is where the story of Zbigniew Herbert's *Collected Poems* becomes more complicated. In a recent essay in *Poetry* magazine, the poet and translator Michael Hofmann argued that not only is the *Collected Poems* inferior to works translated decades ago by the Carpenters (whose efforts weren't included here for obscure reasons) but also that it is "a hopelessly, irredeemably bad book." Hofmann can't read Polish (neither can I), but he makes a vigorous, smart, and hugely entertaining case by comparing the older and newer translations. Admittedly, not all of Hofmann's examples are convincing. He claims, for instance, that the volume's translator, Alissa Valles, "makes a fool of herself" by using the phrase "indifferent plenitude" whereas the Carpenters "knowing or wisely sensing that Herbert demands a mixing of English and Latin—have 'indifferent fullness.'" It's by no means clear why a description whose terms involve "a mixing of English and Latin" is better than one whose roots lie solely in Latin (does "the woe and the ecstasy" sound better than "the agony and the ecstasy"?), to say nothing of the fact that "plenitude" has rich philosophical associations running from Aristotle to Thomas Aquinas to David Lewis.

Still, Hofmann's basic point is sound—this book would've been better if some of the Carpenters' work had been retained. Sometimes, it's a matter of the earlier translations being subtly richer. In "Mr. Cogito—the Return," for example, Herbert's protagonist returns to his occupied homeland to confront its ailments. The Carpenters render one of the threats Cogito faces as "the blow given from behind." In Valles's version, it is "a blow out of the blue," which is tinnier, needlessly cliché, and emphasizes the unexpectedness of the "blow" at the expense of its treacherousness. Other times, the newer translation is simply inaccurate. We are told, for instance, that Mr. Cogito "felt revulsion from the Sphinx" (in context, Herbert clearly means "for the Sphinx"), that a prosecutor has a "yellow indicator finger" (index finger?), and that you can hear "the tolling of scattered walls" (collapsing walls?).

That said, Herbert wrote many poems; mistakes are to be expected. And as always, the central difficulty for any translator lies in conveying words and concepts that lack true analogues in our language. In such cases, is the literal meaning best? Or what you think the poet might've said if he were an English speaker? To understand how complicated these questions can be, consider "The Road to Delphi." In this short prose poem, Apollo is shown idly toying with the severed head of Medusa while repeating a particular line. In Polish, that line is "Sztukmistrz musi zgłebić okrucieństwo," for which a Polish-English dictionary offers this translation: "A performer must get to the bottom of cruelty." The Carpenters, however, render the line: "A craftsman must probe to the very bottom of cruelty." "Craftsman" is surprising, but it makes a certain sense—the poem is exploring the old idea of art as an essentially coldhearted activity (as Yeats said, "Cast a cold eye / On life, on death"), and Herbert has deliberately avoided the Polish word for "artist" (*artysta*) in favor of *sztukmistrz*, which means "performer, juggler, conjuror." In doing so, Herbert is emphasizing the side of art that has to do with performance for its own sake—by extension, he's pointing out the chill at the core of technical excellence. So "craftsman" may help bring that aspect of the poem into English.

But it isn't what Herbert said. Which is perhaps why Valles gives the same line as: "A conjuror must plumb the depths of cruelty." Aside from "plumb the depths," which is overdone, this version is almost certainly a better word-for-word translation. But it doesn't make much sense in English, probably because the figure of the traveling magician doesn't figure prominently in American consciousness. Consequently Valles's version, while accurate, has the unfortunate effect of making the casual reader think of David Blaine, which is plumbing the depths of cruelty indeed.

So if translation is always a matter of approximating, does it matter that Zbigniew Herbert's *Collected Poems* has its weaknesses? Well, yes: a translated poet may, as Auden said, become his admirers, but only after he's become a poet in English who's interesting enough to attract admirers in the first place. Herbert is now a complete poet in English—and he's not as strong as he should be. In "Elegy of Fortinbras," in which the practical Fortinbras eulogizes the romantic Hamlet, Herbert writes that "we live on archipelagos / and that water these words what can they do what can they do prince." Whatever this poet's new words can do, we'll have to hope it's enough to carry him across the estranging sea between his language and our own.

THE POETRY OF NABOKOV

The club of novelist-poets is distinguished but tiny. Thomas Hardy is the founding member, Herman Melville and D. H. Lawrence take turns at the reception desk, and loitering at the door are talented contemporary (or near-contemporary) writers like James Dickey, Margaret Atwood, and Denis Johnson. Any way you count them, though, the true novelist-poets always seem outnumbered by the novelist-essayists, the novelist-memoirists, and the fell horde of novelist–story writers.

This isn't to say novelists don't try to be poets and vice versa. But most writers turn out to be so much stronger at one endeavor than the other that they resemble fiddler crabs: NOVELIST-poets like John Updike and Cynthia Ozick, or novelist-POETS like Philip Larkin and Randall Jarrell. What causes the imbalance? One possibility is that poetry and prose are more like different musical instruments than different musical genres. While we don't expect violinists to be accomplished pianists, we're not at all surprised when a good pianist can play both Chopin and "Boogie with Stu." Similarly, we don't find it unusual when a writer who excels at one prose project also excels at another—both, after all, involve sentences. Whereas poetry supposedly involves . . . something else.

It's an appealing theory, but not completely convincing. In particular, it breaks down whenever the work in question undermines our ideas about its reputed genre. James Joyce is a novelist, certainly, and *Ulysses* is a great work of prose. But it's a great work of prose partly because its prose often resembles poetry. Les Murray's *Fredy Neptune* is a brilliant example of poetry, but do its length and narrative structure really justify its subtitle: *A Novel in Verse*?

Perhaps the most difficult case of all, though, is that of Vladimir Nabokov. And it's difficult for several reasons. Nabokov was multilingual, and an overwhelming majority of his poetry was written early in his career and in Russian. The new *Vladimir Nabokov: Selected Poems*, edited by Thomas Karshan, contains only twenty-three original English poems—essentially his entire output—compared with about three times that number translated from the Russian by Nabokov himself or by his late son, Dmitri (and there were many more to choose from). It's possible, of course, to be an excellent poet in one language and an excellent novelist in another. But leaving aside the linguistic status of Nabokov's own translations, questions of quality in Russian poetry should be left to Russian readers, and those of us who read Nabokov in English are reduced to looking at not quite two dozen mostly short original poems.

They're a decidedly mixed bag. Nabokov's English poems share some of the qualities of his prose, notably its confident lucidity (Nabokov is complex but never garbled) and elegantly unfolding inventiveness. While the poems are slightly simpler in diction than the typical Nabokovian sentence, his fondness for half-dollar words is still much in evidence: over the course of ten pages, we get "prototypic," "anchoret," "scholiastic," and "dendrologists." And as you might expect, Nabokov fixates on—and is sometimes fixated by—formal prestidigitation. Notice the way he not only juggles the potentially heavy rhymes in the tercets that conclude "Lines Written in Oregon" but throws in a little French and German as well:

And I rest where I awoke
In the sea shade—l'ombre glauque—
Of a legendary oak;

Where the woods get ever dimmer,
Where the Phantom Orchids glimmer—
Esmeralda, immer, immer.

The poem, which recalls Nabokov's own visit to Oregon, is about the interaction of Old World and New (thus the French and German, which would otherwise be little more than showing off). But there's an additional, subtle formal touch. The poem's unusual trochaic meter is also used in Longfellow's *Song of Hiawatha,* one of the definitive early poems of America—and that meter in turn was inspired by the Finnish *Kalevala,* one of the great mythic poems of Europe. It's an ingenious fusion of structure and theme.

At his best, Nabokov writes a delicate, knowing poetry of crystalline surfaces and twisty depths, and in work like "Lines Written in Oregon," as well as "A Literary Dinner" and "An Evening of Russian Poetry," his talent is displayed in all its appealing peculiarity. Still, there are very few poems to judge here, and some are fairly light (nor are the lines written by the undergraduate Nabokov likely to impress, unless you like your poetry rich in "o'er" and frosted with "moonlight dim"). If this sample were the total of Nabokov's claim to poetic greatness, it would be hard to call him more than a talented dabbler.

But, of course, it isn't. There is still the elephant in the room, which in this case is also a dead bird beneath a window. Because Nabokov's English poetry arguably includes the 999 lines of *Pale Fire*, the centerpiece of his novel of the same name, whose opening is quoted as frequently as many of the past century's most admired poems:

> I was the shadow of the waxwing slain
> By the false azure in the windowpane;
> I was the smudge of ashen fluff—and I
> Lived on, flew on, in the reflected sky.

In the novel, the poem is attributed to John Shade, a noted poet whose manuscript has been appropriated by a man called Kinbote, who may also be the exiled monarch of a kingdom called Zembla. Kinbote's deranged commentary on the poem provides the substance of the novel, as his remarks become increasingly less about the lines than about his own tattered psychology.

The poem itself is a seemingly clear-eyed discussion of death and natural patterns centered on the poet's loss of his only child, an unattractive and disturbed girl who drowned herself after being scorned by a blind date. The entire poem is written in heroic couplets (Shade is presented as a Pope scholar), and the lines discussing Shade's awareness of his daughter's looming unhappiness are typical of its strange power:

> *At Christmas parties games were rough, no doubt,*
> *And one shy little guest might be left out;*
> *But let's be fair: while children of her age*
> *Were cast as elves and fairies on the stage*
> *That she'd helped paint for the school pantomime,*
> *My gentle girl appeared as Mother Time,*
> *A bent charwoman with slop pail and broom,*
> *And like a fool I sobbed in the men's room.*

Although couplets were the dominant poetic form of the eighteenth century, they sound odd to many modern readers. But they're well chosen in *Pale Fire* for two reasons. First, within the context of the poem, the couplet form has a crisp exactness that enhances the work's reflective surfaces (the opening bird lives on in a reflection, the "azure" sky later appears as the "azure" entrance to the bar at which Shade's child is humiliated, the poem's unwritten last line is probably its first line, and so forth). The paired rhymes are the twin beams of light around which the mirrors revolve. Second, *Pale Fire* is frequently in dialogue with other poems, particularly those of T. S. Eliot. In addition to mockingly poaching some words from Eliot's *Four Quartets*, the poem's third canto rewrites part of the "A Game of Chess" section from *The Waste Land*. Eliot, as Nabokov probably knew, wrote a book on Dryden, the master of the couplet. And, indeed, the original draft of "The Fire Sermon" included a section in couplets (a section Eliot wisely abandoned). It's perhaps brash of Nabokov to have written in such an odd form partly as a challenge to Eliot and his heirs, but the technical achievement is hard to deny.

Still, the merits of *Pale Fire* have been debated over the years, with earlier critics tending to dismiss the poem in favor of its baroque prose trappings. But more recently, the poem has come into its own, so to speak, and the culmination of this process is a recent edition of *Pale Fire* as a stand-alone literary artifact (published by Gingko Press). It is an almost ridiculously lovely package: the poem itself is printed in a small booklet, the note cards upon which Shade "wrote" the poem are re-created (complete with faux ink stains), and an accompanying critical text contains helpful essays from the Nabokov scholar Brian Boyd and the poetry critic R. S. Gwynn (who makes a smart case for Nabokov having used couplets partly as a response to Robert Lowell's early work). If you're a Nabokov devotee, this is comparable to getting a special edition of *Physical Graffiti* with a facsimile string from one of Jimmy Page's custom violin bows inside.

But does it work? Can the poem *Pale Fire* exist without the novel *Pale Fire*? There are reasons to think it cannot. In a *New Yorker* blog post last year, Paul Muldoon conceded that *Pale Fire* is "a quite wonderful poem," but he asked, "Isn't it like one of those tall buildings which incorporates in its core the very crane that raised it?"

This is beautifully put, but there is another way to look at things. When authors write "as" a character, particularly in a third-person novel, we usually understand that the text created by that character is subordinate to the world in which the character exists. In *Persuasion*, for example, Jane Austen brings the novel to its emotional peak with a letter written by Frederick Wentworth—which we understand is really written by Austen and dependent for its resonance on the world of Anne Elliot, the Musgroves, Lady Russell, and so forth. It's hard to imagine anyone reading the letters of Frederick Wentworth for their own sake, just as it's difficult to conceive of anyone separating the e-mails of Denise from their place in *The Corrections*. In general, the writing of fictional characters is dependent on the larger work, and it is the larger work that reflects the author's worldview.

Lyric poems present a slightly different picture (as can first-person novels, though often to a lesser degree). A lyric poem depends on the development of a single sensibility. That sensibility might involve a construction called "I" that could stand in for the poet, but it could just as easily take the form of a Greek warrior (Tennyson's "Ulysses") or a giant toad (Bishop's "Rainy Season; Sub-Tropics"), which is to say: lyric poems don't have

characters; they are characters—and characters with an oddly
doubled aspect. We hear the voice of the poem, but we also understand that we're hearing a filtered version of the poet's own
voice. We're hearing both a giant toad and Elizabeth Bishop;
both Gerontion (who may himself be more than one person)
and Thomas Stearns Eliot; both "I" and Robert Frost. The poet
isn't so much taking on a character as donning a mask.

There is obviously great potential for confusion as to who is
saying what in this arrangement. And this confusion over voice
is central in many ways to the development of early twentieth-
century poetry (the original title of *The Waste Land* was "He Do
the Police in Different Voices"). By placing a long poem at the
center of *Pale Fire*, and refusing to turn Shade into a character
obviously separable from himself (unlike Kinbote or Humbert
Humbert), Nabokov encourages and deepens this confusion.
His most obvious peer in this project is the great Portuguese
poet Fernando Pessoa, whose own poetry is written in the voices
of some seventy different heteronyms, all with different personalities, biographies, and styles—yet all of them inseparable from
Pessoa.

So perhaps it's wrong to ask whether *Pale Fire* can hold up
as a poem on its own, or whether it should really be attributed to
Nabokov. No poem is ever on its own. And the poem is not
Nabokov's any more than it is John Shade's. *Pale Fire* is a voice
within a voice—a mirrored and thoroughly modern sensibility. And that sensibility, whatever name we give it, is one hell
of a poet.

MARY JO BANG'S *ELEGY*

"The art of losing isn't hard to master," Elizabeth Bishop
tells us—and yet artistry can often seem the least appropriate response to the misery of loss. When pain is primitive and
specific, as it is following the death of a loved one, we don't want
an exquisite performance filled with grand abstractions. What
we want is to go beyond art, beyond society and beyond speech
itself, as Lear does when he enters carrying the body of his
daughter and crying "Howl, howl, howl, howl!" We want heav-
en's vault to crack. We want the veil parted and the bone laid
bare. This is what Tennyson meant when he wrote in canto 54 of
In Memoriam his tribute to his friend Arthur Hallam, that his
grief left him "no language but a cry."

Still, *In Memoriam* is over a thousand lines long, which is a
lot of language any way you slice it. This points toward one of
the central paradoxes of the modern private elegy. The closer a
poet is to the subject he elegizes, the more we expect him to

respond in ways that aren't poetic—but it takes craft to make a poem seem uncrafted, and it takes words to show how short our words can fall. As a result, the elegist is forced to go through increasingly complicated contortions in order to sound sufficiently simple. He finds himself in the awkward position of orchestrating a death wail. Now, one might respond that many (too many) poems meditate on the limits of speech, and that would be true. But it's equally true that nobody reads a poem about Lacanian theory the same way one reads a poem about the poet's dead child. Any elegist must confront this fact.

That confrontation can be especially problematic for a certain type of contemporary poet. Stevens accused Frost of writing about "subjects," to which Frost retorted that Stevens wrote about "bric-a-brac." The dominant contemporary American style, with its self-conscious intellectualism, evasiveness, and preoccupation with "language itself" is firmly on the side of bric-a-brac. This style, like all styles, may be put to any use, but it will always approach its goals through the back door via head fakes, double bluffs, rope tricks, and an elaborate system of pulleys. It's a strategy poorly suited to "subjects" in general, let alone the intractable subject that haunts an elegy.

But the best stylists thrive when challenged. This is perhaps why Mary Jo Bang largely succeeds in her new book of elegies for her son, called, simply enough, *Elegy*. Bang's previous four collections are polished and frequently interesting, but they also contain more than their share of overwrought and overthought poetry about poetry. Sure, a poem might be called "Open Heart Surgery," but by line 14 we'd discover that "all the while, the ghost of Gertrude Stein / was whispering in my ear." Bang's last book, *The Eye Like a Strange Balloon*, consisted entirely of poems about works of art ("Always asking, has this THIS been built / Or is it all process?"), which for a bric-a-brac poet is the equivalent of a Wes Anderson movie about a troop of overgrown adolescents who collect meerschaum pipes and have mother issues—in other words, pretty much what you'd expect.

That can't be said of *Elegy*. This is a focused, forthright collection written almost entirely in the bleakest key imaginable. The poems aren't all great, some of them aren't even good, but collectively they are overwhelming—which is both a compliment to Bang's talent and to the toughness of mind that allowed her to attempt this difficult project in the first place.

Like *In Memoriam*, the book is a roughly chronological account of the poet's mourning. The poems return repeatedly to two related themes: the connection between grieving and the perception of time ("Small cog after cog slips into the hour / And razor thin minute slot without stop"), and the idea of elegy as theater ("Come on stage and be yourself, / The elegist says to the dead"). Bang's technique here doesn't depart much from her previous work—she favors free-verse stanzas animated by conspicuous enjambment ("November is more of the usual / November"), clots of assonance and alliteration ("The knife never dulls, / Does it, Dearie, / On the blade side), and peculiar syntactic units ("How very gone / The nothing after"). But that technique is now at the service of a much richer and darker purpose. Consider the end of "Three Trees," in which Bang's fondness for writing about art—in this case the animated movie

Jimmy Neutron: Boy Genius—leads to an unexpectedly raw note:

> *The day is dragged here and there but still*
> *can't be saved. BAM. Immediately*
> *the next second clicks into the skyscape*
> *apocalypse. In the dust, a celluloid woman*
> *mows a multilayered lawn.*
> *The arch overhead reads, O Art*
> *Still Has Truth Take Refuge. Where? There.*
> *There, there, says someone.*

The poet doubts the redemptive power of her own gift while simultaneously using it to find a tone that—in the final line—wavers perfectly between her contempt for consolation and her desire for it. The achievement of art shows the limitation of art, and vice versa. This is the great strength of *Elegy*. No one will ever bring back the dead by writing poetry; indeed, the only certain result of writing a poem is the poem itself. But as Bang proves in this sad, strange book, the conversion of grief into art may be balanced, if not redeemed, by the transformation of art into grieving.

JORIE GRAHAM, SUPERSTAR

I n the cloistered world of American poetry, the revolutions are never televised—which can make them awfully hard to distinguish from coups d'état. For the average reader, nothing is likely to demonstrate this peculiar phenomenon so much as the delicate, secretive, enigmatical process through which a contemporary poetic reputation is consummated (or if you prefer, attained). One day the poetry fan is dozing under a tree with Elizabeth Bishop's collected poems on her lap; the next thing she knows, the road signs have been changed, the post office is now a Banana Republic, and the name of a new major poet has been quietly etched into the stones of Parnassus—or, at any rate, into the syllabi of a thousand MFA programs.

If the current state of affairs is any guide, there's a good chance the name writ therein will be Jorie Graham. Graham is a burnished idol of the poetry world, having at age fifty-five already pulled off the trifecta of American verse: (1) A major prize (the Pulitzer); (2) a faculty position at Iowa, the Death Star of the modern MFA system; and (3) an appointment at one of the Ivies (in this case Harvard, where Graham now occupies a seat previously held by Nobel laureate Seamus Heaney). She's gotten breathless, full-profile attention from the *New Yorker* ("the closest thing American poetry has to a rock star"), been given a "genius" grant by the MacArthur Foundation, and received several ardent reviews—including one-third of a book—from her colleague Helen Vendler, widely considered to be the most influential poetry critic of the past half century. Graham would seem to be, as they say, "made."

But what kind of making goes into being made? While the items on Graham's résumé are impressive, they weren't bestowed by Apollo; they were handed out by regular old human beings, often working in regular old committees. And committees of poets and critics, like committees of pretty much everyone else, are usually less inclined to go for broke than to split the difference. At present, American poetry is a fractured discipline—part profession, part gaggle of coteries, part contest hustle. Its mind may dwell in the vale of soul making, but its common sense is aiming for the Lorna Snootbat Second Book Prize. Above all, as primarily an academic art, poetry is subject to the same insecurities riddling the humanities in general, in particular the fear of being insufficiently "serious" or "useful."

In this uncertain atmosphere, Graham is a uniter, not a divider. For one thing, she's nice. In interviews, Graham comes off as kindhearted and eager to praise—the kind of person you'd want as a colleague or mentor. She has friendly words for avant-gardists like Susan Howe, friendly words for formalists like Anthony Hecht, and friendly words for her tribe of former students ("I love all of them," she says, and it must be true, because they show up as winners of the many contests she judges with remarkable frequency). Plus, as Shelley might say, if Graham fell upon the thorns of life, she'd blurb. A typical Graham book plug is so rhapsodic and inscrutable (one blurbee has "an ear so finely tuned it cannot but register all the finest, filamentary truths the eye discerns") that it practically yodels, "Poooeeet-rrry!" Which doesn't mean she's insincere. As Graham puts it, "There are very few poets whose work doesn't, someplace in its enterprise, stun me." Poooeeetrrry!

So Graham appeals because she doesn't look for trouble in a field that's already troubled enough. And of course, it helps to have the blessings of the major institutional powers of the poetry world. Nor does it hurt—anywhere—to have good looks, sophistication, and aristocratic connections (profiles of Graham inevitably involve *E! True Hollywood Story* sentences like this one from *Harvard Magazine*: "The poet's youth was almost impossibly glamorous and romantic"). But more than anything else, Graham has succeeded because of the kind of poetry she writes.

Graham's work combines two qualities not generally found together—first, it's often sumptuously "poetic" ("a scintillant fold the fabric of the daylight bending"); second, it's ostentatiously thinky (typical titles: "Notes on the Reality of the Self," "What Is Called Thinking," "Relativity: A Quartet"). The former quality appeals to lovers of operatic lyricism; the latter quality not only pleases certain parts of poetry's largely academic audience, but it soothes the art form's nagging status anxiety (anything involving this much Heidegger must be important). When Graham writes well, her rich, quirky phrasing complements the abstractions she often ends up pursuing. "I Watched a Snake," for instance, is filled with airy poeticisms like "a mending / of the visible // by the invisible," but it's also a pretty good poem about looking at a snake.

Yet there's always been something strangely bleary in Graham's writing—as if she's just noticed something interesting and motioned the reader over, only to stand in his light, blocking his view with her own viewing. This tendency has become more pronounced as Graham has gotten older; in recent books she achieves an arty vagueness that has to be (barely) seen to be believed (from *Swarm*: "Explain requited / Explain indeed the blood of your lives I will require // explain the strange weight of meanwhile"). Curiously, this soft spot in Graham's art probably works to her political advantage. She began by writing tight, short-lined free verse; now she writes sprawling, long-lined free verse; along the way, she's tried out about fifteen different styles. Whatever you do as a poet, it'd be hard to say that Graham absolutely rejects it.

In her latest collection, *Overlord*, Graham takes a gamble by tackling a straight subject. The book is largely a meditation on the current political atmosphere as filtered through World War II (thus the title); the poet's general sense is that we're in big trouble. *Overlord* has some interesting poems, most notably the handful involving the voices of veterans, and the collection as a whole is comprehensible, lyrical, and obviously heartfelt. But it's also sadly diffuse. Consider the beginning of "Praying (Attempt of April 19 '04)": "If I could shout but I must not shout. / The girl standing in my doorway yesterday weeping. / In her right hand an updated report on global warming." Well, at least it's an updated report; you'd hate to see her weeping (instead of plain old "crying") over last Tuesday's version. The poem continues in this hopped-up manner until finally plunging into Harvard Yard street preachin': "Let the dream of contagion / set loose its virus. Don't let her turn away. / I, here, today, am letting her cry out the figures, the scenarios, / am letting her wave her down-loaded pages / into this normal office-air between us." Putting aside the redundancies ("contagion" and "virus"?), the infelicities ("downloaded pages"?), and the cartoon setup (whoever "the girl" is, she sure needs to toughen up before she goes to camp), putting all of this aside—what are these lines about? Generalized angst? Adobe Acrobat?

The point isn't that Graham's a bad poet—she's not—but rather that the fogginess, which has been a chronic problem in her work, becomes especially inhibiting in *Overlord* because there's just no leeway for muddling. Graham is trying to write here in response to actual events, in a full lyric voice and in a public manner. It's a worthy project. But this isn't the kind of challenge that can be bowled over with rhetoric, analyzed into submission, or conquered with good intentions. In the achingly cliché "Posterity," for instance, Graham attempts to feed a homeless man chicken out of an aluminum wrapper while calling on "Buber, Kafka, Dr. Robinson—you hunger specialists" (what about Colonel Sanders?)—and somehow she burns the guy's hands. Unfortunately, that sententious, well-meaning blunder is *Overlord* in a nutshell (or, rather, some tinfoil).

So have we gotten a little ahead of ourselves in appointing our major poets? Shouldn't these things be argued over a little more—and a little more publicly—before poetry's slumbering audience yawns, stretches, and looks down to see what titles we've left in its lap? Because if those titles, however illustrious, are compromise choices rather than prized necessities, isn't it likely that readers will rub their eyes, thumb a few pages, and then sigh and go right back to sleep again?

THE NOTEBOOKS OF ROBERT FROST

No one resembles a poet so much as another poet, which is a mixed blessing for American poetry. On the one hand, this kinship helps explain why writers with divergent sensibilities often read one another's work with surprising compassion and skill; on the other, it also explains why certain factions in the poetry world loathe one another nearly as much as *Star Wars* fanatics despise people who have a working knowledge of Klingon. Sometimes this acrimony stems from a genuine aesthetic disagreement that is serious and important and (as one might say in Poetryland) worthy of A Panel Discussion Followed by a Short Reception. Other times, though, it's just a matter of writers carping at each other because they realize that if they didn't, people would have a hard time telling them apart.

The longest-running feud is probably the low-intensity border war between so-called experimental poets and their "mainstream" brethren. Since the distinctions can be hard to parse (to most people, saying "mainstream poetry" is like saying "mainstream tapestry weaving"), it's helpful to turn to the experts. In her book *21st-Century Modernism*, Marjorie Perloff, a professor emerita at Stanford and longtime champion of the avant-garde, claims the "dominant" mode in poetry these days is "expressivist," whereas experimental writing involves "constructivism . . . the specific understanding that language, far from being a vehicle or conduit for thoughts or feelings outside and prior to it, is itself the site of meaning-making." She fleshes out this concept with quotes from several contemporary avant-garde poets, who argue, among other things, that "There are no thoughts except through language" and "As soon as I start listening to the words they reveal their own vectors and affinities, pull the poem into their own field of force, often in unforeseen directions."

Indeed, experimental poetry "finds its own name as it goes" and "may be worked over once it is in being, but may not be worried into being," because ultimately "the whole thing is performance and prowess and feats of association." After all, where a given poem is concerned, "what do I want to communicate but what a hell of a good time I had writing it?" Such poems necessarily disdain lyric sincerity in favor of what one writer calls "the pleasure of ulteriority" and are usually—no surprise—aggressively bookish ("So many of them have literary criticism in them—in them"). Admittedly, this approach may not appeal to more conservative tastes, but as a general description of much of today's most successful experimental writing, it's not too bad.

The problem, however, is that only the first two of those statements were actually made by contemporary avant-garde poets. Everything else, of course, was said by Robert Frost (who is, to put it mildly, rarely described as a forefather of vanguard poetics). The point here is not that our self-consciously avant-garde writers are kidding themselves, or that your ninth-grade English class was sliding along the razor's edge of American culture by reading "Birches." No, the point is that whenever we begin forming up teams in American poetry, we run into the problem of picking sides for such complex and hard-to-place poets as Frost, T. S. Eliot, and Wallace Stevens (not to mention Marianne Moore, Elizabeth Bishop, and Lorine Niedecker). Rather than take these writers as they are—rather than acknowledge, for example, that Frost was as innovative as many poets more often considered "experimental"—we prefer to reduce such figures to a size better suited to the game we want to play. We cut the poet to fit the jersey.

This is an especially easy mistake to make with Frost, whose notebooks, edited by Robert Faggen, have now been published. Frost once said he wanted to be seen as "the exception I like to think I am in everything." The problem with being an exception to every category is that after a while you begin to frustrate the categorizers. Consequently, Frost now occupies a position as unique as it is unstable. He's a definitive great American poet, yet he's never been embraced by the American academy as eagerly as, say, Ezra Pound. (In fact, Frost may be the only poet who is universally acknowledged to be a master but who nonetheless seems to require periodic reputation-buffing essays from the likes of Randall Jarrell and Seamus Heaney.) He's a technician of prodigious agility, yet he generally limits himself to iambics and favors rhymes like "reason" and "season." And then there is the fraught matter of his popularity. Unlike almost every poet of comparable ability, Frost can claim a general reading audience, especially among readers who want poems that "make sense"—yet his aesthetic is evasive, arguably manipulative, and has at its core a freezing indifference that would make the neighborhood barbecue awfully uncomfortable. Still, as the critic Richard Poirier argues, "There is no point trying to explain the popularity away, as if it were a misconception prompted by a pose." It's easy to see how a poet this contradictory might suffer from the unsubtle ways in which we tend to talk about things like experimentalism and "the mainstream." In such arguments, Frost will be simplified at best, ignored entirely at worst.

The new *Notebooks of Robert Frost* won't make things any easier. Not that they aren't entertaining—open any page and you'll find observations like "Seek first in poetry concrete images of sound," and "Reality is the cold feeling on the end of the trout's nose from the stream that runs away," as well as "Art is the last of your childhood and may be followed somewhat irresponsibly," and "An artist delights in roughness for what he can do it." Faggen has chosen to reproduce all of the more than forty notebooks essentially "as is," which is perhaps helpful for scholars but is taxing for regular readers, who will find Frost's chronological shifts confusing (to say nothing of such unenlightening entries as "Come see kill a vase" and "Marriage Japanese Dwarf tree"). Still, any Frost reader will benefit from Faggen's thoughtful introduction and be intrigued by the way in which concepts from these largely aphoristic journals animate the poems and vice versa. When Frost writes in Notebook 29 that "poetry is also the renewal of principles" and that "Principles have got to be lost in order to be found," one thinks of the vision of truth from his poem "The Black Cottage": "Most of the change we think we see in life / Is due to truths being in and out of favor." Frost's speaker then imagines being "monarch of a desert land / I could devote and dedicate forever / To the truths we keep coming back and back to," a land that could only be "sand dunes held loosely in tamarisk / Blown over and over themselves in idleness." Some poets don't seem themselves outside their chosen medium; the Frost of these notebooks, however, is very much the Frost of the poems.

And that's the problem (if it is a problem). Had Frost's journals contained a study of Walter Benjamin or a series of sympathetic and incisive observations about Gertrude Stein's *Tender Buttons*, he possibly could be made to fit into the American experimental lineage. Had they contained a quiveringly sensitive commentary on the flora of New England, maybe he could be seen as reliably conventional. But more than four decades after his death, this most American of American poets still fits uncomfortably into our country's favorite aesthetic categories.

There are signs, though, that this is changing. Experimental poets like Susan Wheeler have begun to appreciate Frost's emphasis on writing as performance, and to treat him as a valuable source rather than an opponent (Wheeler's *Source Codes* contains a very funny riff on Frost's "Provide, Provide"). More important, Frost managed to procure the best set of supporters an American poet can have: non-American poets, especially non-American poets with jobs in American universities. A short list of these would include Joseph Brodsky, Derek Walcott, Glyn Maxwell, and roughly every Northern Irish poet born after 1935. In a turn of events Frost would have relished, the Pulitzer prize (an award he collected a record four times) went in 2003 to the Irish poet Paul Muldoon, who declared Frost to be "the greatest American poet of the 20th century." If this is a peculiar and circuitous way for the influence of Frost's poetry to be felt on his native soil, well, as Frost put it, "the line will have the more charm for not being mechanically straight." And for a poet who has always been a figure of curves and bends, of digressions and turnings, perhaps there is no better reward.

DONALD JUSTICE

I s it better to be great or to be a great example? In most artistic arenas, the answer is easy—who wouldn't rather be Laurence Olivier than someone known for playing a convincing butler? If you're a poet, though, this question isn't so simple. As general knowledge about poetry has faded, so has our confidence about what might constitute a "great" poem in the first place. Anyone trying to make a broad statement about poetry is therefore forced to survey a crowd of self-promoting aspirants—the new formalists, the langpo refugees, the post-avant—which is probably why contemporary American anthologies often read like plays with a hundred parts, all small. And when so many scenes have been set aside for cooks and clowns and angry shopkeepers, would we even recognize a leading man if he showed up to audition?

In the world of American poetry, Donald Justice wasn't a bit player; he was an Olivier. Justice, who died on August 6 (three weeks before this piece ran), was born in Miami in 1925, and like most poets, he spent his life touring American universities. (He was most closely linked to Iowa, where he taught for many years in the Writers' Workshop.) His life wasn't dramatic. He worked on poems; he painted; he studied music; he wrote some criticism. He gave readings and went to conferences. In most ways, Justice was no different from any number of solid, quiet older writers devoted to traditional short poems. But he was different in one important sense: sometimes his poems weren't just good; they were great. They were great in the way that Elizabeth Bishop's poems were great, or Thom Gunn's or Philip Larkin's. They were great in the way that tells us what poetry used to be, and is, and will be. Though its primary subject was the past, his work as a whole is more extraordinarily present—more thrillingly contemporary—than most of the styles that have advertised their commitment to "making it new" over the past half century. It's as if, by looking determinedly backward, he looked further ahead than almost anyone else.

Of course, looking back usually means that you stop going forward, which is why Frank Zappa said the world wouldn't end in fire or ice but in paperwork or nostalgia. Justice's preoccupation with nostalgia—and with the idea of endings—has always been the easiest thing to notice about his poetry aside from its virtuoso technique. The *Collected Poems* begins with his first collection, *The Summer Anniversaries* (1960) and ends with new work, allowing us to see this theme emerge as a progression of titles. The first page gives us "Anniversaries," the last page "There is a gold light in certain old paintings." Along the way, we pass things like "Portraits of the Sixties," "Memories of the Depression Years," "Nostalgia of the Lakefronts," and "Dance Lessons of the Thirties." It's no surprise that when Justice mentions "marvelous clichés," he wryly follows with "Ah, those were the days."

But Justice's poetry doesn't just address nostalgia; it evokes nostalgia through an expert manipulation of form. The typical Justice poem is brief, uses simple diction decorated with the occasional archaism, and is scored to a slow and sifting rhythm that recalls Stevens and the T. S. Eliot of "Preludes." "Dance Lessons of the Thirties" begins:

> *Wafts of old incense mixed with Cuban coffee*
> *Hung on the air; a fan turned; it was summer.*
> *And (of the buried life) some last aroma*
> *Still clung to the tumbled cushions of the sofa.*

> *At lesson time, pushed back, it used to be*
> *The thing we managed somehow just to miss*
> *With our last-second dips and whirls—all this*
> *While the Victrola wound down gradually.*

The measured near-rhyme of "summer," "aroma," and "sofa" is a characteristic Justice touch; his poems often edge toward rhyme, achieve it, and then play with the expectations that have been created. In particular, Justice likes odd chords built on rich rhyme and identical rhyme; each stanza of the poem "Sadness," for example, offers couplets like "And night crept

down with an awful slowness toward the water; / And there
were lanterns once, doubled in the water." Patterns like this appear alongside conventional repetitive forms like the villanelle,
and the effect is like overhearing a song in which all the notes
are echoes and all the echoes notes.

It would be a mistake, though, to assume that writing about
nostalgia makes Justice himself a nostalgist. A nostalgist wants
his present to be part of the past, rather than for the past to
be part of his present; accordingly, the nostalgist's craving for
historical bric-a-brac serves only to push the time he longs for
farther and farther out of reach. If anything, Justice does the
reverse: when he looks back he does so haltingly, with a hand
shading his eyes. He doesn't document the past, he calls to it at
a distance from behind a latticework of style (it's worth noting
that when Justice's poems are less successful, it's not because
they've become sentimental but because they've been polished
into brittleness). This aspect of his work is especially evident in
the way Justice handles one of his favorite flourishes, the apostrophe. Particularly later in his career, Justice was intrigued by
this effect; in one eight-page stretch alone he cries: "O the saintly
forbearance of these mirrors!" "O marvelous early cigarettes!"
and "O counters of spectacles!" Apostrophe is rare now mostly
because it's considered false and gushy, which makes it seem a
strange choice for such a fastidious poet. But for Justice the in-
adequacy of the gesture is what matters most. Each apostrophe
strikes a deliberately off-key note that is both an acknowledgement of limitation and a signal of the great feeling behind that
acknowledgement.

Such an acceptance is exactly what enables the past to enter the present—for absences to become presences. In "From a Notebook," Justice describes a friend who insists that the adjective is the most beautiful part of speech because it is "the most Personal," to which Justice replies, "I, on the contrary, maintain that the Conjunction, being Impersonal, is the most Beautiful, and especially when suppressed." This is the manifesto of an ironist, balanced between two poles but committing to neither, and Justice is perhaps best described as an ironist of nostalgia. It's this combination that allows the time he looks back on to become the time he looks forward to, and that underscores the most inimitable moments in his writing. In his late poem "The Miami of Other Days," Justice summons up a year when "the city was not yet itself," and when bonfires on the beach "were nostalgias for the lights of cities / Left behind." He continues:

> And gods slept under tabernacle tents
> That sprang up overnight on circus grounds
> Like giant toadstools yearning for respectability,
> To be given body by those bell-voiced women
> Who blessed in long white sleeves the multitudes;
> Or dwelt beneath the still pure river, rising
> From time to time, for breath, like great sea cows,
> Mysteriously human.

Notice how antecedents and images begin to blur—have the "gods" been "given body" or the "tabernacle tents"? How can "gods" that are "great sea cows" become "mysteriously human"? Given Justice's painstaking habits, such imprecision isn't carelessness. But neither does it seem (entirely) designed. The best way to read this passage is as an instance in which the strength of the vision—the wave of the past—has risen into the language of the poem, pouring through the poet while being poured out by him, being recovered and lost, lost and recovered. Being written. This is Justice's final signature, and there is nothing like it.

This again raises the question: what could Donald Justice be considered a great example of? The best answer is that he wasn't a great example of anything—he was simply a great poet. And because of that, because he didn't lead a school or start a movement or stand for a theory, his achievements will be for a while easier to overlook than they should be. But a writer like this understands that poetry always means waiting for the right line and waiting for the right time to use it. Readers who are in turn willing to wait for Justice will find a past revealed in all its rich strangeness—and a future as well.

ON CARL PHILLIPS

"People of humor," said Coleridge, "are always in some degree people of genius." It's an arguable proposition, but one that many younger American poets would embrace, some with perhaps too much enthusiasm. Carl Phillips, however, might have reservations. Phillips is a serious person: serious about his poetry, which is a showcase of penetrating, tasteful, well-crafted lyricism; serious about his Sophocles (a trained classicist, Phillips has translated *Philoctetes*); and even serious about his comedy, which he apparently prefers on the thoughtful side. In interviews, for example, Phillips has said he admires the humor of the magisterial English poet Geoffrey Hill (which is sort of like praising the joie de vivre of Eeyore) but that he sees little to recommend in the Three Stooges (Larry, Moe, Curly, we hardly knew ye). It should come as no surprise, then, that Phillips's eighth collection, *The Rest of Love*, is short on postmodern ironic clowning and long on sober, high-minded reflections in which the authority of poetry itself rarely comes into question.

This is not to say these poems are straightforward. In many ways, Phillips's work reaches back to the knotty practice of the modernists, who in turn drew heavily on the violently yoked ideas of Donne and Herbert (the title of Phillips's book recalls Herbert's "The Pulley," which plays on the different meanings of the word "rest"). The thirty-odd short lyrics here are complicated, atmospheric, passionately private affairs in which antecedents are hazy and italicized interjections are plentiful. Words like "light" and "dark" and "release" appear regularly; words like "Schenectady" and "flop" and "boxer shorts" do not. A typical Phillips poem looks painstakingly assembled (which is why this poet is sometimes labeled "formal"), but the logic behind the individual connections is often obscure. For example, "In Stone" begins:

> *Their clothes; their rings as well, until*
> *at last they wore nothing. All was visible:*
> *flourish; humiliation; some things,*
> *more than others, looking almost the same.*
> *As if* Not only torn but lavish let be
> the angle all tearing starts at,
> *as if this were the rule, each*
> *splitting open around, unfolding*
> *from—so as, incidentally, to expose—*
> *its wet center. . . .*

On the one hand, this sounds very fine; on the other hand, "each" what? Insisting on an answer to this sort of question is usually a mistake, though: Phillips's best poems offer impressions, not epigrams. Like many of his peers, Phillips is drawn to ambiguous postures; he likes to float toward a position, edge away, go off at a slant, and come back again. He favors questions ("Is it latchless, or only / unlatched, / that door, / slamming?) and gestures ("as if" gets a real workout here) over assertions, and when he does make assertions, they tend to be phrased as questions: "That much, still, / is true, isn't it?" Though Phillips often skirts the line between indeterminacy and mere vagueness, he usually manages to stay on the right side of it, and his poems are enriched by their ambivalence.

Not every ambivalence is created equal, though. While Phillips can be tender when he wants to be, he's more interested in (and more interesting when) showing us struggles for control. In particular, he likes to play complex syntax against free-verse line breaks, allowing the ostentatious control of the former to challenge the inherent arbitrariness of the latter much the way that waves build and disperse across a beach. This game of clench-and-release prevents many of his poems from solidifying until their closing lines. Consider these early lines from "Like Cuttings for a Wreath of Praise and Ransom":

> *The landscape opening as if no end to it,*
>
> *a longing anywhere*
> *   for some resistance, some*
> *stop: the magnolia, its ring of bird-ravaged*
> *seed-cones,*
> *   the birds themselves, a wind lifting*

a collar of feathers at the neck of each—stiff
courtiers,
                    Elizabethan.

The poem, which is about (among other things) reconciling oneself to a mixed existence, ends by relaxing into an image of confinement: "They say / the legs go here. The straps adjust. / Like so." Phillips is a deft hand with this kind of paradox, another legacy of his Metaphysical heritage.

The best poems in *The Rest of Love* are, appropriately enough, love poems. As a suitor, Phillips doesn't really do sweet and earnest; instead, he's more likely to give us the swirling, hot-and-cold drama of love at its most fraught (in this, as in some of his phrasing, Phillips seems to have been taking notes from current poet laureate Louise Glück). Like Donne, Phillips mixes the divine with the beloved and, in accordance with his interest in control, throws in a suggestion of S and M to boot. Of meeting the Lord in a dream, Phillips writes,

because I've asked he shows me his mercy—
a complicated arrangement
of holes and

hooks, buckles. What else did you think
mercy looked like,
he says and, demonstrating, he straps it on,
         then takes it off.

"Batter my heart, three-person'd God," indeed. In fine poems like "If a Wilderness" and "Here, on Earth," Phillips proves that the great English verse tradition of erotic religious poetry is alive and well, and apparently teaching creative writing in Saint Louis.

That said, there are two significant problems with *The Rest of Love*. The first is that the poems often blur together—not only does Phillips use the same affected voice ("Here's where our mounts, / thirsting, took of the water") throughout the collection, but he's altogether too fond of ending poems with a hushed, would-be profundity ("O what / is the soul? The rest of the boys / sang back"). The second problem here, which is closely related to the first, is that Phillips can be so thoroughgoing in his rejection of ironic whimsy that he crosses the fine line between solemn and pompous ("Is fervor belief's / only measure? Is there // no saving / what betrays itself?"). There's much to be said for unfashionable earnestness, but when a poet sounds like he'd have to struggle to order a taco without sermonizing about "desire" and "the body," his readers are liable to get a little impatient. Phillips might respond to this criticism by saying that a poet has as much right as anybody else to take himself seriously, to which the only reply is: sure, but like anybody else, a poet has to earn it. And in this sense, it's worth remembering something that Mark Twain, our greatest comedic writer, had to say about humor: "The secret source of humor is not joy, but sorrow; there is no humor in Heaven." Here on earth, though, where joy is rare and our sorrow is continually before us, how serious can a truly serious poet afford to be?

RICHARD WILBUR'S

ANTEROOMS

I t's tough to be a grand old man of—well, anything, really.
Surely at this point Leonard Cohen must experience every
trembling imitation of "Hallelujah" as a whip across his back,
wielded by a doe-eyed Satan. In his elegy for Yeats, Auden famously claims that the poet, upon dying, "became his admirers," but it would've been more accurate to say that like most
grand old men (and not just the ones who actually *are* men),
Yeats had much earlier become shorthand for an array of gener-
alizations. Stick around long enough, and to most people you're
no longer an artist; you're a brand.

Richard Wilbur (born in 1921) has been for decades a grand
old man of American poetry, and he's spent most of his career
being alternately praised and condemned for the same three
things. First, he's widely agreed to be a formal virtuoso. One
might think this would be an indisputable virtue, but, in certain

quarters, working in meter can still earn you skeptical looks. Second, Wilbur is, depending on your preference, courtly or cautious, civilized or old-fashioned, reasonable or kind of dull— basically he's the kind of writer who's willing to use the word "sir" in direct address without any irony whatsoever (as he writes in a poem about LBJ: "Wait, Sir, and see how time will render you." Indeed, sirrah, eftsoons shall you know!). Finally, Wilbur is sometimes put forward as a model of resistance to certain tendencies in American poetry, most notably the conspicuous self-dramatization associated with Robert Lowell and Sylvia Plath, and the even more conspicuous self-dramatization associated with Allen Ginsberg. Whether this is entirely true of Wilbur is a complicated question, but it's fair to say that his writing can make even Donald Justice's work seem gushy.

Wilbur's new book of poems, *Anterooms*, is his ninth, not counting a couple of collected editions and various translations. It is, in some ways, a slight production. Its roughly sixty pages contain only twelve full-on poems; the rest is taken up with translations (from Brodsky, Mallarmé, Verlaine, Horace, and Symphosius), a wordplay exercise for children, and song lyrics for a version of Jean Giraudoux's *La folle de Chaillot*. Interesting stuff, maybe, but not really what one is looking for from a writer with two Pulitzers. So it would be tempting to say that what we have here is a scanty manuscript that will nonetheless be extravagantly praised because its author is still deeply respected and, my goodness, isn't it wonderful that he's still making a go of it at his age?

Tempting but wrong. The better work in *Anterooms*, however limited in quantity, is as good as anything Wilbur's ever produced, and upholds certain virtues other poets would do well to acknowledge, even if they travel roads different from the relatively straight one Wilbur has followed. (There are, after all, many roads in American poetry, and they intersect at odd points.) To understand what's so interesting about these poems, it helps to recall that much of modern poetry is built on juxtaposition. This is true even of writers ordinarily thought to have little stylistic overlap: John Ashbery's writing obviously depends on juxtaposed tones and registers, but Elizabeth Bishop's poems can be almost equally reliant on deliberate contrast (think, in "At the Fishhouses," of the difference in register between an early line like "The five fishhouses have steeply peaked roofs" and a later line like "your hand would burn / as if the water were a transmutation of fire / that feeds on stones and burns with a dark gray flame"). Wilbur is an exception to this tendency. His writing is intent on reducing difference—he asks us to see a poem, not as a sum of distinguishable parts, but as a smooth, silvery whole. Even his shadows are meticulously blended. Consider the beginning of "The Undead," from 1961:

> *Even as children, they were late sleepers,*
> *Preferring their dreams, even when quick with monsters,*
> *To the world with all its breakable toys,*
> *Its compacts with the dying.*

Wilbur goes on to make a number of delicately dark suggestions: the undead (who are implicitly associated with a certain kind of artist) come "as all extremists do / In time, to a sort of grandeur"; their "utter self-concern" finally renders them "self-less: / Mirrors fail to perceive them"; and they are ultimately haunted by what they will never have, "rooms with something to lose." In fact, the entire poem can be read as an updating of "The Lady of Shalott" (bet you didn't realize she was a vampire).

But all of these satisfying observations are delivered in the same mode. There's no moment at which the voice of "the un-dead" actually emerges, and even if there were, you can be fairly sure that voice wouldn't say something like "Braaaaiins! WAAAANT!" No, it would probably make a coolly intelligent remark about what it means "To prey on life forever and not possess it, / As rock-hollows, tide after tide, / Glassily strand the sea," which is naturally how the poem ends. This doesn't make "The Undead" unsuccessful; on the contrary, it's one of the finest pieces you'll read from any living poet. But it does ask something slightly unusual from the contemporary reader. It asks us to value poetry that is happy to be read as solid and static, rather than unstable and in flux.

This is an especially tricky thing to ask if you happen to be writing about death, as Wilbur is in the strongest poems in *Anterooms*. Death, rather like Wilbur's poetry, does not easily admit of divisions; it is "the total emptiness forever," as Larkin put it. So what happens when you combine a style so dependent on surfaces with a subject that is, in a sense, nothing but surface? Sometimes you get a plangent simplicity, as in "Ecclesiastes 11:1," in which Wilbur plays on the verse's suggestion that we "cast our bread upon the waters." He says this advice

Helps us to believe
That it's no great sin to give,
Hoping to receive.

Therefore I shall throw
Broken bread, this sullen day,
Out across the snow,

Betting crust and crumb
That birds will gather, and that
One more spring will come.

Other poems have the flat, exacting power of tarot cards. Here is the end of "Galveston, 1961," the strangest poem in this book, in which Wilbur imagines a woman (whom he knew?) as a drowning victim of the great Galveston hurricane, now rising back from the ocean as a combination of deity and vision:

Shake out your spattering hair
And sprawl beside me here,
Sharing what we can share
Now that we are so near,

Small talk and speechless love—
Mine being all but dumb
That knows so little of
What goddess you become

And still half-seem to be,
Though close and clear you lie,
Whom droplets of the sea
Emboss and magnify.

Almost fifty years ago, Randall Jarrell claimed that as a poet, Wilbur "never goes too far, but he never goes far enough." It's an observation that's invariably quoted whenever Wilbur gets reviewed (far be it from me to break the chain). But to write convincingly about death—and also, as Wilbur has increasingly done, about grief—isn't a matter of going anywhere. It's a matter of remaining poised in the face of a vast and freezing indifference. And while the strong, spare poems here are unlikely to strike many readers as the illustrious pronouncements of a grand old man—the kind of figure Jarrell had in mind—they are wholly successful in meeting the darkest of subjects with their own quiet light. Which is a far grander thing, surely.

FREDERICK SEIDEL, SCARY GUY

Many poets have been acquainted with the night; some have been intimate with it; and a handful have been so haunted and intoxicated by the shadier side of existence that it can be hard to pick them out from the murk that surrounds them. As *Poems 1959–2009* demonstrates, Frederick Seidel has spent the last half century being that darkest and strangest sort of poet. He is, it's widely agreed, one of poetry's few truly scary characters. This is a reputation of which he's plainly aware and by which he's obviously amused, at least to judge from the nervy title of his 2006 book, *Ooga-Booga*. This perception also colors the praise his collections typically receive—to pick one example from many, Calvin Bedient admiringly describes him as "the most frightening American poet ever," which is a bit like calling someone "history's most bloodthirsty clockmaker." What is it about Seidel that bothers and excites everyone so much?

The simplest answer is that he's an exhilarating and

unsettling writer who is very good at saying things that can seem rather bad. When a Seidel poem begins, "The most beautiful power in the world has buttocks," it's hard to know whether to applaud or shake your head. But that's not the entire story. There is also the peculiar attraction—and occasional repulsion—of the Seidel persona. Unlike most poets, he's rich, has known a number of famous and semifamous people, and has spent a fair amount of time whizzing around on expensive Italian motorcycles while obsessing over breasts and violence. Yet nobody really knows him. He doesn't do readings, he rarely teaches, and it's almost impossible to imagine him showing up at a writers' conference, unless he was looking for someone who might go well with some fava beans and a nice Chianti.

This separation from the poetry world's institutions doesn't seem to have troubled Seidel's career. True, it's probably kept him out of several anthologies, but on the other hand, it's made him an attractive subject for reviewers (who enjoy pointing out the follies of anthologists) and an irresistible object of fascination for the sort of youngish male writer who has fantasies of striding around the literary world like a combination of James Dean and the Earl of Rochester. Seidel is published by a major house and has enjoyed long, smart, immensely positive write-ups in at least three general-interest magazines—a grim fate for which most poets would happily sacrifice their children, and possibly even their cats.

Of course, none of this has much to do with Seidel's actual work, which has generally gotten better as he's gotten older, regardless of who or what has been paying attention to him. He began his career in the shadow of Robert Lowell, and that shadow appears to have been nearly pitch-black. Certainly there's little original in lines like these, from 1963: "Now the green leaves of Irish Boston fly or wither / Into bloodred Hebrew, Cotton Mather's fall. / When this morning the end-of-it-all / Siren, out of its head, / Turned inside out, hell-red, / Anne, you touched my wrist." By *These Days* (1989), however, Seidel has largely abandoned the mannered Lowellian angst in favor of an approach that, while still technically accomplished, is considerably more ferocious. Here is "That Fall":

> *The body on the bed is made of china,*
> *Shiny china vagina and pubic hair.*
> *The glassy smoothness of a woman's body!*
> *I stand outside the open door and stare.*
>
> *I watch the shark glide by . . . it comes and goes—*
> *Must constantly keep moving or it will drown.*
> *The mouth slit in the formless fetal nose*
> *Gives it that empty look—it looks unborn;*
>
> *It comes into the room up to the bed*
> *Just like a dog. The smell of burning leaves,*
> *Rose bittersweetness rising from the red,*
> *Is what I see. I must be twelve. That fall.*

It seems inadequate to call this a poem of adolescent male sexual desire, although that's exactly what it is. In any case, all the signature Seidel elements are present: the jeweler-exact metaphors (the shark has "a formless fetal nose"), the nightmare, Hieronymus Bosch atmosphere in which images and senses blur ("The smell of burning leaves . . . / Is what I see"), and the deliberate aural clumsiness ("shiny china vagina") coupled uneasily with Swinburnian fluidity ("Rose bittersweetness rising from the red").

This combination of barbarity and grace is one of Seidel's most remarkable technical achievements: he's like a violinist who pauses while bowing expertly through Paganini's Caprice no. 24 to smash his instrument against the wall. Skipping through his poems from *The Cosmos Trilogy* (2003), for instance, one finds the carefully judged quatrain that begins "October": "It is time to lose your life, / Even if it isn't over. / It is time to say goodbye and try to die. / It is October." This within a few dozen pages of the comic and terrible "Venus," which includes possibly the most intentionally awful couplet written by anyone whose last name isn't Geisel or Nash: "Her breasts are prodigious. / Her ass is steatopygous." When people claim to be shocked by Seidel's work, it's not the actual content that disturbs them—if you've seen *28 Weeks Later*, you've seen far worse—but rather these strange juxtapositions of artful and dreadful. This is probably the reason he reminds some readers of Philip Larkin, with whom he otherwise has little in common. The anger that often motivates Larkin's rapid shifts in diction and tone becomes in Seidel a rage that can destabilize the poem entirely.

If anything, Seidel, born in 1936, has gotten less mellow as he's aged. A sampling of lines from the new poems gathered under the title *Evening Man*: "I make her oink" (in reference to sex); "My face had been sliced off / And lay there on the ground like a washcloth"; "And the angel of the Lord came to Mary and said: / You have cancer. / Mary could not think how. / No man had been with her." This is grim stuff, even when meant to be amusing. But what prevents Seidel's work from being simply grotesque or decadent—most of the time, anyway—is his connection to the larger political universe. Adam Kirsch has observed that "among contemporary poets, it is Seidel's social interest that is really unusual." This is exactly right, and the nature of Seidel's social interest makes his work interesting in ways that the work of his closest peer, Sylvia Plath, often is not. Seidel and Plath are our most talented devotees of psychic violence, but whereas Plath co-opts the outside world to make her own obsessions burn hotter ("my skin, / Bright as a Nazi lampshade"), Seidel occupies a more ambiguous territory. He's as likely to be possessed by events as to possess them ("Rank as the odor in urine / Of asparagus from the night before, / This is empire waking drunk, and remembering in the dark").

To be fair, Plath died young; no one knows how her work may have changed. Still, if the Plath we know is Lady Lazarus, the figure Seidel resembles most is the sin-eater, that old, odd, and possibly apocryphal participant in folk funerals in Scotland and Wales. In the late seventeenth century, the Englishman John Aubrey described sin eating like so: "When the Corps was brought out of the house, and layd on the Biere, a Loafe of Breade was brought out, and delivered to the Sinne-eater over the corps . . . in consideration whereof he tooke upon him (ipso facto) all of the Sinnes of the Defunct, and freed him (or her) from walking after they were dead." In Aubrey's telling, the sin-eaters were poor people at society's margin, in particular "a long, leane, ugly, lamentable poor raskal" who lived alone, pre-sumably surrounded by the many sins he had spent a lifetime taking on. Frederick Seidel isn't poor, but it's not hard to imag-ine him in that cottage at nightfall, looking half-longingly, half-contemptuously at the lights of the village while preparing for his lonely supper.

MARIE PONSOT

One of the best things about being an American is that you are free to dislike poetry for any reason you want. You can say it's too clever or too dumb; you can think it's old-fashioned or pointlessly trendy; you can protest that it has nothing to do with real life; or you can complain that it's mostly about Volkswagens and mastectomies. Whatever line you take, there will be room for your opinion in our national antipathy for this snotty, boring, passé art form. And this, surely, is what democracy is all about.

Yet ignoring poetry has its drawbacks. For one thing, it causes us to miss out on the pleasure of seeing our worst expectations exceeded: some poems aren't just bad; they are stupendously awful, and reading them is even more fun than watching drunken confessions on *Cops*. By the same token, though, sometimes a collection of poems appears that isn't actually bad at all; that is, on the contrary, serious, persuasive, and entertaining;

that is—it can happen—a great book. Marie Ponsot's *Springing: New and Selected Poems* is that kind of collection. Ponsot won't be a familiar name to most people (not even to some poets) because she's just turned eighty-one, and her jacket photo, while appealing, lacks the Stevie Nicks–meets–Simone Weil allure that is usually the best way to sell a contemporary poet. On top of that, Ponsot is a pruner. She has published only five books (including this one) in her lifetime, and they're all short.

Short but accomplished. Ponsot is a love poet, a metaphysician and a formalist, but she is neither sappy nor tedious nor predictable. And she isn't cozy. Older poets—particularly older female poets—are often held up as representatives of all that is life affirming, but Ponsot's best work has a dry bite that would make lunch meat out of Oprah, to say nothing of Dr. Phil. Her previous collection, for example, began with a poem entitled "I've Been Around: It Gets Me Nowhere," and Ponsot followed that up with a poem suggesting that the loss of old memories and feelings "will empty me / too emptily / and keep me here / asleep, at sea / under the guilt quilt, / under the you tree." Tough as she is, though, Ponsot's sensibility is generally quirky rather than caustic; like Stevie Smith or Amy Clampitt, she cultivates an eccentricity that allows her to get her points across on the sly, even if it makes the occasional poem the verbal equivalent of a fruit hat.

A typical Ponsot poem decorates a traditional—or at least orderly—formal structure with askew descriptions ("a shine of laughing"), clots of assonance ("blackish package"), and absolutely horrendous puns ("Self-schooled I've been fish"). Though she has a wide tonal range, Ponsot is most likely to be rakish or wounded and least likely to be starchy or cold. When she writes, "The stopped woods / are seized of quiet," you get the feeling it never occurred to her that the phrase could sound pompous— which is a good thing, because in her poem it doesn't. Ponsot also has an attentive ear and likes to show it off with gaudy stress exercises such as the spondee fest that begins her poem "Pathetic Fallacies Are Bad Science But": "If leaf trash chokes the stream-bed, / reach for rock-bottom as you rake / the muck out." Reading a lot of this can be like eating a bucket of peanut butter. But Ponsot's baroque tendencies are usually winning: she seems to be having a good time, to be taking pleasure in her craft, and her enthusiasm is contagious even when the special effects don't quite come off.

In any case, spectacle is secondary to Ponsot's work. No matter how much a poem may strain after play, Ponsot ultimately drives it toward a point or moral, as if Gerard Manley Hopkins were being manhandled midspring by Alexander Pope. Appropriately enough, this impulse often leads her to anchor her work with epigrams. Her sonnets, for example, frequently rely on concluding couplets that sum up in traditional Shakespearean fashion, as in, "Patterns lapse in a bliss of signal mist / which concludes in the swim of the analyst." Even the new poems, which are stranger (and better) than her earliest writing, turn on epigrammatic conclusions, although here the language is looser and the wit more agile ("I think I've got whatever I need / in the overhead compartment"). This classical touch stabilizes Ponsot's work the way rhyme stabilizes Sylvia

Plath's. And like Plath, Ponsot occasionally strays into near dog-gerel; for example, "people penned in the scarred / yard stop at the metal / whistle blown hard." But where Plath uses this exag-gerated form to convey aggression or desire (or both), Ponsot does so out of an assertive curiosity: she likes the sound of "yard," so she repeats it. This tactic doesn't water Plath down so much as pour similar energy into a differently shaped vessel; at her best, Ponsot has Plath's strangeness without her single-mindedness.

Ponsot is least effective when her Hopkinsesque phrasing provides cover for such thrown-together descriptions as "the othering bliss of child" or, worse, "the faithing leap of sex." In these moments, Ponsot sounds less like the vigorous writer she is than like someone who was in far too much of a hurry. She also lapses into fashionable prejudice on occasion; only a few pages away from a beautiful, complex tribute to her mother, en-titled "Late," Ponsot manages to write about men as if they were all modeled on the Great Santini. "Most males," she writes, be-have "as if they confuse / Marking with marring; as if . . . / they smash what they can't use." What's more, "these July boys & men" are "trained not to listen for what their lives mean / But to beat." It's certainly possible, even honorable, for a poet to chal-lenge the ethos of power and competition that pervades contem-porary life, but it would be nice if Ponsot could do it without using clichés about what brutes guys are.

It seems petty to criticize Ponsot for these mistakes, though, because they are the necessary consequence of her ambitious style: if you're going to be vivid, sometimes you're going to be vividly wrong. What's surprising is how often she's right. Ponsot's average work is good, and her strongest work—the work she should be judged by—is terrific. Her villanelle "Northampton Style" begins:

> *Evening falls. Someone's playing a dulcimer*
> *Northampton-style, on the porch out back.*
> *Its voice touches and parts the air of summer,*
>
> *as if it swam to time us down a river*
> *where we dive and leave a single track*
> *as evening falls. Someone's playing a dulcimer*
>
> *that lets us wash our mix of dreams together.*

Ponsot's signature quirkiness is here ("swam to time"), but matched to a quieter, more stately tone. Although the poem risks a cliché mood of bittersweet reflection (contemporary poetry's default mode), Ponsot's lines stand out for their craftsmanship. The hard rhyme ("back," "track") prevents the poem from becoming euphonious, preparing us for a shift toward a more awkward subject—mortality—later in the poem. Here's how Ponsot makes that move:

> A small breeze rises and the leaves stir / as uneasy as we,
> while the woods go black; / its voice touches and parts
> the air of summer // and lets darkness enter us; our
> strings go slack / though the player keeps up his plangent attack. / Evening falls. Someone's playing a dulcimer; / its voice touches and parts the air of summer.

Will this undermine global capitalism or take the pulse of Schrödinger's cat? No, but the challenges the poem takes on are real, and the poet makes her work in overcoming them seem natural. That's an accomplishment. And accomplishments like this, carried over eight decades, five books, and a puzzling absence from contemporary anthologies—all in the face of sales that are dwarfed by the ghostwritten autobiographies of pop stars—are what American art is all about. That may sound like bleak news for artists, but there are advantages to writing poetry with the exhilarating integrity that Marie Ponsot demonstrates in *Springing*. For one thing, long after the last episode of *The West Wing* has vanished, someone might read one of her poems, think, "Now that is interesting," and afterward imagine himself in terms conceived partly through Ponsot's writing. Of course, at that point, many of us may no longer be alive.

Which, when you think about it, is just another reason to hate poetry.

ACKNOWLEDGMENTS

I'M GRATEFUL TO ANN GODOFF, my editor, for her continued support. I'm also indebted to her colleagues Will Heyward, Casey Rasch, Katie Hurley, Norina Frabotta, Sabrina Bowers, Dolores Reilly, Darren Haggar, John Fagan, and Olivia Taussig.

This book owes its existence to the *New York Times Book Review*, and in particular to Greg Cowles and Dwight Garner, who edited the majority of the pieces gathered here. David Kelly, Parul Sehgal, and Jen Szalai also coaxed a couple of these essays into shape. I'm thankful to the *Book Review*'s current editor, Pamela Paul, and its two previous editors, Sam Tanenhaus and Chip McGrath, for allowing me the use of a handsome soapbox.

Chris Wiman and Don Share at *Poetry* magazine, Heidi Julavits and Andrew Leland at the *Believer*, and David Caplan and Jon Peede at the *Virginia Quarterly Review* also shepherded essays in this collection into print with skill and patience.

I'm indebted to several readers who lent a hand to these pieces behind-the-scenes. They are Jane Avrich (whose editing savvy improved at least half a dozen of these essays), James Richardson, Maureen McLane, Michael Donohue, and Matti Eklund.

I'm grateful as always to my agent and friend, Betsy Lerner.

And I'm grateful to Karen, who is my primary reader, and to Lila, who thinks poems are funny.